Quenched Like a Wick

Revealing the Day America Breathes Her Last

By Drew Simmons

... They shall lie down together, they shall not rise; they are extinguished, they are quenched like a wick. Isaiah 43:17

Quenched Like a Wick by Drew Simmons

Cover design by Jason Alexander, ExpertSubjects.com

3rd Edition

ISBN-13: 978-1475038897
ISBN-10: 1475038895

Contents

Introduction

Sometimes we can look back on our lives and see remnants of purpose. I still remember very clearly that final paper I had to write for my senior year of high school English Lit. My first thought was to compare the decline of America to that of the Roman Empire. Why I wanted to write about that I have no idea. But having limited time to research such a broad topic, I went instead with something with which I was more familiar. I had just started reading some popular Christian books about "end time" prophecies. So I decided to write about how we are nearing the end of this age, and all that that entails. To be honest, though, I'm sure I did nothing more than regurgitate what I was reading. I had a lot of zeal, but little true knowledge.

Little did I know then where I'd be today. Some twenty years later I've uncovered the greatest secret a man could find. And it's at the root of that high school paper I attempted to write long ago. It's the very question that multitudes are asking today. What will happen to America and when will it happen? There seems to be a collective undercurrent of fear in America. A fearful expectation for what's coming upon America and the world. And isn't this exactly what Hebrews chapter 10 promises? When a person (or a whole nation of them, in our case) willfully sins, there comes a fearful expectation of judgment, and fiery indignation, no less.[1]

Just look how far we've come in such a short time. Only two hundred thirty years ago we were a nation of rebellious ragtags fighting for our independence. Only one hundred years ago America sat on the sideline for three years before joining the allied forces in World War 1. But today America's military might is surpassed by no other nation on earth. We charge ahead fearlessly into even the most remote corners of the world. We are the lone superpower of

---

[1] Hebrews 10:26-27

the world. We sit as Queen atop all peoples and continents. We are the world's hyperpower. Of only America today can it be said "I am, and there is no one else besides me."[2] No, there is no other nation like America today. But can it continue forever?

Is the end of her reign really just a matter of economics as the secularists would have you believe? Have we merely arrived at a point where we find ourselves living beyond our means? Is it that our debt has caught up with us and now America will be thrust into Third World status, riots and marshal law, as many believe? Or could it be there's more going on than meets the eye? Maybe there is much more in store for America than just "fading into the background" as popular Bible teachers would have you believe.

In this book I want to show you what is really coming to America and when it will arrive. I'm no Nostradamus. Nor have I been staring at a crystal ball. No, I've been staring intently at the source of God's truth to mankind, the Bible. With great care and diligence[3] I've looked into the light[4] that exposes the thief of the Tribulation.[5] It's from this time in the Word of God that I can confidently say to you that, yes, most assuredly America is discussed in the Bible; even so prominently that we can mark our calendars by it. For the very day she will breathe her last is now clearly in sight.

---

[2] Isaiah 47:8
[3] Isaiah 21:7
[4] Psalm 119:105
[5] 1 Thessalonians 5:4-5

Preface

Before we begin there are just a few housekeeping items I feel the need to convey. I am not affiliated with any denomination or sect of Christianity. I am a born-again Christian; period. I believe the underlying Hebrew and Greek texts of the 66 books of the "Old" and "New" Testaments are the inspired, inerrant Word of God. His Word is to be understood within the context of the entire Bible. God does not change. God did not suddenly change his personality when he sent his only begotten Son to redeem mankind. His Word is rightly taught and understood when understood within the context of the entire Bible.

For the most part, I refer to Jesus as Yahshua. From what I've read on the subject, I believe the Hebrew name Yahshua (or Yahushua, or Yeshua, or Yah'shua) is truer to what our Savior would have been called when he walked the earth. Some questions have been raised as to the origins and transliteration of the Greek name Jesus, or Iesous, which makes my decision to use Yahshua that much easier. However, I am not dogmatic about this, nor do I think Jehovah is either, as he allowed countless Bibles to be written using the Greek name Jesus.

I also prefer to use the New King James Version (NKJV) of the Bible and that's the version of all Scripture references in this book unless otherwise stated. I believe the original Hebrew and Greek texts are the inspired, infallible Word of God. However, fallible men translated those texts into various languages with, hopefully, the best of intentions. Therefore it's important to use the tools of our day, like the Strong's Concordance, to research the meanings of the original Greek and Hebrew words used in the Bible. Some translations of the Bible insert words into the text, beyond simple words to enhance readability, because the translator feels they should be there. Those translations should be considered more commentary than translation. Keep this in mind when reading your favorite "translation."

I reference a lot of Scripture in the footnotes on each page. But the passages I reference for each topic are not meant to be an exhaustive list. The Bible presents far more detail than I can include in a book this size. As you look up those passages it may be helpful to start with the NKJV as I may have keyed on certain words found in that version which may not be found in other translations. I say this because if you initially look up the passage in a version other than the NKJV, the connection I'm trying to make to that particular verse may not be as apparent.

That being said, I can't over emphasize the importance of looking up the Scripture references and studying the passages for yourself. You will get so much more out of this book by studying the passages I reference.

This book is meant to be read from front to back, each chapter in the order presented. The arguments presented in each chapter build on the information in the chapters that came before it. Some people like to skip around but it won't make as much sense that way.

If you like this book you may also appreciate reading my blog: www.wakeupbabylon.blogspot.com. May the Spirit of God bless us all with wisdom[6] and spiritual discernment[7] and may he instruct us in right judgment as we rely on him to teach us from his Word.[8]

---

[6] James 1:5
[7] 1 Corinthians 2:14
[8] Isaiah 28:9, 26, 29

Chapter 1 - A Day Like No Other

*The great day of the LORD is near; it is near and hastens
quickly. The noise of the day of the LORD is bitter; there the
mighty men shall cry out. That day is a day of wrath, a day of
trouble and distress, a day of devastation and desolation, a day
of darkness and gloominess, a day of clouds and thick darkness,
a day of trumpet and alarm against the fortified cities and
against the high towers.* Zephaniah 1:14-16

In just the past decade the world has already endured a
staggering amount of pain and hardship. Since 9/11 we've
witnessed devastating and record setting tsunamis, earthquakes,
volcanic ash clouds, snow storms, wildfires, floods, droughts,
tornadoes, nuclear meltdowns, oil spills, hurricanes, cyclones,
pandemics, diseases, famines, landslides, heat waves, mass animal
die-offs, and power outages, just to name a few.[9] Yet in spite of all
this tragedy and heartache, the Bible describes a time at the end of
this age, yet to begin, which will be unparalleled in destruction and
loss of life. While the most catastrophic of these recent disasters has
taken over 200,000 lives, an event yet to come will take upwards of
300 million. And that will be just the beginning. Isaiah tells us God is
going to make man more rare than fine gold.[10] The picture we're
given is one of hell enlarging itself and opening its mouth wide
beyond measure to accommodate so many lost souls at one time.[11]

If I were to take a poll regarding that Day, the time of
Tribulation, I'm sure many believers and unbelievers alike could tell
me about the anti-Christ, the seven years, the horrible plagues, the

---

[9] *World Disasters Timeline.* Retrieved March 14, 2012, from
http://www.mapreport.com/subtopics/d.html
[10] Isaiah 13:12
[11] Isaiah 5:14

battle of Armageddon and finally the return of Christ. And while the earth will see all of these things, there's much more to that Day than many realize. It seems the focus of many Christians, when seeking to learn about the end of days, is limited to the books of Revelation and Daniel, the two most difficult books of the Bible. But after all, isn't that where most of that Day is discussed? I have found the answer to that question to be a resounding "No!"

Unraveling the Mystery

The prophecies regarding the Tribulation are numerous and notoriously difficult to understand. I would be lying if I claimed to understand all of them at this present time. However, in this book I will attempt to explain what I do understand. Proverb 25:2 tells us it's the glory of God to conceal a matter but the glory of kings is to search out a matter. And twice in the book of Revelation we are told that God's people are made kings and priests unto God the Father by the blood of Yahshua (Jesus) the Christ.[12] Should we therefore throw up our hands in frustration because it's difficult to understand? No, but let us rather tune out the distractions of life and forge ahead as kings and priests to God, believing in faith that he will give us understanding[13], by his Spirit[14], as we diligently study his Word. The watchman of Isaiah 21 listened earnestly and with great care.[15] Let's be among those who mark God's words and really hear what he's saying.[16] Perhaps some of us will listen and hear for the time to come.[17] May we be among the wise who will understand the

---

[12] Revelation 1:6, 5:10
[13] Isaiah 28:29, Matthew 23:8
[14] 1 Corinthians 2:14
[15] Isaiah 21:7
[16] Jeremiah 23:18
[17] Isaiah 42:23

message of these last days.[18] Let us be counted among those who have their lamps full of oil when the Bridegroom arrives.[19]

Many will protest, saying: "Isn't it enough that we just ready ourselves spiritually? Do we really need to know all the whys and what-fors? Aren't we told just to watch and be ready?" To these I would respond, how do you know for what to watch? Will you be able to discern between a lie and the truth? Will you be able to sift through all the half-truths of our day? And shouldn't we be found walking in the full truth of God's Word?

For we know that "true worshipers will worship the Father in spirit and truth; for the Father is seeking such to worship Him."[20] But do Christians today really understand all we need to about our God? There's evidence in the Bible that this generation doesn't fully consider all the characteristics of the God we serve.[21] Consider that one of the more frequent phrases in the Bible regarding our day is when Jehovah says: "then you will know that I am the Lord." In Ezekiel he takes it a step further and says: "then you will know that I am the Lord who strikes."[22] Could it be that this generation, after experiencing unparalleled blessing and favor, mercy and graciousness, only understands Jehovah's lovingkindness towards his people?

Perhaps we've forgotten that there's another aspect of God, that of his severity and judgment.[23] Jeremiah instructs those who boast that they should boast only in their full knowledge of God, "that he understands and knows Me, that I am the LORD, exercising lovingkindness, judgment, and righteousness in the earth. For in these I delight," says the LORD.[24] And while this generation is very

---

[18] Daniel 12:10, Hosea 14:9, Matthew 25:2
[19] Matthew 25:4
[20] John 4:23
[21] Isaiah 1:3, Jeremiah 4:22, Hosea 5:4
[22] Ezekiel 7:9
[23] Romans 11:22
[24] Jeremiah 9:23-24

familiar with his lovingkindness perhaps we've forgotten that he has, in the past, removed his lovingkindness and mercies from his people for a time for the purpose of chastising them for succumbing to the sin of the land.[25] Therefore we can conclude that by studying the events of our day, and days soon to come, we are learning about the righteousness and judgment of God, two qualities with which we may not be familiar.

Furthermore, did God give us details of that Day only to ignore them? So many people today seem to be caught up with such utter silliness.[26] Some sincere believers are trying to find end-time meaning in numbers on license plates, receipts and the Dow. Others are trying to make sense out of dreams and visions. Still others fear continually as they witness one catastrophe after another. Should God's people be tossed to and fro by every wind of doctrine regarding the last days? No, but rather let us be grounded in the Word of God and what it really has to say about our day.

But did God really conceal his foreknowledge of the last days from the masses? It would certainly seem so. I'm not sure past generations could even conceive of the things of our day. We have a weapon that can level a city. We can travel faster than the speed of sound. We send rockets into space. We even have robots to clean our floors. But in Daniel we find something very interesting. He is told to seal up the book until the time of the end.[27] Contained within this verse is both a prediction and a promise. A prediction that past generations won't be able to understand the message of our day. But the promise is given to us. The time of the end has arrived and we can understand what the Bible has to say about our day. We can look intently at the Scriptures and then find fulfillment in our day.

Silence in Heaven

---

[25] Jeremiah 16:5
[26] Ezekiel 13:8
[27] Daniel 12:4

We can take a trek through the wilderness but if we don't know how to find our direction we're likely to get lost. We need some basic tools of survival. We need to know on which side of the tree moss grows and where the sun rises and sets. A compass would be nice and a map is handy too. It may not show every detail but it gives us that big picture view of the land. All the major landmarks should be clearly marked. Likewise, without a broad knowledge of the Scriptures we're apt to fall into common traps. If we only focus on Daniel and Revelation then we aren't seeing the whole picture.

> *When He opened the seventh seal, there was silence in heaven for about half an hour.* Revelation 8:1

We come across Scripture like this and we don't know what to make of it. What could it possibly mean? Some have tried to apply the "day equals a thousand years" concept to this.[28] That concept may apply in some places, such as Hosea 8:2, but where is it said we must apply this principle to every prophecy concerning a span of time? However, with calculator in hand they determine this must be about twenty-one days. But what about Revelation 14:7? It says the <u>hour</u> of his judgment has arrived. Could it be that the <u>half hour</u> is a subset of the <u>hour</u>? And if the hour is what we call the Tribulation could it also be that John's vision of the Tribulation is incomplete? How? Because heaven was silent regarding half of it. John was taken up into heaven to see a vision of things to come but he was only shown about half of it. To John, at least, heaven was silent regarding the other half.

John sees:

- Six seals of a scroll opened
- One-half hour of silence when the seventh is opened
- Trumpet and Bowl judgments

---

[28] 2 Peter 3:8

The word silence here is the Greek word sigē, which is a deliberate hushing.[29] If this silence was a result of the events that came before it, or in anticipation of those following, I believe the word siōpaō, an involuntary stillness, would have been used.[30] When the time of silence came to an end John was then allowed to continue his narrative. In the sequence of the opening of the seven seals the silence began at the opening of the seventh. Next, roughly half of the entire vision (or hour) was blacked-out, so to speak. Then the vision speaks of seven trumpets which were preparing to sound. My point is not to examine the book of Revelation but rather to pull out some interesting tidbits. The book of Revelation, as a whole, is not in exact chronological order. However, we can discern some chronology. The seven seals lead up to this mysterious half hour of silence. Then we read of the sounding of seven trumpets. And if you notice, both the trumpets and the bowls end with the return of Christ.[31] Therefore, the trumpet and bowl judgments must occur simultaneously.

But before we get sidetracked too quickly let's finish discussing that silence in heaven. I've made a case, and a rather flimsy one so far, that the book of Revelation only tells us half the story. But which half? To answer that we have to look at what's going on before and after that time of silence. Look at Revelation 6:12-17. Now let me bring your attention to the words just prior to the half hour of silence: "For the great day of His wrath has come." So we see that the opening of the sixth seal relates to an awareness of the people that the Day has begun, the Day of the Lord, the great time of wrath. Then immediately following the opening events of that day we come to a moment of silence. Then after that silence we find ourselves reading about events that most would associate with the final forty-two months[32], or three and a half years, of the Tribulation. So we see that the book of Revelation focuses primarily

---

[29] Strong's Greek Dictionary entry G4602
[30] Strong's Greek Dictionary entry G4623
[31] Revelation 10:7, 11:15, 16:17
[32] Revelation 11:2, 13:5

on the second half of Tribulation. Now, is this a strong enough case? No, not yet. We have to be able to reconcile all the prophetic text of the Bible. We can't read one book of the Bible and expect to know how the events of the Tribulation play out. Everything must agree.

The Nature of Prophecy

Why would God describe future events in such a cryptic manner? Why do prophecies seem to jump around from one event to the next? Why does one prophet skim over or completely ignore an event that another prophet describes in great detail? How are we to make the connections necessary to understand the picture? How can we place the events in a proper sequence? Much has been written of the nature of prophecy. In Barnes' Notes on the Bible, when commenting on Habakkuk 2:1[33], he writes:

> *The general idea of prophecy which is presented in these passages, is that of a scene which is made to pass before the mind like a picture, or a landscape, where the mind contemplates a panoramic view of objects around it, or in the distance; where, as in a landscape, objects may appear to be grouped together, or lying near together, which may be in fact separated a considerable distance. The prophets described those objects which were presented to their minds as they "appeared" to them, or as they seem to be drawn on the picture which was before them....*
>
> *From the view which has now been taken of the nature of prophecy, some important remarks may be made, throwing additional light on the subject.*
>
> *(1) It is not to be expected that the prophets would describe what they saw in all their connections and relations; ...They*

---

[33] *Barnes' Notes on the Bible: Habakkuk 2:1*, Retrieved March 14, 2012, from http://barnes.biblecommenter.com/habakkuk/2.htm

would present what they saw as we describe what we witness in a landscape. Objects which appear to be near, may be in fact separated by a considerable interval....

(2) Some single view of a future event may attract the attention and engross the mind of the prophet. A multitude of comparatively unimportant objects may pass unnoticed, while there may be one single absorbing view that shall seize upon, and occupy all the attention. Thus, in the prophecies which relate to the Messiah. Scarcely any one of the prophets gives any connected or complete view of his entire life and character. It is some single view of him, or some single event in his life, that occupies the mind. Thus, at one time his birth is described; at another his kingdom; at another his divine nature; at another his sufferings; at another his resurrection; at another his glory. "The prophetic view is made up, not of one of these predictions, but of all combined;" as the life of Jesus is not that which is contained in one of the evangelists, but in all combined....

(3) Another peculiarity, which may arise from the nature of prophecy here presented, may have been that the mind of the prophet glanced rapidly from one thing to another. By very slight associations or connections, as they may now appear to us, the mind is carried from one object or event to another; and almost before we are aware of it, the prophet seems to be describing some point that has, as appears to us, scarcely any connection with the one which he had but just before been describing....

(4) It follows from this view of prophecy, that the prophets would speak of occurrences and events as they appeared to them. They would speak of them as actually present, or as passing before their eyes. They would describe them as being what they had seen, and would thus throw them into the past tense, as we describe what we have seen in a landscape, and

speak of what we saw. It would be comparatively infrequent, therefore, that the event would be described as "future."...

(5) From this view it also follows, that the prophecies are usually to be regarded as seen in space and not in time; or in other words, the time would not be actually and definitely marked. They would describe the order, or the succession of events; but between them there might be a considerable, and an unmeasured interval of time....

So, on the one hand we have certain prophetic text which lies before us as a giant jigsaw puzzle; pieces scattered in disarray. Yet on the other hand we have promises that indicate that we should, in fact, be able to assemble that puzzle with the correct understanding.[34] Yet many have tried, only to throw up their hands in frustration. Many others have opted instead to have popular books explain it to them by modern-day seers.

This is exactly the picture we're given. Isaiah 29 speaks of a time when the Lord will pour out a spirit of deep sleep on the prophets and seers of the day. He says the whole vision has become to them "like the words of a book that is sealed, which men deliver to one who is literate, saying, 'Read this, please.' And he says, 'I cannot, for it is sealed.' Then the book is delivered to one who is illiterate, saying, 'Read this, please.' And he says, 'I am not literate.' Therefore the Lord said: 'Inasmuch as these people draw near with their mouths and honor Me with their lips, but have removed their hearts far from Me, and their fear toward Me is taught by the commandment of men...'"[35]

Before we dismiss this prophecy as something that must have already happened long ago we first must come to terms with the context of the chapter. Could it be that the enemies of God's people, spoken of in verse 5, who become like fine dust, like chaff

---

[34] Isaiah 28:29, Daniel 12:9, 1 Corinthians 2:14
[35] Isaiah 29:11-13

before the wind, "suddenly, in an instant," is really speaking of nuclear war? And could it be the "storm and tempest and the flame of devouring fire" mentioned in verse 6 is the same language that is used in the previous chapter, and throughout the Bible, to describe the coming Tribulation? I submit to the reader that it is. So if even the popular teachers of the day have misunderstood the message, what hope is there for the rest of us? Will anyone truly understand the message of the last days in the Bible? Surely God did not put the understanding of the message beyond the reach of all, did he? If the things of the Spirit of God are spiritually discerned[36] certainly there must be a way to understand. There must be a way to unravel the mystery, by the Spirit of God.

Points of Comparison

I have also spoken by the prophets, and have multiplied visions; I have given symbols through the witness of the prophets.
Hosea 12:10

If half of John's vision in Revelation went silent, where can we locate the other half of the story? What is that key that unlocks understanding of the message; or at least gives us that big picture view? The Bible is so cryptic when speaking of our day. How can we know how those events will play out? Look at Hosea 12:10. The word "symbol" in the NKJV is "similitude" in the KJV. Strong's concordance defines it as "to compare."[37] The English definition of similitude includes "a point of comparison."[38] God is speaking through Hosea here saying, "I have told you everything you need to know. I've sent you prophets with my message. And not only that, I made them all agree. You can compare the messages of the prophets against one another to see the whole picture." It's written that God

---

[36] 1 Corinthians 2:14
[37] Strong's Hebrew Dictionary entry H1819
[38] *Merriam-webster.com*. Retrieved March 14, 2012, from http://www.merriam-webster.com/dictionary/similitude

will do nothing unless he reveals his secret to his servants the prophets.[39] And we learn again in Acts that this very message of the last days, the "times of the restoration of all things," was given expressly to the prophets and recorded in Scripture.[40]

But if this is true shouldn't another prophet confirm what Hosea is saying? Shouldn't there be a point of comparison to confirm Hosea's concept regarding points of comparison? In fact there is. Isaiah 28:9 asks, "Whom will he teach knowledge? And whom will he make to understand the message?" Well, what message is he talking about?

All throughout Isaiah 28 we are given hints about the context. Verse 2 talks about a violent storm and a flood of mighty waters overflowing. Or, in other words, like the flood waters of Noah. Verse 5 says that the Lord of hosts will be like a crown of glory to the remnant of his people. Verse 6 speaks of a spirit of justice to him who sits in judgment. (Remember, we are currently in the age of grace, when mercy and "abundant pardon" is readily available.[41]) Verse 8 describes it as a time when God's own people are overrun with sin. Verse 15 mentions an "overflowing scourge" of which the people of the day don't think they'll take part because they'd rather believe a lie. Verse 16 then mentions Yahshua, that precious cornerstone. Verse 17 mentions that mighty storm again, the hail of which will sweep away the lies; or in other words, prove wrong those trusting in lies. Verse 18 says the overflowing scourge will trample the priests and prophets mentioned in verses 1, 7 and 14. Verse 19 says it will be a terror just to understand the report day by day. And finally in verse 22 we read that it's "a destruction determined even upon the whole earth."

Can I tell you that the "overflowing scourge" of Isaiah 28 is the same "overflowing flood" of Nahum 1:8 and the "overflowing of the water" of Habakkuk 3:10? While the deluge brought destruction

---

[39] Amos 3:7
[40] Acts 3:21
[41] Isaiah 55:7

upon the earth in Noah's day, this scourge is a type of the destruction by fire we read about in regards to the end of the age. This world-wide destruction is the same event described in Isaiah 13:11 when God says he will "punish the world for its evil." It's the same day that Joel describes as very great and terrible.[42] And Malachi calls it the great and dreadful day of the Lord.[43] Isaiah 28 is speaking of both the time just preceding the Tribulation and the Tribulation itself.

Therefore, in Isaiah 28:9 when the Lord asks, "Who can I make to understand the message," he's asking: who can I cause to understand the time of the end? We see the same question being asked in Jeremiah when he says, "To whom shall I speak, and give warning, that they may hear?"[44] Now that we've established that the backdrop of Isaiah 28 is the Tribulation, what can we learn? What does he answer? Who will understand the message of the last days?

Then he asks: "Will it be someone who is just weaned from milk?"[45] In other words, will it be someone who hasn't yet progressed beyond the basic doctrines of faith? Someone who is untrained in the deeper messages of the Bible?[46] Then he answers:

> *For precept must be upon precept, precept upon precept, line upon line, line upon line, here a little, there a little.*
> Isaiah 28:10

And what is a precept but a rule for right living? And where do we get these rules for right living but from the Word of God, the Bible? The word line here also means rule, but it goes further in that it's being used to measure something. And we're told these precepts and lines are found little by little. Here a little, there a little. When we study the Word of God and begin comparing the messages of the prophets, this is exactly what we find. In the midst of the historical

---

[42] Joel 2:11
[43] Malachi 4:5
[44] Jeremiah 6:10
[45] Isaiah 28:9
[46] 1 Corinthians 3:2, Hebrews 5:12-13, 1 Peter 2:2

stories of the Bible we find rules by which to live. And when the context is the message of the latter days we're able to compare these messages to arrive at a more complete picture. Verses 12 and 13 confirm that this message is from the Lord. This is how God chooses to teach his people about the last days. Contained within this message is a way for the weary to find rest and refreshing.[47] It's a message of hope for God's people who are burdened down with the cares of this life. But for the naysayers who continue to follow lies, this message is a snare to them.[48]

A Thread Woven In Time

You may have noticed that the end-time prophecies are scattered all throughout the Bible. It's as if God, in his infinite wisdom, has woven a thread throughout the whole Bible which speaks of our generation. And if we look closely enough we can see it. But we have to progress beyond a merely casual approach to the Bible. We must look intently and study with diligence. When we read a text for the tenth time and still don't understand, we must pray for understanding[49] and resolve to read it another ten times. We must come back to the text again and again until Father reveals its meaning. And we must rely on those points of comparison. Countless times I've found myself studying a text and my memory will be triggered regarding an entirely different text with which I've struggled. It's as if a light bulb blinks on and I find myself immediately comparing the two texts for similarities. In addition, today we have excellent tools such as concordances, dictionaries, and commentaries, most now at our fingertips through a web browser, which enable us to delve deeper into the meaning of words and passages. If we truly want to understand, we can't limit our study to our favorite translation of the Bible. Rather, we need to do some research and see what the underlying Greek and Hebrew

---

[47] Isaiah 28:12, 30:15, 55:7

[48] Isaiah 28:13

[49] James 1:5

words mean. In fact, relying on only one translation of the Bible will most certainly cause us to be misled. Some translators have inserted words into the translated text which are not found in the original Hebrew and Greek, and which should definitely not have been inserted.[50]

But for what exactly are we looking? How can we know when a text is speaking of our day? There are certain words and phrases used in the Bible to which we need to pay very close attention. I've already listed some of them, such as the examination of Isaiah 28. While time will not allow to show them all, I will list some here as a small sampling. These types of phrases act as clues when reading the Bible. When we understand that a passage is speaking of our day we can then examine that passage for details. Then we are able to add that landmark to our map; our big picture view of the events of that Day.

Even from the very first book of the Bible we can see this thread begin to be woven. In Genesis 49:1 Jacob calls his sons together for a very curious reason. I'm sure his sons were expecting to hear something specifically about themselves in the day in which they lived. But no, Jacob says come here, let me tell you what will befall you in the last days. Notice that phrase: in the last days. What Jacob gave his sons that day were prophecies that would reverberate throughout history, all the way to the very end of this age, our day.

In Deuteronomy Moses also uses this prophetic phrase when addressing both his generation and our generation. Verse 31:29 says: "After my death you will become utterly corrupt...and evil will befall you in the latter days, because you will do evil in the sight of the Lord." And again in the next chapter, verse 32:29, he laments, "Oh that they were wise, that they understood this, that they would consider their latter end!" And Daniel, when giving an outline in chapter nine of things to come regarding God's people, refers to the

---

[50] See "Cyrus" in Isaiah 48:14 of the New Living Translation; just one of many examples.

Law of Moses. Certainly Daniel must have had the scroll of Deuteronomy in mind when he said "therefore the curse and the oath written in the Law of Moses the servant of God have been poured out on us, because we have sinned against Him."[51] Later we will discover why Daniel, like Moses, was referring to both his generation and ours.

Sometimes we just need to ask ourselves, has what I'm reading already happened? Could it possibly have happened already? Such questions are especially appropriate when we read phrases from Ezekiel like, "Now the end has come upon you."[52] And again, three verses later, "The end has come; it has dawned for you."[53] And again in Ezekiel: "when their iniquity came to an end."[54] Likewise, God says through Amos, "I will not pass by them anymore."[55] And again he says, "The end has come upon My people."[56] Furthermore, in Nahum it's written: "Affliction will not rise up a second time."[57] And Zephaniah speaks of a time when "The remnant of Israel shall do no unrighteousness."[58] Now I put forth the question: Did the end already come, long ago, or are we at the end today? Certainly God's people have experienced affliction, but this time it's different. We're told affliction will not rise up a second time. The implication here is that this is the last and final affliction being spoken of. And did God's people stop sinning? No, God's people still sin today. So we see in the midst of these passages, and many more like them, God is trying to tell us something about our day. Woven within his Word is a message for our generation.

---

[51] Daniel 9:11
[52] Ezekiel 7:3
[53] Ezekiel 7:6
[54] Ezekiel 35:5
[55] Amos 7:8
[56] Amos 8:2
[57] Nahum 1:9
[58] Zephaniah 3:13

And that message is of a time like no other. Isaiah describes it as God's awesome and very unusual act.[59] The Day of the Lord[60] is described as a cloudy and dark day[61], a day of darkness and gloominess, a day of clouds and thick darkness.[62] Amos asks, what good is the day of the Lord to you? In other words, why are you looking forward to it? He says it will be a day of darkness and not light.[63] And if these truly are the last days before that Day James instructs the rich of the earth, we who have heaped up earthly treasure, to weep and howl for the miseries that are coming upon us.[64] And the writer of Hebrews uses very strong language[65] to admonish God's people to provoke and exhort one another to love and good works, even so much more as we see that Day approaching.[66]

There is most assuredly a Day coming when our Lord will arise and be exalted unlike the world has ever seen.[67] It's the time spoken of by the prophets when all eyes will be on Jehovah.[68] On that Day he will stand up to plead with, or contend with, the people.[69] And not just any people, but both Micah and Moses tell us he will contend with his own people.[70] In fact, Micah tells us that "all of this" is because of the sin of God's people.[71] Should this really surprise us? In Peter we read that judgment begins at the house of the Lord.[72] And while we may not presently understand all of what's to come we're told by Jeremiah that at some point in the latter days

---

[59] Isaiah 28:21
[60] Ezekiel 13:5
[61] Ezekiel 34:12
[62] Joel 2:2
[63] Amos 5:18
[64] James 5:1-3
[65] Strong's Greek Dictionary entry G3948
[66] Hebrews 10:24-25
[67] Isaiah 33:10
[68] Zechariah 9:1
[69] Isaiah 3:13
[70] Deuteronomy 32:36, Micah 6:2
[71] Micah 1:5
[72] 1 Peter 4:17

we'll understand it perfectly.[73] (I fear many won't understand perfectly until they see it with their own eyes.[74]) And again he says that in the latter days we'll consider it.[75]

Continue this study with me and we will most definitely consider it. For behold, the Day is coming, burning like an oven.[76] That Day soon to come is bearing down on us like the scorching heat of summer. Jehovah is pleading with his people to wake up and become clean.[77] And he pleads with the world to recognize his power and might; to give him the honor he is due. But there are so many questions yet to answer. How will that Day begin? What events will precede that Day? How will we know when it's about to start? What will happen to the greatest nation on earth? How will America fare? Can we know for certain the time of year it will begin? How about the year itself? The month? The exact day? Just how much information does the Bible give us about that Day? Let's take a good, hard look and see for ourselves.

---

[73] Jeremiah 23:20

[74] Habakkuk 1:5

[75] Jeremiah 30:24

[76] Malachi 4:1

[77] Isaiah 52, Isaiah 1:17

Chapter 2 - Sudden Destruction

For you yourselves know perfectly that the day of the Lord so comes as a thief in the night. For when they say, "Peace and safety!" then sudden destruction comes upon them, as labor pains upon a pregnant woman. And they shall not escape.
1 Thessalonians 5:3-4

As we progress ever closer to the start of that Day people are beginning to develop some very interesting ideas. I'm not exactly sure how these ideas develop and grow but I'm convinced a lot of people aren't spending enough time reading the Bible.[78] As I speak with people and read their books and blogs I get the impression that people are looking at everything except the Word of God. Some people today are even saying that the Tribulation has already started! They rationalize that the first half of the Tribulation will be relative peace and calm. As I will show, this is clearly not the case. Scripture is clear that when that Day begins, the whole world will know it.[79] It will be unmistakable.

Paul, when writing to the church at Thessalonica, confirms what the people apparently already knew. He reiterated that when the people of that day, which is our day, are saying "Peace and Safety," then sudden destruction will come upon us like labor pains upon a pregnant woman: a common word picture in the Bible regarding that Day.[80] And in the verse prior he refers to this event as the day of the Lord which will arrive like a thief in the night. This "thief in the night" phrase gives a picture of how that Day will approach but not what it will be like. This is an important point and worth repeating. The verse says the Day "so comes" as a thief in the

---

[78] Jeremiah 6:10
[79] Revelation 6:17
[80] 1 Thessalonians 5:3

night. But when it actually arrives it'll be like a woman experiencing labor pains. Any woman in labor will tell you that when those pains grip them they're unmistakable!

Peace and Safety

The Greek word used here for peace carries with it a sense of quietness and rest.[81] And when do we feel the most at rest and the most secure? When we're in a deep, restful sleep, tucked away safely in our beds in the middle of the night. We're dreaming the night away. We're not consciously thinking about who may be prowling around outside. It's at this time that we are most vulnerable. Now we know from other passages that the day of the Lord will come upon the entire world.[82] Paul is saying here that when the whole world is at peace and feeling secure, that's when the Day will begin. [83] That Day will start when the world is reveling in a time of unprecedented peace and security.

And just as the start of that Day will be unmistakable, so too will be that time of unprecedented peace and safety. I believe God will use this "peace and safety" prophecy as a very clear sign to even those who have only been partially paying attention. As I discussed at the opening of this book the world today is experiencing an unprecedented time of upheaval. We are today experiencing a series of wakeup calls. God is trying to get our attention. God's hand of judgment is heavy upon the earth today because our wickedness and rebellion is heavy upon the earth.[84] And those lesser judgments[85] will continue to intensify. As these catastrophes continue to wash over the earth like waves it's going to seem as if nothing is stable. But the time is coming when Jehovah will relent. His chastisements

---

[81] Strong's Greek Dictionary entry G1550
[82] Isaiah 13:11, 14:26, 26:21, 28:22, Zechariah 5:3, Luke 21:35, Micah 5:15
[83] Jeremiah 14:19
[84] Isaiah 24:20
[85] Amos 4:6-10, Jeremiah 12:4, 14:1-6, Hosea 4:3, Matthew 24:7

will cease for a time. In Isaiah 1:5 he asks, "Why should you be stricken again?" Jehovah is saying here: "It's of no use to continue to chastise you with these lesser judgments, you'll only continue to rebel."[86] So out of nowhere the dark clouds of judgment will seem to dissipate. Those severe trials will just stop. Nations will declare peace with their enemies. Troops will return home.[87] Natural disasters will quiet down. Many will also be healed of severe infirmities. There will be a time of unprecedented peace and safety and the inhabitants of the earth will think the worst is over. Then, seemingly out of nowhere, sudden destruction will come upon the world like birth pains upon a woman in labor. You see, this is why the approach of that Day is likened unto a thief in the night. At the moment we feel the most safe and secure, when we least expect trouble, that's the very moment that Day will be begin.

> *When I give healing to Israel, then revealed is the iniquity of Ephraim, and the wickedness of Samaria, for they have wrought falsehood, and a **thief** doth come in, stript off hath a troop in the street.* Hosea 7:1 (YLT)

If you notice, Hosea speaks of that time of healing while also speaking of the thief. Many translations of this passage read "When I would have healed Israel." I chose the Young's Literal Translation because I believe it confirms and correctly conveys the end-time scenario described by the other prophets.[88] We see here that during this time of healing there will also be an opportunity for repentance. Why else would one reveal the sin of God's people other than to cause individuals to see their need for repentance? At the same time Jehovah brings healing to his people there is also a declaration of the sin of God's people for the purpose of repentance. After all, often it's the realization of God's kindness that leads us to repentance.[89] The timing of that outpouring of God's healing is crucial. God desires

---

[86] Jeremiah 2:30, 5:3, 6:29, Zephaniah 3:2, 3:7

[87] Isaiah 33:1

[88] Malachi 4:2, Hosea 7:1 YLT, Isaiah 48:14, Isaiah 57:12-58:1, Micah 3:8, John 14:12, Romans 2:4

[89] Romans 2:4

people to repent and believe in him so he can spare them when that Day arrives, just as he spared the three Hebrew boys in the fiery furnace.[90] But look what happens next: "A thief comes in; a band of robbers takes spoil outside."[91] Just after this time of healing the thief arrives.

But You Are Not in Darkness

They run to and fro in the city, they run on the wall; they climb into the houses, they enter at the windows like a thief. Joel 2:9

Interesting analogy used here of the thief. The thief doesn't want to get caught so he must use stealth. He has to be sneaky. He tries hard not to be seen or heard. Get in quietly and get out with the goods, undetected. But God is saying here, "Look, you are not in darkness; you are not ignorant of the coming thief. At least you shouldn't be. Why? Because I've given you my Word. I've given you the light[92] that exposes the coming thief. You can know when that thief is coming." But we have to read his Word. We have to study. There is a clear expectation upon God's people. We are to be found waiting at the window when the thief arrives.

We Christians are admonished over and over again to not let that Day take us off guard. We are told plainly that we are not to be in darkness regarding the Tribulation, that that Day should overtake us as a thief.[93] The third chapter of Revelation, the letter written to the church in Sardis, confirms this principle. God says to that church: "if you will not watch, I will come upon you as a thief, and you will not know what hour I come upon you."[94] The expectation here is that by our watching we won't be taken off guard. Then he takes it a step further and declares that if we don't watch we won't know the

---

[90] Daniel 3:25
[91] Hosea 7:1
[92] Psalms 119:105
[93] 1 Thessalonians 5:1-5
[94] Revelation 3:3

timing of the arrival of the thief. This seems to imply that not only can we know but that we are expected to know when the thief arrives. But how, exactly, are we to know when that Day will arrive as a thief? For what should we be watching? Is it some sort of inner feeling? No, feelings are deceptive.[95] Rather, we should be watching for the things we're told about in the Bible.

How did the Thessalonians "know perfectly" about that Day? They knew the same way the Bereans knew, from the Scriptures, which we refer to as the Old Testament. In Paul's day it wasn't considered "old," whatever that means. Those were the Scriptures the Bereans studied to confirm that Paul was telling the truth.[96] And while the Thessalonians were not as diligent in their study as the Bereans, the teachings came from the same place, the Old Testament. So what Scripture references would Paul have used to teach the Thessalonians about the suddenness of that Day?

In an Instant, Suddenly

Now Paul was no ordinary Jew. When it came to the things written in the law of God he was zealous. He called himself a Hebrew of Hebrews.[97] And he said he was taught according to the strictness of the law and was zealous toward God.[98] When he converted to Christianity I imagine he studied the Scriptures with renewed zeal as he sought to fulfill the great purpose God had for his life. After all, he was sent to many distant lands to proclaim salvation through Yahshua the Christ and to show how Yahshua fulfilled the prophecies of the Scriptures. To say that he was familiar with the Scriptures would be an understatement. It's within this frame of reference that Paul taught about that Day, even reminding them that they "know perfectly" how the day of the Lord is to arrive.[99] Now if Paul could

---

[95] Jeremiah 17:9
[96] Acts 17:11
[97] Philippians 3:5
[98] Acts 22:3
[99] 1 Thessalonians 5:2

speak so confidently regarding his knowledge of that Day how much more should we, the generation to whom the book has been unsealed in these last days?[100]

What did Paul see in the Old Testament Scriptures that would lead him to teach of the sudden destruction at the start of that Day? One of the first things he may have noticed about that Day is the sudden change in the posture of our great Jehovah. We see in Isaiah 42 a contrast between our Lord's first coming and the time leading to his second. The first twelve verses speak of the first coming of Christ: "A bruised reed he will not break. He will not cry out, nor cause his voice to be heard in the street." But the language is diametrically opposed to this starting in verse 13: "He shall cry out, yes shout aloud!" In verse 14 we see this admission: "I have held my peace a long time." And this is exactly what we see Paul teach in Romans 9 regarding the longsuffering of God before the final destruction of the wicked.[101] Furthermore, we see Peter teach the same principle of longsuffering in 2 Peter 3:8-10. So we understand from Isaiah 42 that first Yahshua will arrive as the humble, suffering Servant. Then there's a long, indeterminate span of time. After which he stands up to intervene in the affairs of men in a very direct and obvious manner, even likening his actions to a woman travailing in child birth. And while the NKJV says he will "pant and gasp at once," the KJV uses the much more vivid translation of "destroy and devour at once." This is then followed with: "I will lay waste the mountains and hills," which speaks of utter desolation coming to greater and lesser nations.[102]

Christ or Elijah or the Prophet?

I want to point out an interesting tidbit while we're on the subject of the suffering Servant. When John the Baptist began

---

[100] Daniel 12:4
[101] Romans 9:22
[102] Isaiah 42:14-15

preaching to prepare the way for the arrival of Yahshua, there was much dispute and disagreement among the religious men of the day. In John 1:25 they asked John the Baptist, why are you baptizing if you are not the Christ or Elijah or the prophet? In spite of all their time studying the law the religious leaders of the day, as a whole, were really pretty clueless regarding the prophecies.[103] They knew that Elijah was to return before that Day.[104] They also knew of a triumphant Savior King, the Messiah. And they knew of some obscure reference to a prophet that Moses said would be sent to them. They were told to listen to that prophet and that he would be like Moses.[105] But because of the hardness of their hearts they were unable to put it all together. They didn't understand that Yahshua would first come as that Prophet to whom Moses said they were to listen; the spotless lamb led to the slaughter, wounded for our transgressions.[106] This lack of understanding among the religious leaders of the day is a foreshadowing of our day. Many teachers today believe Yahshua will return to his people first in glory[107] rather than as Judge. But his Word tells us that judgment begins at the house of God.[108] Well, if this is the age of grace then judgment is yet in the future. Therefore that judgment spoken of must be when our Lord rises up to enter into judgment with the people of the earth. This is one reason why it's so important to study the whole Word of God, with the right spirit. Let us not be deceived into thinking we know how things will play out. Rather, may we labor in the Word and study to show ourselves approved.[109]

From Savior to Judge

---

[103] Matthew 16:3
[104] Malachi 4:5
[105] Deuteronomy 18:15
[106] Isaiah 53
[107] Isaiah 66:5
[108] 1 Peter 4:17
[109] 2 Timothy 2:15

At the end of that long period of longsuffering, which we refer to as the age of grace, Yahshua suddenly changes posture from longsuffering Savior to righteous Judge. This is confirmed by other texts as well. Jeremiah 23 speaks of the Branch of Righteousness, whom we know to be Yahshua, coming to execute judgment and righteousness in the earth (verse 5) in the latter days (verse 20). Micah 1:8 says "Therefore I will wail and howl, I will go stripped and naked; I will make a wailing like the jackals and a mourning like the ostriches." Isaiah 3:13 describes a time when our Lord stands up to plead, and stands to judge the people. Notice the picture here of Jehovah, sitting, patiently enduring the increasing wickedness of the people with much longsuffering[110] until the fullness of the Gentiles come in[111]; until all those who want to, find salvation through Yahshua during the age of grace. Then God suddenly stands up to enter into judgment with the world. And we see in the very next verse, Isaiah 3:14, God will enter into judgment even with the elders of his people for the way they led, or rather misled, the people of God.

This word picture is repeated again in Isaiah 33:10 when he says, "Now I will rise, now I will be exalted, now I will lift myself up." And again in Isaiah 31:2 we see that he will "arise against the house of evildoers." Associated with that "rising up" is a time of healing just prior to the beginning of that Day. In Malachi 4:2 we read that he will "arise with healing in his wings," after which his people will "go out" of whatever country to which this healing comes. (The curious student of the Word may wonder why, when, and from where they are leaving and to what destination they are heading.) This is that time of healing I just discussed. In Isaiah 60:2 we see that even as darkness covers the earth and deep darkness the people (the Tribulation), the Lord will arise over his people that his glory may be seen upon them. In Isaiah 51:9 we observe an emphatic prayer of the people (before the Tribulation) that the arm, or strength, of the Lord would awake (or rise up) as in the ancient days

---

[110] Romans 9:22
[111] Romans 11:25

when his mighty works were clearly seen in the earth. In Isaiah 28:21 we see the Lord will "rise up" in anger to do his awesome work and bring to pass his unusual act (the Tribulation). (Habakkuk tells us it's a work so incredible that many will not believe it even when told.[112]) In Zephaniah 3:8 the Lord admonishes us to wait for him until the Day he rises up for plunder, to pour on the kingdoms all his fierce anger, wherein the earth will be devoured by the fire of his jealousy (the Tribulation).

In Fierce Anger

So we see that this rising up of the Lord in fierce anger describes the beginning of that Day which we call the Tribulation. This rising up occurs suddenly and with great destruction after a time of unprecedented peace and security on the earth. Perhaps this is why Yahshua himself said, as recorded in Revelation 16:15, "Behold, I am coming as a thief." It's as if our Lord wants to remove any doubt about how he would make his presence known in the earth once again after a long period of longsuffering and mercy; what we refer to as the age of grace. Now, the context of that quote is in the midst of the final judgments being poured out on the unrepentant wicked of the earth. So, taken together with Revelation 3:3, which is directed towards his people, we see a message that says: if you watch, you'll know when I'm coming as a thief. You will know when that Day is going to arrive. But if you don't watch I'll come upon you unexpectedly as a thief. Either way he's coming as a thief and that Day will begin with sudden destruction. But it's our choice whether we'll be waiting at the window, fully ready and aware in that hour, or still asleep in our beds.

We can easily search for this phrase "fierce anger" and find Scripture discussing that Day. At the opening of Zephaniah 2 we see a command that the people of God are to be assembled before the fierce anger of the Lord comes upon them; before that Day passes

---

[112] Habakkuk 1:5

like chaff.[113] Then in verse 3 we see that the assembling of the people is for the purpose of seeking the Lord, or repentance, discussed earlier. We can assume then that the time of healing and repentance occurs while the people are assembled. And while it's unrealistic to think all the people can be assembled at one time and one place before that Day begins, there is an assembling of people today that makes much more sense. Huge stadiums have been built all across the land which hold up to sixty thousand people, on the low end, and up to a hundred ten thousand on the high end. Perhaps this is why Isaiah predicted it would be a good year before the trouble would come.[114] That's about how long it would take to visit all the major stadiums.

One may perform a search for "fierce anger" and be tempted to immediately dismiss many of the Scripture references, thinking they speak only of a time long ago. And while this may be true of some of them we have to be careful not to overlook the dual nature of prophecy. As we'll see later when discussing Moses, Jeremiah and Daniel many times we're given prophecies in the Bible which are to be applied to two, or even three, generations separated by a great span of time. So while some texts may obviously be addressed to us, such as Jeremiah 30:24 ("The fierce anger of the LORD will not return until He has done it, and until He has performed the intents of His heart. In the latter days you will consider it."), others are not as obvious. Among the less obvious ones are those found in Jeremiah 25 when discussing the sudden and complete destruction of a nation called Babylon, also connected to the start of that Day, which I'll discuss later. The reason these are less obvious is because the connections to our day are a little more involved. But to see the whole picture we have to make those connections.

Babylon's Sudden Destruction

---

[113] Zephaniah 2:1-2
[114] Isaiah 32:10

It's this same Babylonian nation, or city-state, that Isaiah 47 speaks of when describing her desolation and sudden downfall.[115] And Jeremiah, again in chapters 50 and 51, speaks of this nation of Babylon that will fall suddenly.[116] And the book of Habakkuk addresses this great nation of the Chaldeans, but goes one step further, telling us that her creditors are among the troops coming against her suddenly.[117] And as if all these "old" Testament verses regarding the sudden downfall of Babylon are not enough, we find "new" Testament Scripture which says the same thing. But while one could argue the "old" has already happened long ago in history, it's impossible to make the same argument regarding this "new" Babylon mentioned throughout the book of Revelation, which was written shortly after the time of Christ. For in the New Testament we read that the utter and complete destruction of an end-time nation, or city-state, or great city, referred to as Babylon, will take only one hour.[118]

There's one last connection I want to make before moving on. I'm sure for many of us the foremost question on our mind is, quite honestly, ourselves. What happens to us, those whom God says he knows trusts in him[119] when that Day begins with sudden destruction? While many have accepted the pre-trib rapture doctrine as the likely answer to that question I'd like to ask the reader to have an open mind as we take a look at God's Word. The most important thing we can do is honor God. And by diligently studying his whole Word we are showing him honor. We esteem his Word higher than anything else, even our own preferences or desires. May we be like Jeremiah who said "your word was to me the joy and rejoicing of my heart." [120] Or like Ezekiel who ate the scroll and it was like honey.[121] Or like John in the book of Revelation who

---

[115] Isaiah 47:11
[116] Jeremiah 51:8
[117] Habakkuk 2:7
[118] Revelation 18:10
[119] Nahum 1:7
[120] Jeremiah 15:16
[121] Ezekiel 3:3

ate the scroll even though he was told ahead of time it would cause his stomach to feel bitter.[122] With this attitude of reverence toward the Word of God let's press on and see where the connections lead us.

We've already established that the Day will begin with sudden destruction. And we've established that Babylon, whoever she may be, is also completely destroyed in just one hour sometime during the Tribulation. Later I will show in more detail why the sudden destruction of Babylon is connected to the start of the Tribulation. But for now I want to briefly make a connection to God's people.

> *Be in pain, and labor to bring forth, O daughter of Zion, like a woman in birth pangs. For now you shall go forth from the city, you shall dwell in the field, and to Babylon you shall go. There you shall be delivered; there the LORD will redeem you from the hand of your enemies.* Micah 4:10

The forth chapter of Micah begins with these words: "Now it shall come to pass in the latter days..." I put forth to the reader that this is very clear context. This is clearly speaking of our day. And once again we have this recurring theme of a woman in labor. The curious reader would aptly ask what, exactly, does God want to birth in the last days? But putting that question aside for now, I want to show that this Babylon is once again mentioned in the context of the last days. This is the same Babylon spoken of in Revelation 17 and 18. The connection I want to make here is that between Babylon and the daughter of Zion, or the people of God. It's saying that the people of God, in the last days, will be delivered out of Babylon.

Now I realize what many will say, that God's people are being delivered out of some sort of ungodly world system. To these I would only point out that in many places Babylon is spoken of as a great city (i.e. City-state), Kingdom, nation, land and mountain (symbolically, a nation) who has cities and other characteristics

---

[122] Revelation 10:9-10

associated with what we would refer to today as a sovereign nation.[123] More on that later.

It's clear from passages like this one in Micah 4 that God is concerned about his people who dwell within this latter-day Babylon. Jeremiah is in perfect harmony when he records in Jeremiah 50:4 that both Israel and Judah will depart a burning Babylon in the last days. Revelation 18:4 repeats this call to God's people to flee Babylon in the midst of her destruction. The prophecies seem to indicate that a significant percentage of God's people are dwelling in Babylon when she meets her one-hour demise.

To tie all of this together I submit yet another mention of end-time Babylon in Zechariah chapter 2. There we find these words: "Up, Zion! Escape, you who dwell with the daughter of Babylon."[124] And just a few verses later we encounter these words, as we've established in this chapter, which clearly speak of the beginning of that Day when Jehovah stands up to enter into judgment with the world:

> *Be silent, all flesh, before the LORD, for He is aroused from His holy habitation!* Zechariah 2:13

What is it about this nation of the last days, called Babylon, that would garner so much attention from the prophets?

---

[123] Jeremiah 50:12, 50:32, 51:25, 51:43, Habakkuk 1:6, Isaiah 13:19, 47:5
[124] Zechariah 2:7

Chapter 3 - It Will Not Tarry

But know this, that if the master of the house had known what hour the thief would come, he would have watched and not allowed his house to be broken into. Matthew 24:43

In the previous chapters we saw how that Day, the Tribulation, "so comes" as a thief. And we saw how it will arrive with sudden destruction, as birth pains suddenly grip a woman in labor. If we were to combine these two pictures for the sports fan we might say it'll be like a linebacker blitzing past the defenders to wallop the quarterback from his blind side. He didn't even see it coming! Now had that quarterback glanced behind him he could have rolled out of the pocket before the linebacker arrived. Sounds easy enough, right? Wrong. It's actually very hard to do when looking down field for an open receiver. It's just as hard trying to understand what the Bible really says about our day. It's easy for all the armchair quarterbacks to talk about but very hard to get right in reality.

But that's exactly what's expected of us. We are expected to study his Word intently and with great care. We're expected to know when the thief will arrive and be ready for him. But we can't skim over the Scriptures and expect to rightly understand the meaning. Now, scores of people can quote the verse that says no man knows the day or hour.[125] But what does it really mean? Many people quote that verse and say, well, that's that, we can't know when he's coming so why even bother? Others, so confident and zealous of their understanding, take it a step further and become indignant when they hear of anyone mentioning a date regarding the end of days. But is that really what that passage is talking about?

---

[125] Matthew 24:36, Mark 13:32

Matthew 24:43 says: "But know this, that if the master of the house had known what hour the thief would come, he would have watched and not allowed his house to be broken into." It's sort of like saying, well, if the quarterback had eyes in the back of his head he wouldn't have gotten walloped! Wow, if we can't know when the thief arrives then we have to admit that Yahshua (Jesus) is taunting us!

Does that sound like something he would do to his people? Would Yahshua taunt his own people with impossibilities? Or is there more depth to this passage than meets the eye? Many of Yahshua's teachings were in the form of parables which are difficult to understand. And we already know that the prophecies for our day are notoriously difficult to understand. So let's take a look at that passage more closely.

The Righteous and the Wicked

In the previous chapter I spoke of the two references in the book of Revelation that mention how Yahshua will stand up in judgment "as a thief." One was written to God's people[126], the other appeared in the context of the judgments being poured out upon unrepentant sinners.[127] (What an odd place to remind us to watch. It seems to stick out like a sore thumb.) I tried to show that Scripture directly links this approach as a thief with the arrival of sudden destruction. The thief and sudden destruction go hand in hand. And in Matthew 24 we see another reference to the thief which also is associated with the wicked. Verses 48 through 51 speak of the evil servant who decided that the Master was taking too long to return. So that evil servant began to mistreat the people around him and take part in activities which are not befitting a child of God. Now look at what we're told about that evil servant. Verse 50 says: "the master of that servant will come on a day when he is

---

[126] Revelation 3:3
[127] Revelation 16:15

not looking for him and at an hour that he is not aware of." Look closely. The servant is not looking and he's not aware of the hour.

Without question he's not looking. But he's also not aware of that hour?! Wait a minute. Stop the presses! Would it not have been sufficient to just say he's not looking? Why tell us he's not aware of the hour? I thought we weren't supposed to know the hour. This is exactly what Revelation 3:3 is saying as well. It says, "...if you will not watch, I will come upon you as a thief, and you will not know what hour I will come upon you." See that? You won't know what hour I will come upon you, IF you don't watch. Out of all the many hours that Day could begin, you won't know which one it will be. Not only that, you won't know when he will come "upon" you.

If you're not ready spiritually when that Day arrives, you're going to be sorry. Matthew 24:46 calls the wise and faithful servant "blessed" upon his arrival, much the same way Shadrach, Meshach, and Abed-Nego were blessed to survive the furnace heated seven times hot.[128] In fact, the first thing king Nebuchadnezzar did when he saw they miraculously survived was to bless their God, the only true God, Jehovah. This is a foreshadowing of things to come. Zephaniah 3:20 tells us that God will give his people "fame and praise among the people of the earth" during the time of his fierce anger.[129] After all, we are his witnesses in the earth.[130] The wicked servant is not so fortunate. They will become as the dust before the wind on that Day.[131] Many may consider this "dust" to be just so much poetry. But the weapon exists today to fulfill this literally. He says he will "come upon" or "come against" the evil servant.[132] In Isaiah we find similar language when speaking of the same point in time, the beginning of the Day of the Lord. Isaiah 3:10-11 says: "Say to the righteous that it shall be well with them, for they shall eat the

---

[128] Daniel 3:28, Isaiah 43:2
[129] Zephaniah 3:8
[130] Isaiah 43:10, 43:12, 44:8, Acts 1:8
[131] Malachi 4:3, Zephaniah 1:17
[132] Revelation 3:3

fruit of their doings. Woe to the wicked! It shall be ill with him, for the reward of his hands shall be given him."[133]

Now, that Day will arrive as a thief, with sudden destruction, to both the righteous and the wicked. But we see that there's a distinction in the outcome. In that Day it will be obvious to everyone who served the Lord and who did not.[134] When that Day begins the righteous are found bearing good fruit by their doings. It will be well with them, relatively speaking. But the wicked will receive the reward of his hands, his doings. Yahshua taught this principle in Matthew 7:19 when he said every tree that does not bear good fruit will be cut down and cast into the fire. James also confirmed this principle when he acknowledged that we are saved by grace, through faith, but there will always be outward evidence of every true heart change.[135] Our religion is worthless if we don't do those things that please God.[136]

"That" Day

But of that day and hour no one knows, not even the angels of heaven, but My Father only. Matthew 24:36

So if we can't know the day or hour, why are we being taunted for something that's impossible to know? But if we can know the timing why does it say we can't know the day or hour? The correct answer to that question has escaped some of the greatest minds the world has known. But when we compare all the messages of the prophets the pieces start to come together. "Who can I cause to understand the message? Line upon line, precept upon precept; a little here, a little there."[137]

---

[133] Jeremiah 17:10, 21:14, 32:19
[134] Malachi 3:18
[135] Ephesians 2:8, James 2:17-18
[136] James 1:27
[137] Isaiah 28:9-10

We've already established that the Day begins like a quarterback that's about to be walloped from his blind side. But when the Scripture says we can't know the day or hour, is it speaking of the beginning of that Day when Yahshua stands up to enter into judgment with the world? I submit to the reader that no, it's not talking about the beginning of that Day. Rather, it's talking about the end of that Day, which culminates with the physical return of Christ to earth. But how can we know for sure? Try reading through Matthew 24 with all of this in mind. When you get to verse 36 where he says "but of that day and hour no one knows," do you know which day he's talking about? What is "that" day? In the previous verse, 35, he talks about heaven and earth passing away. Is that the day he's talking about? Or how about verse 34 in which he says: "until all these things take place." Is that the day to which he's referring, the culmination of all the things he spoke of prior to verse 34? Or how about the event described in verses 29 through 31, which is the physical return of Christ, the sounding of the great trumpet, and the gathering of his elect? Is that the day and hour no one knows? Or does his statement in verse 36 answer one of the three questions asked in verse 3?

Matthew 25 sheds a little more light on this subject. The parable being taught here is that of the ten virgins. Five were wise and five foolish. Five were accepted by the Bridegroom and the other five were not. Verse 10 tells us that the five who were wise were accepted into the wedding and then the door was shut. But in verse 12 the Bridegroom tells the five who were foolish, "I don't know you." Finally, in verse 13, we find this same statement: "Therefore keep watch, because you do not know the day or the hour." It can be concluded, then, that the exact day or hour we can't know about is when the door is finally shut. While we are alive and have breath, the door stands open for us. Until the day we die we can choose to repent and believe in Yahshua for salvation. That was true for the two sinners who were executed with our Lord. One repented and believed and inherited eternal life; the other refused and died in his sin. For those alive during the Tribulation this holds true as well. Those who refuse the mark still have opportunity for repentance.[138] But when Yahshua the Christ appears in heaven the angels will gather those who are his but the door will be shut to the rest. The wicked of the earth who are alive at that point and who fought in the battle against God's elect will be "killed with the sword which proceeded from the mouth of Him who sat on the horse."[139] So we see there is also a clear connection between the return of Christ and the day and hour no one knows. But is this enough? Perhaps there's another layer to this that many don't realize.

The Day and Hour No One Knows

In every culture throughout time people have had certain ways of saying things which, if taken literally, may not make much sense. These are called figures of speech, or idioms. Today when we ask someone if the cat has their tongue we're not asking about a real cat. It's a cute way of pointing out that someone is having trouble speaking. The same was true of the Jewish culture when Christ walked the earth. He was a Jew who spoke like a Jew using the Jewish idioms of the day. It's for this reason that some of the things he said are so confusing to us today. Over time we've lost the meanings of some of those expressions.

However, some have pointed out that this phrase, "the day and hour no one knows," is a Jewish idiom pointing to the Feast of Trumpets, also known as Rosh Hashanah.[140] In Leviticus 23 Jehovah set forth, through Moses, eight "feasts of the Lord" which were to be observed as holy convocations.[141] Seven were to be observed at the appointed times throughout the year. The eighth was the weekly Sabbath rest on the seventh day of each week. Now, one of those

---

[138] Revelation 14:9-11

[139] Revelation 19:21

[140] Avi Ben Mordechai, *Signs in the Heavens* (Millenium 7000 Communications Int'l, 1996), p.293.

[141] Leviticus 23:2

annual feasts was different from the other six. The Feast of Trumpets was to begin on the first day of the month.[142] But their method of counting days and months and seasons was very much unlike ours. Their months always began at a new moon. And a new moon was declared when it was formally verified by two witnesses that the first sliver of the new moon was visible in the sky. Therefore no one knew when the Feast of Trumpets would begin until it was formally verified and declared. It was, without doubt, the hour and day no one knew.

Set It Aside For Now

And He said to them, "It is not for you to know times or seasons which the Father has put in His own authority." Acts 1:7

Before we can continue we have to deal with this potentially troubling verse in Acts. After Yahshua was raised from the dead he remained on the earth another forty days and continued to teach his disciples.[143] But the people still didn't understand the doctrine of longsuffering that we discussed earlier. They still believed that Yahshua would quickly usher in his kingdom. They didn't realize that the start of that Day would still be another two thousand years in the future. So the first thing they asked him about was the restoration of the lost tribes of Israel. The disciples knew from the Scriptures that the northern kingdom, the northern ten tribes, would be restored to the land of Israel at the end of the age.[144] So, naturally, they wanted to know when his kingdom rule would begin. And here in Acts 1:7 he gives them the answer they needed to hear at the time. He tells them, look, you don't need to know about that right now. Then verse eight begins with "But." He's saying in verse eight: but here's what you do need to know about. You will receive power when the Holy Spirit comes upon you and you're going to be my

---

[142] Leviticus 23:24
[143] Acts 1:3
[144] Ezekiel 37

witnesses in this city, Jerusalem, in Samaria (the northern kingdom they just asked about), and to the farthest parts of the earth. He was telling them what they were to be focused upon during the age of grace.

To further illustrate this point I want to point out a couple things about that last phrase from verse seven: "put in His own authority." The word "put" is Strong's G5087. Its definition carries with it the thought of laying or setting something aside. And the word "authority" is Strong's G1849. It's defined as, simply, the liberty to do as one pleases. It has a sense of privilege associated with it. With this understanding we can say he was instructing his people that they didn't need to be concerned with the end of the age at that time which the Father, in his wisdom, had set aside for a time because it was fully within his liberty to do that which pleases him. And now at the end of the age we can truly see with 20/20 hindsight that "God so loved the world that he gave his only begotten Son, that whosoever believes on him should not perish but have everlasting life."[145] It pleased the Father to set aside his Kingdom rule for a very long time that a great number of lost sheep would be found by him.

One Specific Day

> *For the vision is yet for an appointed time; but at the end it will speak, and it will not lie. Though it tarries, wait for it; because it will surely come, it will not tarry.* Habakkuk 2:3

I'm sure you've heard people say the Tribulation can start at any time. While it's true we should always be watching and praying this notion that the Tribulation can start at any time is just not true. Scripture is very clear that the days are numbered. So let's put aside all of the opinions we've heard about the Tribulation and see what the Bible actually says. The first notion we have to address is why Yahshua said the days would be "shortened."

---

[145] John 3:16

*And unless those days were shortened, no flesh would be
saved; but for the elect's sake those days will be shortened.*
Matthew 24:22

Many people read this and think that somehow God's original
plan had to be changed. They surmise that perhaps our great, all-
knowing Jehovah, who saw everything from the beginning of time
and declared how things would be[146], somehow miscalculated the
severity of those days. Maybe God had to scrap his plan A and turn
to plan B and end those days sooner than he would've liked. No, the
truth is that this word "shortened" is not the best translation. The
original Greek word is Strong's G2856, which means "to dock or
abridge or curtail."[147] The phrase "to shorten" makes it sound like it
was afterthought. But, as we'll see, this couldn't be further from the
truth. Rather, what this is saying is that had Yahshua not abridged,
or curtailed, or put an end to, those days, everyone would perish; all
life on earth would die out. And that is clearly not in God's plans for
our earth anytime soon. This curtailing of those days was not at all
an afterthought. Jehovah knows exactly when that Day will begin
and end.

It Will Not Tarry

*For the vision is yet for an appointed time; but at the end it will
speak, and it will not lie. Though it tarries, wait for it; because
it will surely come, it will not tarry.* Habakkuk 2:3

Another curious phrase we have to address is found in
Habakkuk 2:3. He says the vision is "yet for an appointed time." But
then he says "though it tarries, wait for it." And yet again he declares
"it will not tarry." Confused? Once again it sounds like Jehovah may
have to fall back to plan B. First he says the day is appointed, then it
seems to say it may tarry. So which one is it? Will that Day arrive on

---

[146] Isaiah 46:10
[147] Strong's Greek Dictionary entry G2856

time or will it be delayed? I believe what we see here is a prediction that it will seem to tarry, not that it will actually tarry. We're living in the days just preceding the start of that Day. Things are getting worse and worse. The people of the earth are experiencing disaster after disaster just as Yahshua said we would. These are the days of the beginning of sorrows.[148] Things are beginning to get so bad that many can't fathom that the start of that Day would tarry even a few more years. And some have become so impatient that they are beginning to teach that the Tribulation has already begun. But although it seems like that Day should've began by now, continue to wait for it, for it has an appointed day when it will begin which will be unmistakable. There is one specific day when that the Day will begin. This is confirmed over and over in Scripture.

Daniel's and John's Appointed Times

In Daniel 8 the angel Gabriel tells Daniel that "at the appointed time the end shall be."[149] This word "appointed" is defined just as you would expect. It means at a fixed time or season.[150] It's the same concept as our appointments today. You schedule an appointment with your dentist for a particular day at a particular time. It's an agreement between you and your dentist that you'll both be there on that day, at that time. In Daniel 9 a specific time frame is revealed to Daniel.[151] The events described in that time frame, which I'll discuss later, are encompassed by seventy "weeks." The word for week used here denotes a very specific duration of time. It means seven years, just as we would say a decade equals ten years. Therefore when Daniel 9:24 says, "seventy weeks are determined," the meaning we derive from this is that there is an appointed duration of time for everything that must be accomplished.

---

[148] Matthew 24:8
[149] Daniel 8:19
[150] Strong's Hebrew Dictionary entry H4150
[151] Daniel 9:24-27

In Daniel chapter 10 Daniel is made to understand that "the appointed time was long." In other words, a long time would transpire before that specific appointed day. And twice in chapter 11 Daniel is reminded that the vision he is being given for the time of the end will occur at the appointed time.[152] And finally in chapter 12, as if to remove all doubt that the events of the last days will operate against a very precise clock, Daniel is given two different counts of days. In verse 11 he's told that "from the time the daily sacrifice is taken away, and the abomination of desolation is set up, there shall be one thousand two hundred and ninety days." And in verse 12 he's told "Blessed is he who waits, and comes to the one thousand three hundred and thirty-five days." And twice in Revelation we're told about a period lasting forty-two months.[153] And twice more in Revelation we're told about a period lasting one thousand two hundred sixty days.[154] That the days are numbered should not come as any surprise to us. In John's vision recorded in the book of Revelation he is shown four angels "who had been prepared for the hour and day and month and year."[155]

In a Year and Some Days

In Isaiah 32:10 we come across this very curious statement: "In a year and some days you will be troubled, you complacent women; for the vintage will fail, the gathering will not come." Now here is where things get a little more complicated. While it's obvious that both Daniel and John are speaking of the time of the end, the context is not as clear in other places. However, after making some connections, I think we can see that to which Isaiah is referring. I will attempt to make those connections in this book, but let me point out a few things regarding Isaiah 32.

---

[152] Daniel 11:27,35
[153] Revelation 11:2, 13:5
[154] Revelation 11:3, 12:6
[155] Revelation 9:15

In this very same verse, verse 10, we see that the prophet not only has foreknowledge about the specific day that "trouble" begins but he also knows in which season it arrives. After all, he describes it as the season when the vintage, or grape harvest, will fail. This implies that the grapes are on the vine in some form or other but they don't get harvested. The astute reader will say, of course, if he knows the day of year then he also knows the season. So why do I mention this? And more importantly, why does Isaiah include something so obvious? As I've stated before, throughout the Word of God we are given points of comparison. God is allowing us the opportunity to make connections to other passages. And without these connections it's impossible to understand the message of the last days. What I'm attempting to do in this book is make the correct connections and understand the message. Setting aside Isaiah 32 for the moment, I want to bring your attention back to this concept that the days of the end are fixed. They will begin and end at exactly the appointed time our great Jehovah has predetermined.

Jeremiah's Seventy Years

> *'Then it will come to pass, when seventy years are completed, that I will punish the king of Babylon and that nation, the land of the Chaldeans, for their iniquity,' says the LORD; 'and I will make it a perpetual desolation.'* Jeremiah 25:12

Here in Jeremiah 25 we have probably one the most famously overlooked passages of the Bible. While so many hold to the belief that this is only speaking of a time long ago, by so doing they must admit that Jeremiah was a false prophet. But rarely do we hear of any such admission from one who believes that the whole Bible is the inerrant Word of God, which it is. And Jeremiah was not a false prophet. But as it stands, ancient Babylon was not made a perpetual desolation as Jeremiah states here. Yes, Babylon was conquered and people died but it was not wholly overthrown as described here and also in Jeremiah 50 and 51. Nor were the slain of the Lord from one end of the earth to the other, as we see in Jeremiah 25:33. However, there is a Day spoken of by the prophets when such unprecedented catastrophe strikes that literally the entire earth will be affected. And while I will go into this in more detail later I want to point out here that there is a specific, allotted time frame for the rule of Babylon, both ancient and present day. We see here that the number of years she is to reign supreme over the nations of the earth is limited to seventy.

I hope I've successfully dispelled some of the false notions some may have acquired about the Tribulation. This is important because if we are to truly understand that Day we must put aside the rumors and half-truths that hinder us from understanding what the Bible really has to say about that Day. After sifting through the prophecies we can see that Christ will first stand up to enter into judgment with the people of the earth after a long time of graciousness. As I'll show, the door of his patience and graciousness is about to close. And while we can't know the exact day or hour of his physical return to earth at the end of that Day, we can know, and are expected to know, when that Day will begin. Our Savior will not taunt us with ideals that are impossible to attain. Nor did he speak this proverb in vain. Rather, the promise holds true still today. "If the master of the house had known what hour the thief would come, he would have watched and not allowed his house to be broken into."[156] Whether or not we allow our house to be broken into is completely up to us. It's our choice to be spiritually alert and ready, fully aware of that hour and bearing good fruit, or still sleeping the night away. If you knew the thief would arrive tonight at midnight would you still go to sleep or would you make the changes necessary to prevent your house from being broken into?

> *Let the wicked forsake his way, and the unrighteous man his*
> *thoughts; let him return to the LORD, and He will have mercy*
> *on him; and to our God, for He will abundantly pardon.*
> Isaiah 55:7

---

[156] Matthew 24:43

Chapter 4 - Daniel's "Ah, ha!" Moment

Several times already in this book I've alluded to a city-state, or nation, in the Bible referred to as Babylon. That she played an important role in the lives of the people of Jehovah throughout history should be apparent. The Bible mentions her often. This name "Babylon" is mentioned no less than two hundred ninety-one times in the Bible. A quick glance at the history books will reveal that there was, in fact, a great empire called Babylon. It's believed she was at the height of her power some five to six hundred years before the time of Christ. But the Bible also speaks of a Babylon in the context of the last days. As I stated earlier, like ancient Babylon before her, this latter day Babylon meets her demise suddenly after seventy years of supreme rule over the other nations of the earth.

As you conduct your own study of that ancient empire, I want to point something out which may not be obvious. The years given for certain dates in the past may not be perfectly accurate. Historians sometimes agree and sometimes disagree. Often times the leading historians will disagree by as much as a few years when attempting to pinpoint the exact year of an event. The truth is that when studying events that transpired long ago, historians and archaeologists do the best they can with the artifacts they find. Many times the records just aren't sufficient to prove beyond all doubt the specific year of each major event. I might remind the reader that even the year of our Lord's birth, which occurred roughly two thousand years ago, is hotly disputed. Keep this in mind when reading Bible teachings of the last days. Any teaching that uses a date from long ago to predict a future event should be taken with a grain of salt.

When speaking of both ancient and present-day Babylon it is the height of her powerful empire that serves as a backdrop for much text in the Bible. Jeremiah lived in the time preceding the taking of Judah captive to Babylon. He warned the people of Judah, the southern kingdom of Israel, many times that they would be defeated by, and carried away captive to, Babylon for turning away from God and worshipping idols. He even told them how long they would remain in Babylon. It wouldn't be just a few years, nor even just a generation. No, their captivity in Babylon was to last a lifetime for many. They were to remain in Babylon for seventy years, at which time they would be set free to return to the land of Judah.

This Babylonian captivity also serves as the context for the book of Daniel. Daniel was one of the children of Judah in whom was found no blemish and who also was found to be knowledgeable and intelligent, who was chosen to serve in the king's palace.[157] It is this same Daniel who was very much loved by God[158], and who recorded for us in his book many of the prophecies which concern our day. Now, Daniel was just a youth when he was taken captive to Babylon to serve in the king's court. During his lifetime he learned many things, was considered one of the wisest men alive[159], and was given incredible dreams and visions which are recorded in his book. But it wasn't until he was nearing the end of his life that he fully understood one particular prediction as it actually happened. It was as if a light bulb blinked on in his head and for the first time he understood the destiny of God's people both for his day and for the end of the age, our day. But like all Scripture speaking of our day it's somewhat concealed from view.

Three Distinct Periods

> *Seventy weeks are determined for your people and for your holy city, to finish the transgression, to make an end of sins, to make reconciliation for iniquity, to bring in everlasting*

---

[157] Daniel 1:3-6
[158] Daniel 9:23, 10:11, 19
[159] Daniel 1:16-20

righteousness, to seal up vision and prophecy, and to anoint the Most Holy. Daniel 9:24

Daniel chapter 9 contains one of the most fiercely debated passages of the Bible and, as I'll show, one of the most overlooked passages as well. The context of this chapter is that of the overthrow of ancient Babylon and the end of Judah's Babylonian captivity. Daniel was now an old man who had been expecting this event his entire life. He knew Jeremiah's prophecy which foretold that Judah's captivity would last seventy years.[160] And I'm sure he knew of Isaiah's prophecy that Judah would be released by a king named Cyrus.[161] So it's at this point in time, soon after these prophecies came true, that Daniel experienced the events of this chapter. And within this text is potentially the answer every true believer today desires to know: When will Christ return? Recorded in this chapter is a passage which seems to give a timeframe for several major events throughout history. Among them is Yahshua's first appearance on earth as suffering Servant and his return as all-powerful Messiah at the end of this age. For in verse 24 we see that the conclusion of the "seventy weeks" will usher in everlasting righteousness.

This chapter lays out three periods of time: the sixty-two, the seven and the one. These time periods have been interpreted in different ways. Some have even combined the sixty-two and seven to get sixty-nine. The Hebrew word for "weeks" is shabuwas[162], which means "sevens." The English translators use the word "weeks," meaning seven days or seven years. I believe this word is being used to describe a period of seven years just as we use the word decade to describe a period of ten years. Therefore, sixty-two shabuwas would be 434 years (62 x 7 = 434 years). Seven shabuwas would be 49 years (7 x 7 = 49). One shabuwa would be 7 years (1 x 7 = 7 years). In fact, this is why people say the Tribulation will last

---

[160] Jeremiah 25:11-12, 29:10
[161] Isaiah 44:28, 45:1
[162] Strong's Hebrew Dictionary entry H7620

seven years. They note that this period of one shabuwa must be the
last seven years before Christ returns.

> 25 *Know therefore and understand, that from the going forth*
> *of the command to restore and build Jerusalem until Messiah*
> *the Prince, there shall be seven weeks and sixty-two weeks; the*
> *street shall be built again, and the wall, even in troublesome*
> *times. 26 And after the sixty-two weeks Messiah shall be cut*
> *off, but not for Himself; and the people of the prince who is to*
> *come shall destroy the city and the sanctuary. The end of it*
> *shall be with a flood, and till the end of the war desolations are*
> *determined. 27 Then he shall confirm a covenant with many*
> *for one week; but in the middle of the week he shall bring an*
> *end to sacrifice and offering. And on the wing of abominations*
> *shall be one who makes desolate, even until the consummation,*
> *which is determined, is poured out on the desolate.*
> Daniel 9:25-27

While verse 24 establishes an overall timeframe of seventy
weeks, we learn in verses 25-27 that those seventy weeks are
divided into three distinct periods: the sixty-two, the seven, and the
one. Now, here's a riddle for you: how many commands do you see
in verse 25, one or two? Many teachers have taught that verse 25
speaks of only one command. But in fitting with the dual nature of
prophecy, I believe there are two. With this understanding here's
how it could be understood: from the going forth of a command to
restore Jerusalem, there will be 434 years. And from the going forth
of another command to restore Jerusalem, there will be 49 years. Is
it possible to prove there were 434 years between the release of
Judah and the cutting off of Messiah? No, as I said earlier, dates that
long ago are often in dispute. But, as I'll show, there's no need to go
that far back in history. We have all the information we need by
looking at modern history.

The Missing Marker

It's interesting to note that if you read through Daniel 9 you might notice there's a missing marker. If we look closely we can see there are beginning and ending markers, or events, for each of these time periods, except one.

Verse 25:
- The sixty-two will begin with a command to restore Jerusalem, even in troublesome times
- The seven will begin with a command to restore Jerusalem, even in troublesome times

Verse 26:
- The sixty-two will end with the crucifixion of the Messiah.

Verse 27:
- The one will begin when someone confirms a covenant
- In the middle of the one someone will bring an end to sacrifice and offering
- The one will end at the consummation, or completion, of the matter.

So we have two markers to denote the sixty-two. The sixty-two has both a beginning and an ending marker, or event, associated with it. Let's jump ahead and look at the period of one seven. We see its beginning marker is the covenant with many. Further, its middle marker is the breaking of the same covenant. And we see the last marker given is the end of this period of one, or seven years, which concludes the whole matter, which is the return of Christ our Savior.

62 Start - Restore Jerusalem
62 End - Messiah cut off
7 Start - Restore Jerusalem
7 End - ???
1 Start - Covenant with many
1 Middle - Abomination of desolation
1 End - 70 weeks concluded, Return of Christ

Here's where the confusion comes in. The seven has a beginning marker, which is another command to restore Jerusalem. But where's the marker for the end of the seven? People read this passage and they think to themselves "the 49 years end and then the last 7 years begin the very next day." And then entire books are written with this in mind. And people have this in their mind when they read the Bible and all the end-time books and think "it just makes perfect sense." And it all made perfect sense to me until I started reading my Bible, the whole thing. And then it stopped making sense. But then the more I read the more I began to understand; precept upon precept, line upon line.

So where's the missing marker? Can I tell you that God is not stupid? God, in his infinite wisdom, decided that he was not going to allow any one of his servants the prophets to reveal the whole story. The mysteries of God and of the end of the age are revealed line upon line, precept upon precept. If you want to understand then you must study the whole Word of God and you must rely upon God for understanding. Someone once said to me "I re-read Revelation 17 and 18 and it's clear that Babylon is a city, not a nation." Do you see the fallacy in this statement? Where one prophet uses the word city or great city, another uses the word nation. It's only by studying the whole Word of God that we begin to understand how the pieces fit.

Daniel 9 gives us very important clues regarding the last days. And it gives us markers for each time period, except one. There's one marker which is hidden. And this is the pattern of all the prophets. Take your pick: Hosea, Daniel, Isaiah, Jeremiah, Ezekiel, Zephaniah, Micah, Malachi, etc. Each one gives a part of the picture but none describe the whole picture. This is why Isaiah 28 explains that we must set precept to precept and line to line; a little here a little there. And the end of that chapter explains that we must rely on God to help us understand.

God could have told us how it would all play out, A to Z, step by step. He could also have made it easy for everyone to find gold and diamonds. But he didn't. He decided that he would not make it easy to understand his description of the latter days. And finding gold is hard work too. That's how it is. The precious things are hard to come by. But if you really want to know, you can know. It's possible to understand.

One Prophetic Word to Two Generations

When reading some of the prophetic passages we have to realize something. We have to understand that sometimes God is speaking to two generations separated by a great span of time. History does repeat itself. Not in exactly the same way but in similar enough ways for God to be able to say the same things to two different generations. I believe this is no more evident than in the book of Jeremiah.

> *Therefore I will yet bring charges against you, says the LORD,*
> *And against your children's children I will bring charges.*
> Jeremiah 2:9

So he has a problem with those people and their grandchildren? I guess their children are OK. No, I believe what he's saying here is exactly what I've been talking about. He's going to pronounce judgment on that ancient generation and he's going to pronounce judgment on the last generation, our day. Is this really a stretch? Go all the way back to Moses' day. Even before the children of Israel entered the Promised Land after their flight from Egypt, look what Moses said:

> *For I know that after my death you will become utterly*
> *corrupt, and turn aside from the way which I have commanded*
> *you. And evil will befall you in the latter days, because you will*
> *do evil in the sight of the LORD, to provoke Him to anger*
> *through the work of your hands.* Deuteronomy 31:29

Moses was speaking prophetically about the people of his day and the people of our day. And he was given a revelation of nuclear war. Look at the very next chapter:

> *How could one chase a thousand, and two put ten thousand to flight, unless their Rock had sold them, and the LORD had surrendered them?* Deuteronomy 32:30

He's asking, look, how is it possible ten thousand of my people will be chased away by only two enemy soldiers unless the Lord was the One who allowed this? And how is it that two people could cause ten thousand to flee (or be killed)? How many pilots does a nuclear bomber have? Two.

Jeremiah's Two Visions

Let's look at this a little bit further. What happens in the first chapter of Jeremiah? Can I tell you that the first chapter is going to set the stage for the whole book? He's given two visions, which I will paraphrase:

> 11 What do you see? I see a branch of an almond tree.
> 12 Good job. I'm ready to perform my word.
> 13 Now what do you see? I see a boiling pot facing away from the north.
> 14 Out of the north calamity shall break forth...

The branch of an almond tree is speaking of the people of Jeremiah's day. Verse 12 explains verse 11. The branch, OK, I'm ready to perform my Word. This is exactly the scenario we see in Isaiah 48:3. In that verse Jehovah explains to our generation things he did long ago. "I have declared the former things from the beginning; they went forth from My mouth, and I caused them to hear it. Suddenly I did them, and they came to pass." This is the same concept as Jeremiah 1:11-12. He's telling us that long ago, when his prophets walked the earth, he told them what to say and then soon after that he did them.

Now, the boiling pot must be ancient Babylon coming to attack Judah, right? Well, that's only half the story. That did, in fact, happen during Jeremiah's day. But there's a dual prophecy here. Notice the language used in verses 14 through 16. Babylon is not directly referenced there. To paraphrase, it says "I am calling all the families of the kingdoms of the north" against My people because of their sin and rebellion. People take this to only mean ancient Babylon coming against Judah. But the language used is very broad rather than very specific. It's as if the door is being left wide open for this passage to mean more than one thing. And this is the pattern of judgment we see all throughout the Bible. When God's people as a whole, wherever they may be living, become inundated by the sin of that land, God will send against them a destroyer to chastise them for their rebellion. When we begin to examine all the prophetic text written of Babylon (such as Jeremiah 25, 29, 50, 51; Isaiah 13, 18, 47; Revelation 14, 17, 18 to name a few) we soon realize that this nation coming against God's people "out of the north" is speaking of both an ancient event as well as a present-day event; an event to take place in our day. It's said that ancient Babylon came from the north against the land of Judah. But we're also given a picture of latter day Babylon; that her destroyer will also come out of the north. Why is the pot facing away from the north in Jeremiah 1:13?

> *For out of the north a nation comes up against her (Babylon), which shall make her land desolate, and no one shall dwell therein. They shall move, they shall depart, both man and beast.* Jeremiah 50:3[163]

It could be stated that ancient Babylon's destroyer (the Medo-Persian Empire, led by King Cyrus) came out of the north to defeat Babylon. And while this is true, it's also equally true that Jeremiah was not speaking of just one Babylon, but two. This is only possible because God had foreknowledge that both ancient Babylon and present-day Babylon would be destroyed by a military force coming against them from the north.

---

[163] Text in parentheses mine.

Many Nations and Great Kings

> *So I will bring on that land all My words which I have*
> *pronounced against it, all that is written in this book, which*
> *Jeremiah has prophesied concerning all the nations. (For*
> *many nations and great kings shall be served by them also; and*
> *I will repay them according to their deeds and according to the*
> *works of their own hands.)* Jeremiah 25:13-14

It should be understood that God is actively involved throughout history in the setting up and tearing down of entire nations. This point is illustrated in Jeremiah 25. The context of this passage (verses 12-14) is the downfall of Babylon at the end of the seventy year captivity of the people of Judah. But when we look closely at this passage we see that it's not speaking just of ancient Babylon but also of a future Babylon. There are two things to which I'd like to bring your attention. The first is the phrase: all that is written in this book. God is reassuring the reader that everything written about Babylon will surely take place. This is something we should not skim over or take lightly. Deuteronomy 18 informs us that if the words of the prophet do not come to pass we are not to listen to that prophet because those words are not from the Lord.[164] Claiming to speak on the Lord's behalf is a very serious undertaking. The reason I mention this is because all the words Jeremiah spoke concerning Babylon did not come to pass. Yes, Babylon was overthrown by the Medo-Persian empire at the end of the seventy years, but not like Jeremiah seemingly described. As we'll see, this caused quite a bit of confusion in that day.

The second thing I want to bring to your attention is the statement made in verse 14. "For many nations and great kings shall be served by them also; and I will repay them according to their deeds and according to the works of their own hands." On the heels of God reassuring the reader that everything spoken against Babylon

---

[164] Deuteronomy 18:22

will surely come to pass, he then tells the reader that the scope of the prophecy is greater than we might think. He's telling us to look beyond the obvious. Look beyond the history books. He says that many nations and great kings will be served by them also. Who is the "them" to whom he's referring? Is he speaking of Babylon? No. Look at the previous verse. The context of this passage is the prophetic words spoken against the nations. He's saying many nations and great kings will be served by those same prophetic words that Jeremiah is speaking. He's reassuring us that Jeremiah's words do not apply just to ancient Babylon but also to another, yet future, nation called Babylon.

Jeremiah speaks to two different generations that span a great distance in time. We saw how Jeremiah was commissioned to speak not only to the people of his day but also to us in the last days; the generation to usher in the return of Christ. It's important because there are two extremes that we want to avoid. We can't just apply any and every prophetic text to our day without careful consideration. But the other extreme is just as detrimental. If we don't apply a prophetic text to our day, even though it should be, we won't have the complete picture.

Daniel's Hidden Clue

> 62 Start - Restore Jerusalem
> 62 End - Messiah cut off
> 7 Start - Restore Jerusalem
> 7 End - ???
> 1 Start - Covenant with many
> 1 Middle - Abomination of desolation
> 1 End - 70 weeks concluded, Return of Christ

If you remember we're looking for the missing marker of Daniel 9. All three time periods, the sixty-two, the seven, and the one, have markers, or events, associated with them. But the seven is only given a starting marker, which is a command to restore

Jerusalem. Maybe we're looking in the wrong place. Most people concentrate on the last part of Daniel 9. After all, isn't that where the important part is located? The first part of the chapter is just window-dressing, right? Let's see.

> *In the first year of his reign I, Daniel, understood by the books*
> *the number of the years specified by the word of the LORD*
> *through Jeremiah the prophet, that He would accomplish*
> *seventy years in the desolations of Jerusalem.* Daniel 9:2

It's easy to fly right by this verse. After all, isn't he just talking about the seventy years of captivity the people of Judah endured in ancient Babylon? But if there are, in fact, two Babylons, could it also be that there are two commands to restore Jerusalem as I've already shown? And if there are two commands to restore Jerusalem, could it also be that there are two "desolations" of Jerusalem? And if this really is the case, shouldn't we look for the fulfillment of this seventy year prophecy in our day? So where should we look? We're told in verse 2 where to look: "through Jeremiah the prophet." I want to bring something to your attention that multitudes have overlooked. In all the commentaries I've read regarding Daniel 9 I have yet to see anyone discuss what I'm about to show you. Look closely at Daniel 9:1-2.

"Ah, ha!"

When did Daniel understand "by the books...of Jeremiah?" It says he understood in the first year of Darius, which was just <u>after</u> Babylon fell to the Medes. I'm sure prior to this year Daniel had read the prophecies of Jeremiah many times. And from that study he knew that Babylon would ultimately fall, which would result in the return of Judah (the Jews) to the land of Judea. But it's no coincidence that Daniel mentions the year he understood about the desolations (plural) of Jerusalem. Why? Because Daniel was expecting Babylon to be completely and utterly destroyed at the end of the seventy years. Daniel was expecting Babylon to be made a

complete and utter desolation. He was expecting such complete
desolation that the land would no longer be inhabitable, even for the
animals. "And no one shall dwell therein. They shall move, they shall
depart, both man and beast."[165] But it wasn't. The Medo-Persian
Empire conquered Babylon, people died, but life in Babylon
continued. In fact, Daniel himself was in no hurry to leave Babylon.
We learn in Daniel 10:1 that he was most likely still living in Babylon
well after her fall. Some of the people of Judah did eventually leave
Babylon and return to Judea to rebuild[166], but rebuilding was a
young man's task. Daniel was nearing the end of his life at this point.
It's very likely Daniel lived out the remainder of his days in Babylon,
serving in the king's court. In fact, we learn in Daniel chapter 6, after
the old man Daniel survived the lion's den, that he continued to
prosper in the reign of Darius and Cyrus.[167]

But let's return to the first year of Darius, when Babylon was
overthrown by the Medo-Persian Empire. Daniel was undoubtedly
confused at this point. Things were not happening as Jeremiah
described them. I can imagine Daniel rushing home to search
through the scrolls of Jeremiah. Daniel must have been thinking, was
Jeremiah wrong? Was Jeremiah a false prophet? It was as if a light
bulb blinked on for Daniel. "No, Jeremiah was not a false prophet!
Now I understand!" Daniel, at that point, began to understand that
contained within Jeremiah's prophecies are two desolations of
Jerusalem, two seventy-year periods, two Babylons, two commands
to restore Jerusalem, and two restorations of God's people to God's
holy land, Zion. We see that God hides things right in plain sight. But
does Daniel give us another place to look? In verse 11 he mentions
the Law of Moses:

> *Yes, all Israel has transgressed Your law, and has departed so*
> *as not to obey Your voice; therefore the curse and the oath*
> *written in the Law of Moses the servant of God have been*

---

[165] Jeremiah 50:3
[166] See the books of Ezra and Nehemiah
[167] Daniel 6:28

> *poured out on us, because we have sinned against Him.*
> Daniel 9:11

Is our destiny somehow tied to the Torah, the first five books of the Bible? As we saw earlier, it absolutely is. Moses, in the book of Deuteronomy, speaks concerning both his day and our day. In Deuteronomy 31:29 he writes that "evil will befall you (God's people) in the latter days, because you will do evil in the sight of the LORD, to provoke Him to anger through the work of your hands."[168] He even pens a song about our day[169] which we find the angels singing in the book of Revelation.[170] After searching through the scrolls of Jeremiah and Moses, Daniel had an "Ah, ha!" moment. For the first time he fully understood that they both were speaking to two generations separated by a great span of time. When things didn't happen like he thought they would he finally understood that Jeremiah and Moses were speaking of God's people, both of his day and our day, who live in a land that God refers to as Babylon in both cases. We weren't given a specific ending marker for the 49 years in Daniel chapter 9. But we were given something even better. We were given a picture that describes what will befall God's people in the latter days. By making this connection between Babylon and the end of her seventy-year reign we can see what will befall God's people who are living in Babylon at the time of the end of this age. And later I'll show that there is a connection between the end of the 49 years and the end of Babylon's seventy-year reign.

---

[168] Text in parentheses mine.
[169] Deuteronomy 31:19-32:44
[170] Revelation 15:1-3

Chapter 5 - The Beginning of the End

The key to understanding the Bible's message for the last days rests in our ability to make and understand the right connections. In the previous chapter we saw how Babylon plays an important role in the last days. Even Daniel, who was more wise than most, didn't understand just how important until he saw predicted events play out before his very eyes. This should give the rest of us hope. The message of the last days is divided among the prophets like pieces of a puzzle. But if we pay very close attention we can begin to put those pieces together. It is possible to understand.

Already we've seen, by comparing many varying texts of the Bible, how that Day will come upon an unsuspecting world like a thief. While all the world is enjoying an unprecedented time of peace and security that Day will strike us all like pains grip a woman going into labor. But God's people are not to be unaware of when that Day will arrive. After all, we are children of light, not darkness.[171] Just as Daniel was anticipating the end of Babylon's seventy-year reign, so too can we. We can know beyond any doubt that the Day is fixed in time and when it will arrive. The Day coming upon the world is appointed and will arrive at the expected hour. But there is something we must first understand. We have to know how that Day begins.

Jeremiah's 70 Years

And this whole land shall be a desolation and an astonishment, and these nations shall serve the king of Babylon seventy years.

---

[171] 1 Thessalonians 5:5

Then it will come to pass, when seventy years are completed, that I will punish the king of Babylon and that nation, the land of the Chaldeans, for their iniquity, says the LORD; and I will make it a perpetual desolation. Jeremiah 25:11-12

For thus says the LORD: After seventy years are completed at Babylon, I will visit you and perform My good word toward you, and cause you to return to this place. Jeremiah 29:10

I ended the previous chapter discussing Babylon's seventy-year reign and I find it an appropriate place to begin this discussion. We've already seen how the beginning of that Day, the Tribulation, will be unmistakable. It will truly be a day like no other. But how? As one sincere believer asked me, will the world just sort of implode? Sometimes when reading the Bible we can get that impression. The language describing that Day, at first glance, seems more fitting for a big-budget Hollywood movie. But the more we study the more we begin to recognize certain key words and phrases. As we study we begin to become familiar with the patterns. People are great at recognizing patterns. But to see the patterns we have to put in the time.

Let's take a closer look at Jeremiah 25. As I pointed out we find here a prediction that Babylon will rule the earth for seventy years, during which Judah will be in subjection to her. (Israel, the northern kingdom, had already been carried away captive to Assyria by this time.) At the end of the seventy years Babylon will be conquered and God's people will be released to return to Zion. OK, fair enough. That already happened once. But will it happen again? Is this really a dual prophecy, speaking of our day as well? Notice what else is being discussed in Jeremiah 25. There's no doubt the context of this chapter is the taking of Judah captive to Babylon. The first eight verses deal with the sin of God's people. Through Jeremiah God tells the people, "Look, you haven't been listening to Me; therefore, this is what's going to happen." Verses 9 through 11 then explain that God's people will be overthrown, conquered, and taken captive to Babylon. This pattern of judgment is discussed in

Deuteronomy.[172] This is the part of the curse that God will send against his people who become overrun with the sin of the land. After all, God's people are to reflect the God we serve. We are to be holy for he is holy.[173] We are to be light and salt in the earth.[174] We are to be his witnesses to a dying world.[175] What does the world think of our God when the people of God are overrun with sin? All throughout Scripture God declares that this thing will not stand. In Amos he asks, can two walk together unless they are agreed?[176] Something has to change and we know it won't be God doing the changing.[177]

In the previous chapter I discussed verses 12 through 14. That passage informs us that there is a fixed period of time that Babylon will reign. At the end of that time God's people will be set free. Now look at the next section, verses 15 through 26. God tells Jeremiah to take the cup of fury from his hand and cause all the nations to drink of that cup; all the nations to which he is sent and names in that passage. The reader at this point might be tempted to consider this great judgment to have occurred long ago. Before you do, let me draw your attention to verse 27. In that verse we find this phrase: "fall and rise no more." As is the pattern we see time and again in the Scriptures this chapter begins describing events of the day but eventually leads us into a discussion of the time of the end. Clearly then this chapter begins discussing the Tribulation. But the Tribulation is discussed not only in a generic sense but in a very specific way.

The Beginning of Calamity

---

[172] Deuteronomy 28:15-68
[173] 1 Peter 1:16, Leviticus 11:45, 19:2, 20:7
[174] Matthew 5:13-16
[175] Isaiah 43:10, 43:12, 44:8, Acts 1:8
[176] Amos 3:3
[177] Numbers 23:19, Psalm 102:27, Malachi 3:6, James 1:17

"For behold, I begin to bring calamity on the city which is called by My name, and should you be utterly unpunished? You shall not be unpunished, for I will call for a sword on all the inhabitants of the earth," says the LORD of hosts.'
Jeremiah 25:29

In verse 29 we find this phrase: "I begin to bring calamity." I can't overstate how important this clue is. This is exactly the type of phrase we need to begin to put the pieces together. Jehovah is telling us that what's being discussed in this passage is the <u>beginning</u> of that calamity. And by reading a bit further we realize that this beginning is coming to the city (or encampment, in the widest sense[178]) which is called by God's name. In other words the beginning of this calamity is coming to the place where God's people live, whose nation is known to largely contain the people of the one true God. Or said even more plainly, the national religion of that country is rooted in a Judeo-Christian heritage but is also deserving of punishment. He says that particular country will be punished and he will call for a sword on all the rest of the inhabitants of the earth as well.

And at that day the slain of the LORD shall be from one end of the earth even to the other end of the earth. They shall not be lamented, or gathered, or buried; they shall become refuse on the ground. Jeremiah 25:33

This passage, verses 29 through 33, clearly speaks of the beginning of the Tribulation. And we see within this passage several clues to indicate that what's being spoken of here is the very beginning of that Day. Verse 29 says "I will call for a sword." The language used here is that of something being initiated. Likewise, verse 30 says he will "roar from on high, and utter His voice...; He will roar mightily against His fold. He will give a shout..." Verse 31 says "a noise will come to the ends of the earth." Verse 32 says "disaster shall go forth...and a great whirlwind shall be raised up." Verse 33 confirms that this will be a worldwide event. Verse 38 says

---

[178] Strong's Hebrew Dictionary entry H5892

God has left his lair like a lion. It should be evident to the reader that this kind of language speaks of the initiation, or beginning, of worldwide calamity known as the Tribulation. The great whirlwind mentioned in verse 32 is a common word picture in the Bible when speaking of the start of that Day.

So while the beginning of the Tribulation is clearly being discussed I might remind the reader that the backdrop, or context, of Jeremiah 25 is the complete and utter destruction of end-time Babylon. This is not by happenstance or coincidence but by divine design. Our great Jehovah is trying to show us, at least those willing to study, that the complete and utter destruction of end-time Babylon begins the Tribulation. It's the very first event. Furthermore, we learn from this passage that that "city," or encampment, is inhabited by many of God's people and is called by his name; or as we saw, has a Judeo-Christian heritage. But in spite of being called by his name she is worthy of punishment. For we know that end-time Babylon is called the mother of harlots and of the abominations of the earth. And while this is more than enough proof for some, others may be more skeptical. For these I would encourage to read on.

Babylon Is Fallen, Is Fallen

Then I saw another angel flying in the midst of heaven, having the everlasting gospel to preach to those who dwell on the earth— to every nation, tribe, tongue, and people— saying with a loud voice, "Fear God and give glory to Him, for the hour of His judgment has come; and worship Him who made heaven and earth, the sea and springs of water." And another angel followed, saying, "Babylon is fallen, is fallen, that great city, because she has made all nations drink of the wine of the wrath of her fornication." Revelation 14:6-8

The question we're trying to answer, beyond all doubt, is when does Babylon fall relative to the Tribulation? Perhaps

Revelation 14 gives us a clue. Way back in chapter one I discussed this passage. I proposed that the hour of judgment in verse 7 is related to the half-hour of silence in Revelation 8:1. When we view this passage as an overview, or big picture view of things to come, it begins to make much more sense. The angel in verse 6 has "the everlasting gospel to preach to those who dwell on the earth." We can see a parallel to this when we consider the Great Commission. In Matthew 28 Yahshua instructs his disciples to go out into all the earth, teaching all people to keep the commandments they learned from him.[179] And we see this repeated again in Acts when he tells them they should be his witnesses in Jerusalem, Judea, Samaria, and unto the farthest most parts of the earth.[180] So we see verse 6 is speaking of the age of grace.

> 6 The gospel is preached throughout the world. This is now.
> 7 Announcement: The time of Tribulation, the hour of his judgment, is here.
> 8 Babylon is fallen, is fallen!

However, when this angel begins to speak in verse 7, with a loud voice he announces that the hour of God's judgment has arrived. It can be concluded that at this time salvation can still be found through that everlasting gospel. He's still encouraging people to fear God, give him glory and worship him who made all things. But his announcement establishes that something has changed. The time of God's judgment is now here. In the very next verse we see that an angel follows him. By this "following" we can safely conclude that there is a chronological sequence to the things we are reading. In verse eight this angel informs us that "Babylon is fallen, is fallen." That the phrase "is fallen" is stated twice tells us that she received a double judgment. She is not merely being judged, only to rise again at a later time. No, Babylon is now fallen, never more to rise. From these two verses we are allowed to see an overview of the beginning of that day. When the age of grace comes to an end, the hour, or

---

[179] Matthew 28:16-20
[180] Acts 1:8

time, of judgment has arrived. The first thing that occurs when the Tribulation begins is the utter and complete destruction of Babylon.

The astute reader may notice the events mentioned in verses 9 through 20. One may ask: how does the destruction of Babylon at the beginning of Tribulation fit with the events described in the rest of the chapter? If you notice, the events being described from verse 9 on, such as the mark of the beast, are associated with the final forty-two months of the Tribulation. So will the Tribulation only last forty-two months? No. The answer comes to us when we begin to see what's missing, not what's there. Between the end of verse 8 and the beginning of verse 9 there is a half-hour of silence. This is the same half-hour of silence I discussed in chapter one; which is mentioned in Revelation 8:1. The reason this overview jumps from the beginning of Tribulation (verse 8) to the middle of Tribulation (verse 9) is because John's vision was silent about the first forty-two months.

Babylon's Watchman

> *Babylon is fallen, is fallen! And all the carved images of her gods He has broken to the ground.* Isaiah 21:9

This phrase "Babylon is fallen, is fallen" is only found in three places in the Bible: twice in Revelation and once in Isaiah 21. And while many may be tempted to write off the events of Isaiah 21 as only occurring long ago, the downfall of ancient Babylon at the hands of the Medo-Persian warriors, they would be remiss to do so. For in that chapter there are a few phrases with which we must first come to terms. In verse 16 we're told that all the glory of Kedar (the descendants of Ishmael) will fail, or come to an end. Is this speaking of a temporary end to their glory, or a permanent end; such as that found in other text regarding the last days, wherein we're told of the ultimate demise of the Arabian people?[181] Also, one might ask about

---

[181] Ezekiel 27:21, Jeremiah 49:28-33

the pair of horsemen this watchman saw just before the Babylon falls. Are these the two witnesses we read about in Revelation?[182]

> *The watchman said, "The morning comes, and also the night. If you will inquire, inquire; Return! Come back!"* Isaiah 21:12

Furthermore, what's the meaning of the curious statement made in verse 12? This watchman is unlike any other watchman we read about. Typically a watchman will warn the city only after the approaching military force is well within view. However, this watchman seems to know well in advance of the approaching danger. He says: If you want to ask more about this danger then go ahead and ask. Come back as often as you like! What a curious thing to say. He's inviting all interested parties to keep coming back to him to learn more about that Day.

> *...Then behold, at eventide, trouble! And before the morning, he is no more.* Isaiah 17:14

And it's not just any Day, for he says "the morning comes, and also the night." What could that mean? What is the morning to which he's referring? Could he be speaking of one particular day which will be so devastating that when the next morning arrives everything will have changed? The change will be so severe that years to follow will seem like the blackness of night. In fact, there is a period of time described by Amos as a time of darkness which he refers to as the Day of the Lord.[183] The watchman informs us that, indeed, the morning is coming. Babylon is going to be destroyed in one hour and in the morning she is gone. But then night comes. What is the night? The Tribulation. The first event of that night, the Tribulation, is the utter and complete destruction of Babylon.

The Burden of Babylon

---

[182] Revelation 11:3
[183] Amos 5:18

Wail, for the day of the LORD is at hand! It will come as destruction from the Almighty. Isaiah 13:6

Behold, the day of the LORD comes, cruel, with both wrath and fierce anger, to lay the land desolate; and He will destroy its sinners from it. Isaiah 13:9

I will punish the world for its evil, and the wicked for their iniquity; I will halt the arrogance of the proud, and will lay low the haughtiness of the terrible. Isaiah 13:11

Few chapters in the Bible give us more explicit detail of the destruction of end-time Babylon than Isaiah 13. In this chapter we find definitive proof that the beginning of the Day of the Lord is directly linked to Babylon's downfall. And while some may still argue that this refers only to ancient Babylon, we only need to read the words before us to see this could not have only been spoken of a time long ago. Just as we saw when discussing Jeremiah 25, the slain of the Lord were not from one end of the earth to the other when ancient Babylon fell to the Medo-Persian Empire.[184] Isaiah 13:11 confirms that the time of judgment yet to come will come upon the entire world. Furthermore, we see clearly the final downfall of today's Babylon will occur at the same time the Tribulation begins. In both verses 6 and 9 we see that that Day will be ushered in with the utter and complete destruction of a nation that exists today, whom the Bible refers to as Babylon.

"Up, Zion!"

Up, Zion! Escape, you who dwell with the daughter of Babylon. Zechariah 2:7

And the LORD will take possession of Judah as His inheritance in the Holy Land, and will again choose Jerusalem. Be silent,

---

[184] Jeremiah 25:33

*all flesh, before the LORD, for He is aroused from His holy
habitation! Zechariah 2:12-13*

We saw in chapter 2 that Paul was able to teach the
Thessalonians about that Day with confidence, noting that it begins
with sudden destruction.[185] It's very likely Paul was familiar with
the Scriptures that depict Jehovah standing up to enter into
judgment with the world. It's this same pattern we see here in
Zechariah 2. In verse 13 we see that Jehovah is aroused from His
holy habitation. And while some may say that this could occur more
than once in the history of mankind, I bring to your attention the
preceding verse. In verse 12 it's stated that the Lord will take
possession of Judah. This taking possession of Judah is a theme
associated with the end of the age. In the book of Romans Paul
teaches that when Yahshua came as suffering Servant some of the
branches of Judah were broken off because of their unbelief.[186] This
was predicted much earlier when it was written that he would come
to his people and "they received him not."[187] But Paul also predicts
that Judah will be grafted in again if they continue not in their
unbelief.[188] And we learn from other prophets that this is the
scenario of the last days. Judah will, during the Tribulation,
recognize Yahshua as the Messiah.[189] And this will occur when they
see their "children" in their midst.[190] And all of this happens after
God's people escape from a burning Babylon, which is the very first
event of the Tribulation.

The Flying Scroll

---

185 1 Thessalonians 5:3
186 Romans 11:17
187 Isaiah 53:3, John 1:11
188 Romans 11:23
189 Zechariah 12:10, Jeremiah 23:6
190 Isaiah 29:23

Just a few chapters later we see yet another confirmation that Babylon is destroyed at the beginning of that Day. Allow me to paraphrase from Zechariah 5:

> 2 "I see a flying scroll..."
> 3 This scroll represents, or records, the curse going forth to cover the earth. The result of the curse is to cut off all evil doers.
> 4 "I will send out the curse..."

What is the scroll? It represents the judgment of the Tribulation. What time is being spoken of? When it is sent out; the start of the Tribulation. The context has been established. The backdrop of this vision is the start of the Tribulation. Now let's get to the heart of the matter:

> *Then the angel who talked with me came out and said to me, "Lift your eyes now, and see what this is that goes forth." So I asked, "What is it?" And he said, "It is a basket that is going forth." He also said, "This is their resemblance throughout the earth: "Here is a lead disc lifted up, and this is a woman sitting inside the basket"; then he said, "This is Wickedness!"[191] And he thrust her down into the basket, and threw the lead cover over its mouth.* Zechariah 5:5-8

The Hebrew word "shalak"[192] is used twice in this verse. It's a violent action meaning to cast away or cast down, throw away, throw down. It's also a double judgment. As we've seen before "Babylon is fallen, is fallen."; stated twice to signify a double judgment.

> *Render to her just as she rendered to you, and repay her double according to her works; in the cup which she has mixed, mix double for her. In the measure that she glorified herself and lived luxuriously, in the same measure give her torment and sorrow; for she says in her heart, 'I sit as queen, and am no widow, and will not see sorrow.'* Revelation 18:6-7

---

[191] Compare with Revelation 18:2
[192] Strong's Hebrew Dictionary entry H7993

Notice the word "basket" in Zechariah 5:8. The Hebrew word is ephah which is a unit of measure.[193] Revelation 18:7 actually uses the word measure to describe the severity of her judgment. The connection here should be obvious. The wicked woman is being judged and she is positioned inside her judgment. First she's violently cast down. Then a lead disc is violently thrown over her. She is receiving a double judgment which results in her being hidden, or covered, never to be seen again.

> 10 ... "Where are they carrying the basket?"
> 11 And he said to me, "To build a house for it in the land of Shinar; when it is ready, the basket will be set there on its base."

What does Shinar mean? It's Hebrew for Babylon. Notice she's being flown to a different location. While ancient Babylon is located in modern-day Iraq, this latter day Babylon, at the appointed time, will reside in a very distant land. No less than four times in Zechariah 5 we're told this scroll is being sent out. This "sending out" clearly indicates the initiation, or beginning, of the curse that effects the entire world. It's within this context that we see that Babylon is cast down, never to rise again for her many abominations. The destruction of latter-day Babylon is clearly being linked to the beginning of Tribulation.

Desolation at the Threshold

> *The herds shall lie down in her midst, every beast of the nation. Both the pelican and the bittern shall lodge on the capitals of her pillars; their voice shall sing in the windows; desolation shall be at the threshold; for He will lay bare the cedar work.* Zephaniah 2:14

A threshold, often associated with a doorway, is defined as a point of entry, or beginning. Therefore we can read this passage

---

[193] Strong's Hebrew Dictionary entry H374

with the understanding that desolation will be at the beginning. But of which desolation is Zephaniah referring. Zephaniah is only three chapters in length. So to see the proper context we must start at chapter one. In verse 2 God says he "will utterly consume everything from the face of the land." But of which land is he referring? Verses 7 and 14 clearly establish this time as the "great day of the Lord"; a phrase we've seen many times when discussing the Tribulation. In verse 18 we read that the land will be devoured by the fire of his jealousy and that he will "make speedy riddance of all those who dwell in the land." So we see that whatever land he's speaking of will become an utter and complete desolation very quickly. And while the phrase "fire of my jealousy" may seem like just so much poetry, we would do well to consider the strength of the language being used. For we know that many places in the Bible, when speaking of that great Day, speak of fire being used to judge the wicked. While water was used to judge the world first, fire is used at the last.

> *This is the rejoicing city that dwelt securely, that said in her heart, "I am it, and there is none besides me." How has she become a desolation, A place for beasts to lie down! Everyone who passes by her shall hiss and shake his fist.* Zephaniah 2:15

The context of Zephaniah is the Day of the Lord, called the Tribulation, during which one land in particular will very quickly be made completely desolate; void of both man and beast. Furthermore, Zephaniah speaks of the desolation coming to this land at the threshold, or beginning, of that Day. But which land? While we already know that the destruction of Babylon will take only one hour[194], which is very quick, how can we know for sure this land is referring to Babylon? As I've stated, God gives us opportunities to make connections from one passage to another. Just after Zephaniah mentions that threshold in verse 14 he goes on to give us more detail about that land. In verse 15 he establishes that he's referring to the rejoicing city that dwells securely, who says in her heart, "I am it, and there is none besides me." It's clear that this

---

[194] Revelation 18:10

land, or nation, thinks she is the lone superpower of the earth. And when she is finally done in anyone who passes by her will hiss at her; for her great treachery in the earth will have finally been exposed. Where else do we see these themes?

> *"Therefore hear this now, you who are given to pleasures, who dwell securely, who say in your heart, 'I am, and there is no one else besides me; I shall not sit as a widow, nor shall I know the loss of children'."* Isaiah 47:8

> *Because of the wrath of the LORD she shall not be inhabited, but she shall be wholly desolate. Everyone who goes by Babylon shall be horrified and hiss at all her plagues.* Jeremiah 50:13

We see these exact same themes in two of only a handful of chapters in the Bible which deal exclusively with the utter and complete desolation of an end-time nation referred to as Babylon. And where Zephaniah 2 leaves off, chapter 3 picks up. It goes into much more detail about that filthy, polluted, oppressing[195] city or land or nation who, in the face of severe chastisements refused to turn back to her Lord.[196] Zephaniah, in a round-about way, confirms for us that Babylon the Great, mother of harlots, will be destroyed at the beginning of the Tribulation.

There You Will Be Delivered

> *Be in pain, and labor to bring forth, O daughter of Zion, like a woman in birth pangs. For now you shall go forth from the city, you shall dwell in the field, and to Babylon you shall go. There you shall be delivered; there the LORD will redeem you from the hand of your enemies.* Micah 4:10

---

[195] Compare with Revelation 18:2
[196] Zephaniah 3:1-2

As I showed in chapter two, the context of Micah 4 is established from the very first verse with the phrase "Now it shall come to pass in the latter days...." And eight verses later we read of this latter-day Babylon once again. Verse 9 establishes this as the time when those birth pains grip her who is in labor. This is that same day of sudden destruction that Paul spoke of in 1 Thessalonians.[197] This is the beginning of that Day. Then in verse 10 we find a curious statement. He says God's people will go forth from the city, dwell in the field, and she'll end up in Babylon. From there, Babylon, the Lord will redeem his people.

This is a big-picture view of the migration of God's people. After all, didn't God promise Abraham that his descendants would be as the stars of the sky and as the sand of the sea? And doesn't history show that the people of Israel, the northern kingdom, and the people of Judah, the southern kingdom, were dispersed out of their lands of Samaria and Judea? And while some of the people of Judah began returning to Palestine en masse in 1946, what about the rest of God's people? Where did many of them end up? And doesn't Jeremiah 50:4 confirm what we're being told here in Micah 4, that a people called Israel and a people called Judah will be forced to leave a burning Babylon at the end of this age? These are the questions before us. But now we see that the Bible makes it plain that when the Tribulation begins end-time Babylon will be destroyed the very first day. And in the coming chapters we'll see just what the Bible has to say about God's people who live in Babylon today.

---

[197] 1 Thessalonians 5:3

Chapter 6 - Who's the Fairest of Them All?

Sit in silence, and go into darkness, O daughter of the Chaldeans; for you shall no longer be called The Lady of Kingdoms. Isaiah 47:5

As someone who has spent countless hours studying the Bible, and seeing within it something the popular teachers tell us just isn't so, I find myself swimming against the current of popular thought. It's as if I'm staring at an orange while others see an apple. But even in the face of overwhelming opinions to the contrary I feel compelled to make the best case I possibly can and let the chips fall where they may. After all, we are instructed to "convince, rebuke, exhort, with all longsuffering and teaching."[198] And we also are taught that the things of the Spirit of God are "spiritually discerned."[199] Therefore, while I may be fighting an uphill battle I realize it's not really my fight. Other authors have gone into much more detail, even devoting entire books trying to convince people that America is Babylon.[200] If this chapter leaves you still unconvinced, I encourage you to research it further. But, ultimately, people will only see what they are ready to see. For we understand that that same Spirit, called the Helper, was sent into the world when Yahshua (Jesus) departed nearly 2000 years ago.[201] And not only does He "convict the world of sin, and of righteousness, and of judgment,"[202] but he is also called the Spirit of truth who will guide us into all truth and tell us of things to come.[203] So while the Spirit of

---

[198] 2 Timothy 4:2
[199] 1 Corinthians 2:14
[200] R. A. Coombes, *America, The Babylon : America's Destiny Foretold in Biblical Prophecy*, May 1, 1998
[201] John 16:7
[202] John 16:8
[203] John 16:13

truth is available to us who believe, may the ears of our
understanding also be unhindered as we study God's Word.[204]

They Won't Know

I say all of this because one of the many things we're told
about the inhabitants of end-time Babylon is their inability, or
perhaps unwillingness, to understand their destiny. Consider that in
Isaiah 47:11 we're told that when evil comes upon her she won't
know from where it arises. And when trouble comes upon her she
won't be able to put it off. Despite her fierce military strength she
won't be able to fight back that trouble. Perhaps this is why Moses
asked how all this could be possible unless the Lord was behind it.[205]
Furthermore, 47:11 also tells us that desolation will come upon her
suddenly but she won't know. Perhaps some of this can be
attributed to the attitude she has about herself which can be
summed up in one word: pride.[206] For we learn in just a few verses
before this, in verse 8, she says in her heart, "I am, and there is no
one else besides me." She has convinced herself that there is no
other nation on earth that can be compared to her. Filled with pride
she acknowledges herself as the lone superpower of the world. In
the previous chapter I showed that this same line of thinking is
described in Zephaniah 2:15 when describing the land that will be
made completely desolate at the start of Tribulation.

Also in Isaiah 47:8 she tells herself that she will never "sit as
a widow" nor "know the loss of children." While every war has
casualties on both sides we see here something much greater being
spoken. A widow is a woman who outlives her husband. Described
here is a woman who has lost both husband and children. She is a
woman who has reached rock bottom and has become desolate and

---

[204] Jeremiah 6:10
[205] Deuteronomy 32:30
[206] Isaiah 13:19

left alone; all her strength is gone.[207] In the same vein that she considers herself to be the lone superpower of the world she also refuses to believe, nor even considers it a possibility, that she could ever be defeated by another nation. This thought is confirmed when describing that same Babylon in Revelation 18. In verse 7 "she says in her heart, 'I sit as queen, and am no widow, and will not see sorrow.'" We can liken this prideful attitude to the makers of the Titanic, calling her "unsinkable" before her maiden voyage, which we all know ended in horrific tragedy. It seems pride has lulled many into a deep sleep at the very time we should be most alert.

That the citizens of Babylon will be caught completely unaware is further illustrated in Jeremiah. In 50:24 we read that she has been found, trapped, and caught and that she was not aware. She was taken in that trap completely off guard. In Isaiah 13:7 we're shown that when that terrifying Day arrives no one will be ready. Rather, all hands will be limp and every man's heart will melt. We see in Jeremiah 51:17 the problem is not only the complete lack of knowledge of these events to come but also a lack of mental and spiritual readiness. The New King James Bible calls them "dull-hearted." Just as those on the Titanic were completely unaware of the fate that would soon befall them the same is predicted for the inhabitants of last-day Babylon.

Land of My Fathers

When the Bible mentions Babylon my ears perk up and my hair stands on end. For it's speaking of my country, the land of my father, and of his father, and of just a few fathers before him, traced back to that one singular decision by my ancestors to leave their homeland, to leave everything they knew, and immigrate to America. And that decision, made by scores of families just like mine, from varying times and places and circumstances, would come to define who we are and set in motion a destiny long foretold. That promise

---

[207] Lamentations 1:1

given to Abraham so many thousands of years ago that his descendants would become a great, uncountable multitude[208] and be pushed to the farthest ends of the earth[209] was literally fulfilled. And we stand now at the end of this age as living proof that the immutable words of our great Jehovah are living and faithful and true. And while Ephraim, who was placed before younger brother Manasseh[210], was to become a great multitude of nations (the United Kingdom, at one point the largest Empire in history[211]), it was said that Manasseh would become a singular great people, or nation.[212]

While the history and migration of the lost tribes, the ten tribes of the northern kingdom of Israel[213], is beyond the scope of this book, we can examine the characteristics we're told of Babylon to identify her today. And without a doubt we can identify her today, for it takes no great stretch of the imagination, nor any superior powers of deduction to see and comprehend that end-time Babylon is America today, lone superpower of the earth, sea to shining sea.

The People at Her Demise

While it's safe to assume the wicked, who ignore God and his Word, will be caught off guard, what about God's own people living in America today? Will they know what's happening when that Day strikes? We'd like to think so but that's not the picture we're given. Even though we're told that the people will hear of the coming trouble[214], in Jeremiah 50:6 God refers to his people as lost sheep who have been led astray by their shepherds. And in 51:23 we're told that even the shepherd and his flock, which is often

---

[208] Genesis 26:4, 32:12

[209] Isaiah 41:8-9

[210] Genesis 48:17-19

[211] *United Kingdom.* Wikipedia.org. Retrieved March 14, 2012, from http://en.wikipedia.org/wiki/United_Kingdom

[212] Genesis 48:19

[213] J. H. Allen, *Judah's Sceptre and Joseph's Birthright,* A. A. Beauchamp, Boston, Mass. 1918

[214] Jeremiah 6:24, 30:5, Hosea 7:12

characteristic of a pastor and his congregation[215], will be broken in pieces. But while a remnant of God's people will survive her downfall[216], as I'll show, not everyone who says "Lord, Lord"[217] will survive that Day. Perhaps this is why God assures us, within the context of the downfall of Shebna, who was a minister set over the house, that even the nail fastened in a secure place will be removed and cut down and fall. And that which the nail holds will fall as well.[218] Things we've come to take for granted today won't seem so sure when that Day arrives. Later I'll discuss God's people in more detail. But for now let me show you who else is mentioned in all the many discussions of end-time Babylon.

Foreign Migrant Workers

> *Cut off the sower from Babylon, and him who handles the sickle at harvest time. For fear of the oppressing sword everyone shall turn to his own people, and everyone shall flee to his own land.* Jeremiah 50:16

At first glance it would seem this verse is talking about farmers because they are described as planting and harvesting. But I want to point out that these are migrant workers from other countries who do not think of Babylon as their permanent home for the simple fact that they are seen returning to their own lands sometime before Babylon's downfall. America today employs migrant workers to perform the difficult labor to which the majority of us are unaccustomed and even unwilling to take on.

Multi-cultured Population of Babylon

---

[215] John 21:17
[216] Jeremiah 5:10, 5:18, 30:11, 46:28, Amos 3:12, 9:8, Joel 2:32, Amos 4:11, Zechariah 3:2, Isaiah 1:9, 6:13, Ezekiel 7:16
[217] Matthew 7:21
[218] Isaiah 22:25

Then he said to me, "The waters which you saw, where the harlot sits, are peoples, multitudes, nations, and tongues." Revelation 17:15

A sword is against their horses, against their chariots, and against all the mixed peoples who are in her midst; and they will become like women. A sword is against her treasures, and they will be robbed. Jeremiah 50:37

Just as ancient Babylon brought diverse people from other nations to serve the Empire, so too we find modern-day Babylon to be a veritable melting pot of diversity. Our creed, mounted on the Statue of Liberty, is to accept immigrants from all over the world. "Give me your tired, your poor, your huddled masses yearning to breathe free, the wretched refuse of your teeming shore."[219]

Forerunners

Move from the midst of Babylon, go out of the land of the Chaldeans; and be like the rams before the flocks. Jeremiah 50:8

I see two possible interpretations for the phrase "rams before the flocks"; one spiritual and the other natural. On the one hand God will always set out in front a chosen few to proclaim his truth to the people. These are God's true leaders and they speak the whole truth of God's Word uncompromisingly. But in the natural we also may see here a prediction that some will begin to leave Babylon before she is destroyed; even encouraging others to follow suit.[220]

---

[219] Emma Lazarus, *The New Colossus*, 1883
[220] Mark Ehrman, *Getting Out: Your Guide to Leaving America*, February 1, 2009

Invaders / Destroyers[221]

> *The noise of a multitude in the mountains, like that of many people! A tumultuous noise of the kingdoms of nations gathered together! The LORD of hosts musters the army for battle. They come from a far country, from the end of heaven-- the LORD and His weapons of indignation, to destroy the whole land.* Isaiah 13:4-5

Nearly every passage that speaks of Babylon also speaks of her utter destruction at the hands of a great army "the like of whom has never been; nor will there ever be any such after them, even for many successive generations."[222]

America's Military[223]

> *Their horses also are swifter than leopards, and more fierce than evening wolves. Their chargers charge ahead; their cavalry comes from afar; they fly as the eagle that hastens to eat. They all come for violence; their faces are set like the east wind. They gather captives like sand. They scoff at kings, and princes are scorned by them. They deride every stronghold, for they heap up earthen mounds and seize it.* Habakkuk 1:8-10

In the next chapter we'll see how the greatest military the world has known can be defeated in a single hour. But here I'd like to bring your attention to Habakkuk. In that book we find described the current foreign policy of the United States of America. When America wants something that another nation possesses all we have to do is send our military "from afar; they fly as the eagle that hastens to eat."[224] Because of our military might America's share is

---

[221] Jeremiah 4:17, 12:9, 50:14-15, 29, 41-42, 51:2, Isaiah 13:4-5, Joel 1:6, 2:2, 4, 5, 7-9, 11, 20, Nahum 2:3, 3:2-3, Habakkuk 2:6-7, Amos 3:11

[222] Joel 2:2

[223] Jeremiah 50:23, 51:30, Jeremiah 51:56, Habakkuk 1:6-11,1:15-17, 2:5

[224] Habakkuk 1:8

"sumptuous" and our "food plentiful."[225] Our food is plentiful today but, as I'll show, "cleanness of teeth" is coming to our cities before our final destruction.[226]

Nations Oppressed by America[227]

> *I see a terrifying vision: I see the betrayer betraying, the destroyer destroying. Go ahead, you Elamites and Medes, attack and lay siege. I will make an end to all the groaning Babylon caused.* Isaiah 21:2 (NLT)

I would be remiss to speak of our military without mentioning the nations and peoples we have oppressed.[228] While it's beyond the scope of this book to delve into this in great detail, I encourage the skeptical patriot to do a little research regarding our country's activities. Websites such as Cryptogon.com have become popular because they publish stories our mainstream media, for whatever reason, choose not to. I guess reporting on the daily drama of the Kardashians is more important. To give you an example of the kinds of things to which I'm referring, I quote a soldier, a reporter, and a Nobel Prize winner, respectively:

The Soldier

> *"We have been speaking to whoever will listen, telling them that what was shown in the Wikileaks video only begins to depict the suffering we have created. From our own experiences, and the experiences of other veterans we have talked to, we know that the acts depicted in this video are*

---

[225] Habakkuk 1:16
[226] Amos 4:6, 4:11
[227] Isaiah 21:2, Habakkuk 1:6,10-11; Habakkuk 2:5-8; Jeremiah 51:25
[228] See also Isaiah 14:7-8

everyday occurrences of this war: this is the nature of how U.S.-led wars are carried out in this region.

"We acknowledge our part in the deaths and injuries of your loved ones as we tell Americans what we were trained to do and what we carried out in the name of "god and country."[229] *The soldier in the video said that your husband shouldn't have brought your children to battle, but we are acknowledging our responsibility for bringing the battle to your neighborhood, and to your family. We did unto you what we would not want done to us."* [230]

The Reporter

Somewhere on this planet an American commando is carrying out a mission. Now, say that 70 times and you're done... for the day. Without the knowledge of the American public, a secret force within the U.S. military is undertaking operations in a majority of the world's countries. This new Pentagon power elite is waging a global war whose size and scope has never been revealed, until now. [231]

The Nobel Prize Winner

The United States supported and in many cases engendered every right wing military dictatorship in the world after the end of the Second World War. I refer to Indonesia, Greece, Uruguay, Brazil, Paraguay, Haiti, Turkey, the Philippines, Guatemala, El Salvador, and, of course, Chile. The horror the

[229] Habakkuk 1:11
[230] Kim Zetter, U.S. Soldier on 2007 Apache Attack: What I Saw, April 20, 2010, Wired.com
[231] Nick Turse, *The Secret War in 120 Countries*, August 4, 2011, TomDispatch.com

United States inflicted upon Chile in 1973 can never be purged and can never be forgiven.

Hundreds of thousands of deaths took place throughout these countries. Did they take place? And are they in all cases attributable to US foreign policy? The answer is yes they did take place and they are attributable to American foreign policy. But you wouldn't know it.

It never happened. Nothing ever happened. Even while it was happening it wasn't happening. It didn't matter. It was of no interest. The crimes of the United States have been systematic, constant, vicious, remorseless, but very few people have actually talked about them. You have to hand it to America. It has exercised a quite clinical manipulation of power worldwide while masquerading as a force for universal good. It's a brilliant, even witty, highly successful act of hypnosis. [232]

America's Creditors

Will not your creditors rise up suddenly? Will they not awaken who oppress you? And you will become their booty.
Habakkuk 2:7

Habakkuk 2:7 informs us that America's creditors will be among those coming to destroy her. While it's difficult to say to which country this might be referring, we know that China is one of our biggest creditors today. Perhaps this is why Isaiah mentions God "calling a bird of prey from the east, the man who executes My counsel, from a far country."[233] But is America in debt today? One could say America is in debt up to her eyeballs. It will never be, or even could be, repaid.

---

[232] *Nobel Lecture - Literature 2005.* Retrieved January 24, 2012 from http://www.nobelprize.org/nobel_prizes/literature/laureates/2005/pinter-lecture-e.html
[233] Isaiah 46:11

By the 1980s, the inevitable happened. As generations of accumulated wealth disappeared, a line was crossed. America now owed more to the rest of the world than the world owed to it. The United States had become a debtor nation, and it has continued to run up the tab in the decades since.[234]

Merchants of the Earth[235]

And the merchants of the earth will weep and mourn over her, for no one buys their merchandise anymore. Revelation 18:11

Connected with the thought regarding America's humongous indebtedness, we're given a picture in Revelation 18:11 of her role as supreme buyer of the world. At the time of her end, Americans will still be buying so much stuff from other lands that the merchants of the earth will actually weep and mourn at her demise, "for no one buys their merchandise anymore." There is no greater importer of goods today than America.[236]

America's Mother

Your mother shall be deeply ashamed; she who bore you shall be ashamed. Behold, the least of the nations shall be a wilderness, a dry land and a desert. Jeremiah 50:12

Jeremiah 50:12 explains that Babylon's mother will be deeply ashamed of her when she's finally destroyed. This also implies that her mother will still be alive, or existing, on the day America is destroyed. When people immigrate to another land they often refer

---

[234] James Turk, *Debtor Nation*. Retrieved March 22, 2010 from http://www.fgmr.com/debtor-nation.html
[235] Nahum 3:16
[236] *The World Factbook*. Retrieved September 19, 2008 from https://www.cia.gov/library/publications/the-world-factbook/rankorder/2087rank.html

to their original land as their homeland, or motherland. While Americans today can trace their roots back to many different lands, our founding fathers came predominately from Great Britain.

America's Allies

> *Thus shall they be to you with whom you have labored, your merchants from your youth; They shall wander each one to his quarter. No one shall save you.* Isaiah 47:15

Speaking of Great Britain, you might be wondering how is it that America's allies won't rescue her from utter annihilation. Isaiah 47:15 ensures us that America will have no friends willing to come to her aid on that Day.[237]

Sorcerers and Astrologers

> *Stand now with your enchantments and the multitude of your sorceries, in which you have labored from your youth--Perhaps you will be able to profit, perhaps you will prevail. You are wearied in the multitude of your counsels; let now the astrologers, the stargazers, and the monthly prognosticators stand up and save you from what shall come upon you.* Isaiah 47:12-13

In what may or may not come as a surprise to some, Isaiah 47:12-13 calls out America for her blatant reliance on sorcery; even indicating that sorcery (occult practices) has been a part of America since she was founded. This is indeed the truth. One only need look at the symbols on our currency and within our public buildings to see that even from the founding of America our leaders have been involved in pagan and occult religious practices.

---

[237] See also Isaiah 14:6

The Rich, Famous, and Powerful

> *"And I will make drunk her princes and wise men, her*
> *governors, her deputies, and her mighty men. And they shall*
> *sleep a perpetual sleep and not awake," says the King, whose*
> *name is the LORD of hosts.* Jeremiah 51:57

As would be expected when discussing the most wealthy and powerful nation on earth, we read here of those who would be considered the who's who of high society. Have you ever wondered when and where so many important people are gathered together in one place to eat and drink?[238] Consider that in Isaiah 21:5 we read: "Prepare the table, set a watchman in the tower, eat and drink." The word table used here is referring to the king's table. Today in America the king's table is set when a State Dinner is being prepared. Only the rich and famous and powerful are invited.

The Nation of Babylon

> *For indeed I am raising up the Chaldeans, a bitter and hasty*
> *<u>nation</u> which marches through the breadth of the earth, to*
> *possess dwelling places that are not theirs.* Habakkuk 1:6

> *The most proud shall stumble and fall, and no one will raise*
> *him up; I will kindle a fire in his <u>cities</u>, and it will devour all*
> *around him.* Jeremiah 50:32

As I mentioned before, some have bought into the lie that the latter-day Babylon must be some sort of system. I don't know who started that teaching but I only need to point the reader back to the Bible. Scripture is very clear that just as ancient Babylon, being what we would call a nation, was the lone superpower of the earth during her day, so too is present-day Babylon, America. And just as we

---

[238] See also Jeremiah 51:39

would expect, we see that America is described as having one individual set over her. The writers of the Bible used the language of their day even to convey concepts of our day. The meanings of those concepts are adequate for us to understand the intent of the symbol. While Jeremiah and Isaiah refer to this person as the king of Babylon[239], the equivalent modern role is known to us as president. And we know every king must have a court; people to serve underneath him. We see not only those who rule with him but also those with whom powerful men must rub elbows. As you would expect of any great and wealthy nation, there invariably must be rich and powerful and scholarly individuals within that nation. These all are mentioned in the context of a great feast that our president will host the same night America falls, never again to rise.[240]

Many people get hung up on one word here or there. While I have no doubt the original Greek and Hebrew Scriptures are written using the words Jehovah intended, I have much less faith in the English translations of those texts. Besides this, if we take Scripture out of context, it's a moot point. This is one major reason for failing to rightly understand prophecies of our day. Some people read Revelation 17 and 18 and come away thinking Babylon is merely a city. It's the equivalent of the blind man feeling the elephant's leg, thinking it to be a tree. Only when we see the whole picture can we see the whole picture. If you think that was a misprint, let me state it another way. We can't truly understand Babylon until we've read everything about her.

The book of Revelation only gives us part of the view. While Revelation uses the phrases "great city" and "mighty city" to describe Babylon[241], is that the full meaning? How can a city have cities? A city doesn't have cities. A nation has cities just as a nation has a ruler, leaders, soldiers, scholars and even migrant farmers. And this is exactly what we find when we examine what the rest of the Bible

---

[239] Isaiah 14:4, Jeremiah 50:18, Jeremiah 50:43, Jeremiah 51:23
[240] Isaiah 21:5, Jeremiah 51:39, 51:57
[241] Revelation 14:8, 17:18, 18:10, 16, 18, 19, 21

has to say about America. America has a motherland that, figuratively, gave birth to her.[242] America is of the hindermost or last or youngest nations when she is destroyed.[243] America has cities.[244] America is referred to as a land mass inhabited by wild animals.[245] America is symbolized by a mountain, which indicates she is a nation or kingdom.[246] America is called the Lady of Kingdoms, the glory of kingdoms; she is the greatest nation on earth at the time of her demise.[247] America is called a nation, as well.[248]

Some still may refuse to believe that the Bible could refer to a nation as a city. To these I would only point out certain passages in the Bible where we see the word city being used in a generic sense to describe a nation. One such place is Ezekiel 22. In verses 2 and 3 we read of a "city" coming under God's judgment because of her sin. But in verse 6 we read not of the rulers of a city but of the rulers of a nation. In verse 18 we see the object of God's judgment is the "house of Israel," which, historically, would have been known as the northern kingdom of Israel inhabiting the land of Samaria. Although verse 19 says God will gather the people into the midst of Jerusalem, which is sometimes used to refer to people rather than an actual city, we see the broader context of this judgment is against the whole land. This is confirmed by verses 24, 29, and 30 which convey that the judgment is coming to the "land" of the house of Israel, wherever they may be living at the time of the fulfillment of this judgment. While this chapter is clearly speaking of a time long ago, notice that there's nothing in this chapter which prevents these words from alighting on God's people today. In fact, if we look at this passage with an open mind perhaps we can see ourselves. What nation today, though filled with God's people, is, as verse 7 says, making "light of father and mother" by passing laws legalizing same-sex

---

[242] Jeremiah 50:12

[243] Jeremiah 50:12, Strong's Hebrew Dictionary entry H319

[244] Jeremiah 50:32, 51:43

[245] Jeremiah 51:43, Zephaniah 1:2, 2:15

[246] Jeremiah 51:25

[247] Isaiah 13:19, Isaiah 47:5

[248] Jeremiah 50:12, Habakkuk 1:6

marriages? And what about verse 8? Do Christians in America rest on the seventh day of every week, ceasing from all commerce and labor. Or do we continue to do whatever we please on the Sabbath?[249] Aren't we supposed to keep all Ten Commandments? Or should there only be nine?

Founded on Bloodshed

> *Woe to him who builds a town with bloodshed, who establishes a city by iniquity!* Habakkuk 2:12

Despite the countless times I've heard people say that America is not mentioned in the Bible, not only is she mentioned but she's described in detail and plays a very important role in the end times. While Zephaniah spends much of his three chapters devoted to the downfall of America at the beginning of Tribulation, so does Habakkuk. As I just mentioned, the greatness of our military and our aggressive foreign policy is clearly described there. And, as it turns out, even from our humble beginning we've taken what belonged to others. While history shows that our forefathers almost completely wiped out the Native Americans, this was predicted long before it actually happened.

Habakkuk 2:12 pronounces woe on the subject of his book, America, and to some degree ancient Babylon. And while ancient Babylon is not the focus of this book, it's clear that America is being referenced when he describes her as a town built with bloodshed and a city established by iniquity. Some may protest, still not agreeing that the Bible uses the words town, city, land and nation to describe America. But was ancient Babylon a town? Was she even a city? No, ancient Babylon was a great, sovereign world power, just as America is today. To me it's of no consequence how ancient Babylon came to be. But we can easily search the history books and see that present-day Babylon, America, was indeed built upon

---

[249] Isaiah 58:13

bloodshed and established by iniquity. As is often the case, we can find at least one other prophet that agrees. Isaiah 18:7 describes her as a "people terrible from their beginning onward."

Weaponized Space Program

Though Babylon were to mount up to heaven, and though she were to fortify the height of her strength, yet from Me plunderers would come to her," says the LORD.
Jeremiah 51:53

From a 2010 article published by the U.K.'s "The Week":

A top secret robotic space plane has blasted off from Cape Canaveral, and the involvement of a US military agency in the project has Iran - and maybe China - worried about the possibilities of what could be a prototype 'space bomber'.

Officially, the X-37B...is on a test flight to evaluate the vehicle's performance. But the space plane's pedigree as an offshoot of the shuttle programme has led some to suggest it could eventually conduct espionage missions in orbit - and is another step on the road to the "weaponisation of space."[250]

Military Strongholds and Storehouses

Because the plunderer comes against her, against Babylon, and her mighty men are taken. Every one of their bows is broken; for the LORD is the God of recompense, He will surely repay.
Jeremiah 51:56 [251]

---

[250] Tim Edwards, *Top secret space plane has America's enemies scared*. The Week, April 26, 2010
[251] See also Jeremiah 50:26, Nahum 3:13-15

Notice that the bows are broken. A bow is a weapon that launches a projectile. The modern-day arrow is a missile and the modern-day bow is a rocket launcher or missile silo. The following is a quote from Dumitru Duduman:

> He said, "Remember this, Dumitru. The Russian spies have discovered where the nuclear warehouses are in America. When the Americans will think that it is peace and safety - from the middle of the country, some of the people will start fighting against the government. The government will be busy with internal problems. Then from the ocean, from Cuba, Nicaragua, Mexico,,.." (He told me two other countries, but I didn't remember what they were.) "...they will bomb the nuclear warehouses. When they explode, America will burn!"[252]

Divided by Rivers and Situated by Much Water

> In that time a present will be brought to the LORD of hosts from a people tall and smooth of skin, and from a people terrible from their beginning onward, a nation powerful and treading down, whose land the rivers divide-- to the place of the name of the LORD of hosts, to Mount Zion. Isaiah 18:7

> O you who dwell by many waters, abundant in treasures, your end has come, the measure of your covetousness.
> Jeremiah 51:13

Those who think ancient Babylon (in modern-day Iraq) will be rebuilt into last-days Babylon should think twice. In addition to numerous smaller rivers, America's major rivers include the Columbia, Colorado, Rio Grande, Brazos, Missouri, Mississippi, and Ohio. Besides this, much of America's borders touch the seas or Great Lakes. Isaiah 18:7 also describes America as a tall people.

---

[252] Duduman, Dimitru. (September 1984). *The Message for America.* Hand of Help Ministries. Retrieved March 14, 2012 from http://www.handofhelp.com/vision_1.php

While America doesn't have the tallest average height, she is among the tallest; a good five inches taller than the average Iraqi.[253]

Great Influence in World Affairs

All inhabitants of the world and dwellers on the earth: when he lifts up a banner on the mountains, you see it; and when he blows a trumpet, you hear it. Isaiah 18:3

I'm not sure many would dispute America's status and influence in world affairs today.

Ah, the Good Life!

Therefore hear this now, you who are given to pleasures, who dwell securely, who say in your heart, 'I am, and there is no one else besides me; I shall not sit as a widow, nor shall I know the loss of children.' Isaiah 47:8

Thus says the LORD: "Though they are safe, and likewise many, yet in this manner they will be cut down when he passes through. Though I have afflicted you, I will afflict you no more. Nahum 1:12

For all the nations have drunk of the wine of the wrath of her fornication, the kings of the earth have committed fornication with her, and the merchants of the earth have become rich through the abundance of her luxury. Revelation 18:3

The picture we're given of end-time Babylon is that of a nation who exceeds all other nations in nearly every way. She is the

---

[253] *Height Chart of Men and Women in Different Countries.* (October 13, 2008). Disabled World. Retrieved March 14, 2012 from http://www.disabled-world.com/artman/publish/height-chart.shtml

cream of the crop. She sits as Queen of the earth. She is the Lady of kingdoms. She is described as reigning over the kings of the earth[254] and polluting the rest of the world with her wickedness and harlotry. She possesses great wealth and lives in luxury. She seeks pleasures and leisure at every turn. Habakkuk describes her as a nation that oppresses other nations and invades them and takes what doesn't belong to her. But back at home her people feel safe and secure and can't imagine that feeling of security ever coming to an end.

---

[254] Revelation 17:18

Chapter 7 - America is fallen, is fallen!

And another angel followed, saying, "Babylon is fallen, is fallen, that great city, because she has made all nations drink of the wine of the wrath of her fornication." Revelation 14:8

When I consider these words which speak of the complete ruin of my country, the land where I call home, I find it difficult to truly comprehend, let alone convey. I suppose this is why we find written in Habakkuk: "for I will work a work in your days which you would not believe, though it were told you."[255] Isaiah tells us it's a very strange work and unusual act.[256] Those of us who haven't experienced the horrors of war, who haven't had to flee a worn-torn homeland, who have only known peace and safety all our lives might struggle with this concept as well.[257] After all, in America we've come to believe that those kinds of things only happen in other countries. Surely our country is above all of that. There's no other nation like America. We don't suffer like other people do. Sure, we have trials and hardships, but not like that. Besides, America is just too powerful. Our military is too strong to be defeated. Why dwell on something that could never happen, right?

This is exactly the sentiment we see described in the Bible at the time of America's demise. But it all just seems too unreal. It seems preposterous. It's an idea we can't even wrap our minds around. This great land is filled with people and cities and universities and corporations and churches and homes and stories and history; people going about their lives, day in and day out under one banner for nearly two hundred forty years. But now we find ourselves at a time unlike our fathers have known, or their fathers

---

[255] Habakkuk 1:5
[256] Isaiah 28:21
[257] Isaiah 47:8, Nahum 1:12

have known. The last world war ended nearly seventy years ago. And while we know the world is not void of threats, certainly we don't have to worry. After all, the only other superpower we had to fear was the U.S.S.R. and her strength collapsed more than twenty years ago. (Or so we thought.)

So, here America sits, at the height of her power: Queen of the Earth, Lady of Kingdoms, the Glory of Kingdoms, the Mighty City.[258] We are, today, that rejoicing city that dwells securely, or carelessly.[259] We dare anyone to knock us off our throne. And while it seems implausible, even unlikely, that America could be so thoroughly destroyed, this is exactly what the Bible predicts. We read of a day so devastating that no strength will be left in her. All hands will be limp, all knees like water and all faces pale, drained of color. Everyone's heart will melt.[260]

Unless Their Rock Had Sold Them

But how is this possible? Won't our great military protect us?[261] Psalm 127:1 tells us that unless the Lord protects the city, the watchman stays awake in vain. And Moses, at the end of his life, prophesies of two generations separated by a great span of time. Just like Jeremiah, he speaks to his generation and the generation of the latter days, our day. In Deuteronomy 31:29 he says "evil will befall you in the latter days" because of the sin of God's people. Then he implores God's people to consider their latter end.[262] Just as I showed in the previous chapter that God's people in America will be caught off guard when that Day begins, Moses says the same thing. In 32:28 he says the nation is void of counsel and completely lacking understanding. But in 32:30 we find the answer to this question:

---

[258] Isaiah 13:19, Isaiah 47:5, Revelation 18:10
[259] Zephaniah 2:15
[260] Isaiah 13:7, Ezekiel 7:17, 21:7, Nahum 2:10
[261] Ezekiel 33:26
[262] Deuteronomy 32:29

how is this possible? "How could one chase a thousand and two put ten thousand to flight, unless their Rock had sold them."[263] Just before he dies, Moses is given understanding of what will befall God's people, or a good majority of them congregated in one particular nation in the last days.

The Word of God is consistent from Genesis to Revelation. Our great Jehovah sets up kingdoms and tears down kingdoms.[264] He forms the light and creates darkness. He makes peace and creates calamity.[265] Nothing he does is without purpose and nothing is unjustified. He does not willingly afflict or grieve mankind.[266] It is not his desire to bring a great nation to nothing. In fact, we're told we could have avoided such severe punishment; that our righteousness could have been like the waves of the sea.[267] But instead, this is the destiny we chose. And God will allow this great calamity to come upon America in the near future. And we're told that he not only allows it but he also directs these events.

Jump Up and Down, Wave Your Hands Around

There is no question that an army is coming to destroy America. In fact, not just one, but a coalition of nations will join forces to defeat us.[268] But the picture we're given is not of a great battle. No, the picture we're given is that of a no-contest. We're told it won't even be a fight. It will be a one-sided slaughter. Our military won't even put up much of a fight.[269] But how is all of this possible? How does the enemy know the best time to strike? Surely our radar defense system will see them coming!

---

[263] Deuteronomy 32:30
[264] Jeremiah 1:10
[265] Isaiah 45:6-7
[266] Lamentation 3:33
[267] Isaiah 48:18-20
[268] Isaiah 13:4, Jeremiah 50:7, 50:9, 51:27-28
[269] Ezekiel 7:14, Jeremiah 51:30

2 Lift up a banner on the high mountain, raise your voice to them; wave your hand, that they may enter the gates of the nobles. 3 I have commanded My sanctified ones; I have also called My mighty ones for My anger--those who rejoice in My exaltation. Isaiah 13:2-3

I suppose many may not realize the incredible amount of detail we're given about the last days. While it seems ridiculous that the great American superpower could be so easily defeated, not only are we told she will but we're told exactly how it will happen. And you might be surprised to learn that the Bible, or the foreknowledge it contains, plays a role in America's downfall. Look at this amazing detail we're given in Isaiah 13. Starting with verse 3 he says "I've commanded my sanctified ones." He's not talking about the army yet. Sanctified here means clean, holy, set apart.[270] The heathen armies coming to destroy America are not God's holy ones. "Those who rejoice in My exaltation." The heathen nations do not care about or rejoice in Jehovah's exaltation. No, he's saying, I've commanded my holy ones, my mighty champions, to do my work, for the day of my anger. These are God's chosen ones who understand what he intends to do in the last days. God says, I have called and appointed them for the work at hand. And what is that work? What is he calling his sanctified champions to do?

Look at verse 2. It says "Lift up a banner on a high mountain." Mountains in the Bible usually refer to nations. And what nation is higher, or more exalted, than America? It says "raise your voice to them" from this high mountain. Shout out loudly to the heathen. Shout and wave your hands, that the enemy may enter the gates of the nobles (America). He's telling his sanctified ones to give the destroying army the signal. Tell them about the most opportune time to strike. And it's evident this message is being given from the very nation that is to be struck. We've all seen movies or shows that depict a man stranded on an island in the middle of nowhere. He hears a plane off in the distance. As it approaches he does whatever

---

[270] Strong's Hebrew Dictionary entry H6942

it takes to get their attention. That's the picture we're given in Isaiah. The picture here is that of a man jumping up and down, waving his arms and shouting loudly to get the attention of those preparing to destroy America.

But notice that the point of this signal is not to inform the enemy where to attack. The enemy already knows how to attack America. This is not a last-minute, hasty decision. No, I suspect the enemies of America have been plotting her downfall for quite some time. The enemy does not need any encouragement. The enemy does not need to be incited to attack America. No, the real question is "when?" When is the best time to attack America? What point in time will give the enemy the greatest advantage? What set of unique circumstances will allow the enemy to ensure decisive victory over her foe? This is what that signal is about. The one giving the signal knows the best time to strike.

But how? How is that possible? He knows because it's written in the Word of God. Look at what we're being told here: "I have commanded My sanctified ones." Who's speaking? God is speaking through Isaiah. God is the one giving the command to his sanctified ones. Furthermore, we learn in verse 4 that "The LORD of hosts musters the army for battle." God is the one directing these events.

But is someone betraying his own country? Is this the workings of some sort of double agent? No, for we know that the Word of God cannot be stopped. If one fails, God will raise another in his place. The words that go out of his mouth will not be stopped unless he chooses to relent.[271] Should this message be kept secret? How can it? If God wills it, who can withhold it?[272] We know that God will do nothing unless he reveals his secrets to his prophets.[273] And we know that the watchman is allowed to declare what he sees

---

[271] Jeremiah 18:7-10
[272] Isaiah 14:27
[273] Amos 3:7

regarding America.[274] And that which he sees is from looking intently at the Word of God, with great care.[275] And furthermore he's instructed to make the vision plain, and write it down, that they may make haste who read it.[276] We're not told who will make haste. We're only told those that read it are to make haste. I suppose included in those making haste is this army of which Isaiah 13 speaks.

While it seems impossible America could be defeated, it seems even more unlikely the enemy would pay attention to anything written in the Bible. After all, most Christians don't even pay much attention to the Bible. Nevertheless, this is the scenario we find. Jeremiah confirms Isaiah by writing: "Set up a banner in the land, blow the trumpet among the nations! Prepare the nations against her, call the kingdoms together against her."[277] Like Isaiah he calls for a banner, or signal, to be setup in the land. He calls for the trumpet alarm of war to be sounded. It was typical that the watchman would blow the trumpet to alert the city of impending danger. This trumpet, however, is for the nations preparing to destroy America. This is the same "loud voice" that Isaiah describes. Isaiah speaks again of this same banner in an earlier chapter. In chapter 1 he speaks of the land of God's people being completely overthrown.[278] In chapter 2 we see this narrative is being associated with the latter days.[279] And again in chapter 6 he tells us that all her cities will be burned with fire.[280] But in chapter 5 he says "He will lift up a banner to the nations from afar, and will whistle to them from the end of the earth; surely they shall come with speed, swiftly." In Isaiah 5 God is claiming full credit for this banner, or signal. He's saying he is the one responsible for telling the nations of the best time to destroy America. And Isaiah 13:3 informs us that he calls

---

[274] Isaiah 21:6
[275] Isaiah 21:7
[276] Habakkuk 2:2
[277] Jeremiah 51:27-28
[278] Isaiah 1:7
[279] Isaiah 2:2, 2:12
[280] Isaiah 6:11

certain individuals, through which he performs the intents of his heart.[281]

I don't dispute for one minute that the first twelve chapters of Isaiah can be applied to events that transpired long ago. But when we examine the full body of prophetic text we see that much of that text is speaking of two generations separated by a great span of time. History does not repeat itself in exactly the same way but it does repeat itself in similar enough ways to allow the same text to be applied to two distinct generations. The first implementation of Isaiah 1-12 was addressed to God's people living in Palestine some six hundred years before the time of Christ. But the second implementation of the same passage must be applied within the context of what all the prophets say about God's people in the last days, line upon line, precept upon precept.[282] It's only by comparing all the messages of the prophets that we can begin to see a clear picture of the last days. Just as Isaiah describes a remnant of God's people who will survive the utter desolation of their country[283], Jeremiah, in perfect harmony, predicts the same thing regarding end-time Babylon, America.[284] I contend that Isaiah 2, which mentions the "latter days" and the "day of the Lord,"[285] is not to be disconnected from the rest of the passage. Quite the opposite is true. Those phrases connect the entire narrative to our day.

Furthermore, one only need read those first twelve chapters to understand that one consistent story is being told about God's people. The predicament that God's people fell into long ago is the same situation we find ourselves in today. The way God describes his people of that day can and does describe God's people today. The same types of things that befell God's people long ago in Palestine will befall us today in America. This should be no great surprise. After all, we are told that in the last days God will gather his people

---

[281] Jeremiah 30:24

[282] Isaiah 28:10

[283] Isaiah 1:8,Isaiah 6:13, Amos 5:3, Jeremiah 5:10, 5:18, 30:11, 46:28, Amos 3:12, 9:8, Joel 2:32, Amos 4:11, Zechariah 3:2, Isaiah 1:9, 6:13, Ezekiel 7:16

[284] Jeremiah 50:4, 51:10

[285] Isaiah 2:2, 2:12

from the ends, or farthest extremities, of the earth.[286] The farthest extremity from Palestine includes America, or end-time Babylon, which is positioned on the opposite side of the globe. Micah 4, whose very first verse establishes the context of that passage as the "latter days" says of God's people, "And to Babylon you shall go. There you shall be delivered."[287]

The Enemy Strikes Gold

For the stars of heaven and their constellations will not give their light; the sun will be darkened in its going forth, and the moon will not cause its light to shine. Isaiah 13:10

The earth quakes before them, the heavens tremble; the sun and moon grow dark, and the stars diminish their brightness. Joel 2:10

What, exactly, is that signal being shown to the enemies of America, by God's sanctified ones, from America? What is that unique set of circumstances that will occur on one specific day which will give the enemy unprecedented opportunity to destroy America? It just so happens the Bible tells us. Not only that, it also tells us the time of day those circumstances will commence. Furthermore, we're told the times of day those enemy nations, who come from a distant land[288], will leave their base and arrive at our borders. Few may believe we're given such detail, but we are nonetheless.

When we take a serious look at what the prophets tell us about that Day certain characteristics begin to stand out. Notice how the sky is described from our vantage point on earth. Isaiah 13:10 tells us that "the stars of heaven and their constellations will not give their light; the sun will be darkened in its going forth, and the moon will not cause its light to shine." Remember, Isaiah 13 is one of those

---

[286] Isaiah 43:6
[287] Micah 4:10
[288] Isaiah 13:5

107

chapters that deals exclusively with the destruction of America at the beginning of the "day of the Lord," or the Tribulation. So we see on this particular day certain changes take place which are out of the ordinary. Something blots out the light coming from our sun. This is not describing night time. It says the sun is darkened "in its going forth." Joel 2:10 confirms that the light from the sun, moon, and stars will be blotted out. But the verse also tells us that the "earth quakes before them; the heavens tremble." Something very strange will happen at that moment unlike anything we've experienced in recent history. There are two key words I want to bring to your attention. It says this event, whatever it is, will take place "before them." If you read this verse in context you'll see the "them" is referring to the army coming to destroy that prominent nation where a sizable portion of God's people dwell, America. The events being described precede that great army coming to destroy America.

> *"And it shall come to pass in that day," says the Lord GOD,*
> *"That I will make the sun go down at noon, and I will darken*
> *the earth in broad daylight."* Amos 8:9

I hope the picture is starting to develop in your mind as we overlay these passages. At some point during that day the sun will be blotted out and there will be a great quaking on the earth and the sky will also tremble. But what time of day? Amos 8:9 gives us even more detail regarding that day. It says God "will make the sun go down at noon, and...darken the earth in broad daylight." From this passage we see that the sun will be blotted out at midday. But why does it say the sun will go down instead of just be darkened like the other passages? Typically when the sun "goes down" we don't expect it to come up until the next morning. I believe this is telling us that whatever that thing is that blots out the sun will be big enough to blot out the sun for at least eight or so hours, or until night time when the light of the sun is no longer noticeable. This will not be a momentary occurrence lasting only minutes, like a solar eclipse. When the sun "goes down" on that fateful day it won't be seen again until the following morning. After being pressed for more information about that fateful night, America's watchman of Isaiah

21 confirms this when he says "the morning comes, and also the night."[289] He's speaking prophetically of that night when America is destroyed in only one hour[290] on one particular day.[291] The next morning will come but night, the Tribulation, will follow.

The Longest Eight Hours of Your Life

From these passages it becomes clear that America is directly facing the sun when that great "thing" moves between the earth and sun. Whatever it is will not only block out all light from the sun but also cause earthquakes and trembling in the sky. When I read that the sky will tremble my mind immediately thinks of great storms and thunder. Does the Bible mention anything about storms on that day? One of the more frequent descriptions we're given of the beginning of that Day is that of a great storm. In chapter 5 I showed how the latter half of Jeremiah 25 speaks of the complete destruction of end-time Babylon at the beginning of Tribulation. In Jeremiah 25:32 we read that "a great whirlwind shall be raised up from the farthest parts of the earth." From the vantage point of the Middle East / Near East region where this prophecy was recorded, the farthest parts of the earth would be speaking of our side of the world, North and South America. Whether this great whirlwind is an actual whirlwind or merely symbolic is beside the point. (I believe the phrase "great whirlwind" is used here to denote a specific set of circumstances.) As we continue to study the passages that speak of that day we find language that goes far beyond just the lights being turned out at midday and a random earthquake. Perhaps we should not take it lightly when his Word tells us Yahshua (Jesus) "will come with fire and with His chariots, like a whirlwind, to render His anger with fury, and His rebuke with flames of fire."[292] Malachi 3:2 wonders out loud who will be able to endure the day of his coming. As I'll show, it

---

[289] Isaiah 21:11-12
[290] Revelation 18:10
[291] Isaiah 47:9, Revelation 18:8
[292] Isaiah 66:15

seems he was wondering about the beginning of that Day, not the end of that Day when Christ physically returns to earth.

If we make just one more connection from Jeremiah 25 additional understanding opens up to us in chapters like Ezekiel 13. In Jeremiah 25:34-37 we read of a judgment coming against the leaders of God's people when that Day begins. In a later chapter I'll go into much more detail about that judgment. But for now I want to show you a connection. Ezekiel 13:5 sets the context of that chapter as "the day of the Lord." But the day of the Lord, or the Tribulation, or Jacob's Trouble[293], consists of a period of time lasting many months. So how can we know when, within that period, this prophecy occurs? Within that chapter there is only one direct reference to timing. Verse 9 tells us they, the prophets of peace to whom the chapter is dedicated, will not enter into the land of Israel. The judgment spoken of in Ezekiel 13 befalls them before all the people of the land return to Israel. And we're told that when America is destroyed God's people in America find their way to Zion; the land region known as Palestine.[294] But how else does Ezekiel 13 describe that day? Ezekiel decries the rather flimsy wall those prophets of peace built with their lies and half-truths. A wall is representative of a defense. He's saying the prophets of peace failed to properly teach the people the ways of the Lord; instead, their teachings end up deceiving the people. One only need compare Ezekiel 13:5 with Jeremiah 6:27 and 23:22 to see that a strong, solid wall will cause the people to turn from their sin and serve God with pure hearts and clean lives. But of their wall he says, "There will be flooding rain, and you, O great hailstones, shall fall; and a stormy wind shall tear it down."[295]

Notice the references to a great storm. Is this the same storm which will blot out the sun and cause earthquakes and sky trembling? Consider what I've shown thus far. Jeremiah 25 links the

---

[293] Jeremiah 30:7
[294] Jeremiah 50:4, 51:10, and Isaiah 18:7
[295] Ezekiel 13:11

downfall of America with the beginning of that Day. That Day will begin at midday when the sun is over America. Whatever blots out the sun has earthquakes and sky trembling associated with it. Connected with the calamity of all this is a judgment against the leaders of God's people. Then we turn to Ezekiel 13 and find the same woe falling on the leaders of God's people during the day of the Lord; namely the prophets who speak on God's behalf concerning things future. Their judgment happens before God's people return to Zion and is associated with a great storm which consists of a flooding rain, great hailstones, and a stormy wind.[296] This chapter is crystal clear as it adamantly declares that their wall will be torn down by this great storm. But is it possible that a figurative wall, the teachings of those prophets of peace, could be torn down by an actual storm? It is possible and that's exactly what will happen. The same thing happened to the builders of the Titanic who said the ship could not be sunk. When the ship did actually sink, on its maiden voyage no less, their wall of pride and overconfidence, in which the passengers trusted, came crashing down all the way to the ocean floor.

But do we see this picture of a great storm anywhere else in Scripture? In fact, we see it often. Isaiah 28, also in the context of sweeping away the lies of the leaders of God's people in the latter days, speaks of a mighty tempest of hail, a destroying storm, and a flood of mighty waters overflowing.[297] Micah 1:4 speaks of mountains melting and valleys splitting apart like wax before the fire and like waters poured down a steep place. Nahum says "His fury is poured out like fire, and the rocks are thrown down by Him."[298] Both Isaiah 29 and 30 speak of a time of punishment consisting of thunder, earthquake, great noise, hailstones, storm and tempest, and the flame of devouring fire.[299] Amos describes that same tempest

---

[296] Ezekiel 13:11, 13:13
[297] Isaiah 28:2, 28:17
[298] Nahum 1:6
[299] Isaiah 29:6, 30:30

(violent storm) in "the day of the whirlwind."[300] Hosea ensures us that "a wind from the Lord" will come upon the most fruitful of God's people at the time sorrows of a woman in childbirth shall come upon him.[301] Zechariah speaks of a time when God's people will have to leave their pleasant land because it's made desolate by God's whirlwind during a time of great wrath from the Lord of hosts.[302]

If you remember from chapter five I showed how Zephaniah prominently associates America with the beginning of Tribulation. He proclaims that the whole land (America) will be devoured by the fire of God's jealousy, and it'll happen speedily.[303] We know that God is a jealous God, despising all idols that come between him and his people.[304] But is this "fire of his jealousy" real fire or figurative fire? It's easy to see how an entire city can be demolished instantly in the extreme fire of a nuclear detonation. But I haven't even discussed yet when that army will arrive. Is it possible there's fire raining down from that great thing that blots out the sun? It would seem so. Joel, who gives us much detail about the beginning of that Day, tells us that fire will devour the open pastures and a flame will burn up all the trees of the field.[305] In addition to this the grain crops are ruined because the "harvest of the field has perished." And not just grain crops but it seems all the crops of the land will be ruined on that day.[306] What's described here is the complete desolation of the land, shore to shore. While we know that nuclear fallout can devastate a large area, it's hard to comprehend the vast open land of America could completely wither from a single attack lasting only an hour.[307] Furthermore, fallout isn't going cause a fire which "will devour the open pastures." I believe what we're being shown here is that whatever that thing is coming to blot out the sun will also cause

---

[300] Amos 1:14

[301] Hosea 13:13, 13:15

[302] Zechariah 7:12, 7:14

[303] Zephaniah 1:18, Revelation 18:8, 18:10

[304] Exodus 20:4-5

[305] Joel 1:19-20

[306] Joel 1:10-12

[307] Revelation 18:10

earthquakes, tornadoes, floods, hail, great winds, and balls of fire which will set the land of America ablaze even before the army arrives with their nuclear arsenal. This is in perfect harmony with the second chapter of Joel which informs us that the fire will devour the land before them; before that army arrives.[308] When we properly overlay the Scriptures a clear picture begins to develop. Coming soon to America is something so terrifying it will seem like the longest eight hours of our lives. But the worst is yet to come. When Jehovah says he's going to stand up in the fierceness of his anger to judge the earth, we should take it seriously.[309]

That Mysterious Cloud

You might be wondering, as I am, what, exactly, is that great cloud.[310] Consider what we're told. That Day will surprise a sleeping world like a thief in the night. A fierce celestial object will pass between the earth and sun, blot out all light, and wreak havoc on America, causing earthquakes, great hailstones, winds, thunder, and floods. Fire will rain down from the sky and a great noise will be heard across the land.[311] Just as Zephaniah 1 describes the land being utterly wasted, we find a parallel passage in Isaiah 24. That chapter speaks of great turmoil coming to the earth itself. Verse 19 says the earth is shaken exceedingly. And verse 10 establishes the context as the same time that the "city of confusion is broken down." The very definition of the word Babylon is confusion.[312] Isaiah 24 is speaking of the great terrestrial disturbances caused by that celestial "cloud" as it passes.

As I discussed in chapter 2, it will arrive on one specific day and its arrival will not be delayed in the least. In addition, that

---

[308] Joel 2:3
[309] Nahum 1:6
[310] Lamentations 2:1
[311] Isaiah 29:6, 33:3, Jeremiah 10:16, 11:22, 25:31, 50:46, Ezekiel 19:7, Zephaniah 1:14, 2 Peter 3:10
[312] Strong's Hebrew Dictionary entry H894

"thing" will interfere with radar and satellite communication systems. Much of our superior technology will be rendered useless as it passes over us. The enemy will need to send piloted bombers instead of guided missiles because their guidance systems will not function properly either. We are not given any indication that the celestial object will collide with earth. Rather, it seems to approach suddenly, pass by for about eight or so hours, leaving utter desolation in its wake. Notice that Isaiah tells us that after this event God's people, those who were spared[313], will lift up their voices, sing and glorify the Lord in the dawning light.[314] That "dawning light" is referring to the morning after America is destroyed, technically the beginning of the second day of the Tribulation.

So, what is that celestial object which will wreak havoc on our planet? While I can't say with certainty, there are a number of theories floating around today which sound eerily similar to the description found in the Bible. Consider that astronomers have, only as recently as 1995, discovered a type of sub-stellar object called a brown dwarf.[315] Brown dwarfs, which emit almost no light, are reported as being very difficult to detect.[316] Perhaps this is why the Bible describes the world as being taken off guard by the sudden arrival of that cloud.

Speaking of stellar objects, the internet has been ablaze for years with rumors of a hidden planet referred to as Planet X, Nibiru, and a slew of other names. While government officials continue to deny the existence of that planet, many have written books on the subject, even linking ancient Sumerian texts to Planet X. Those who teach about this planet believe it has a very large orbit and passes by the earth every few thousand years causing chaos and destruction.

---

[313] Isaiah 1:8, 6:13

[314] Isaiah 24:14-15

[315] *Brown dwarf*. Wikipedia.org. Retrieved March 14, 2012 from http://en.wikipedia.org/wiki/Brown_dwarf

[316] Brown Dwarf Detectives. Nasa.gov. Retrieved March 14, 2012 from http://www.nasa.gov/vision/universe/ starsgalaxies/brown_dwarf_ detectives.html

Many also believe the Mayan calendar predicted its return in 2012. For reasons I'll explain in the next chapter, I'm not at all concerned about this becoming a reality in 2012.

There's one last theory I'd be remiss not to mention. It's reported that an ancient secular manuscript, called "The Kolbrin," survived throughout the ages and was recently rediscovered and published for our modern day. It speaks of a great celestial object, called the Destroyer that, in times past, caused untold death and destruction on past civilizations. The excerpts I've read from that republished manuscript, though written in a different style than the Bible, sounds nearly identical to the great cloud I described. If it does turn out to be a hoax one can only wonder why someone would go through so much trouble to describe a celestial nightmare already detailed in the Bible. While I have no way of proving the authenticity of "The Kolbrin," and I certainly don't put any other text on par with the Bible, I mention it now because of its uncanny similarity to the things described in this chapter.

Like Taking Candy from a Baby

Despite what some may think, we are given enough information to discern the sequence of events of the Tribulation from start to finish. But it takes work to really see what's going on. We have to study diligently and make the connections God has made available in his Word. By comparing the messages of the prophets we can see a day is coming to America unlike any other. And while it may read just like so much fantasy, we can look at what has transpired in the world thus far to see that the stage is set for the final fulfillment of the remaining prophesied events. That Day of dread, of great darkness and gloominess, of clouds and thick darkness coming to America will alter the current course of history. That day will set the world on the path of severe trials and Tribulations which will culminate with the return of Christ and the long-promised establishment of his Kingdom on earth. And that day will provide an unprecedented opportunity for America's enemies to crush her like fine dust, never again to rise.[317] After all, just like the Titanic, America will eventually be covered by the ocean waves.[318] And now that we have a clear picture of what that day will be like we can begin to understand how the greatest nation on earth, with the strongest military ever known to man, can be defeated in a single hour. We won't even see them coming.

Just as the quarterback is walloped from his blind side by the blitzing quarterback, America will be blind to the onslaught of the approaching enemy nations. Whatever blots out all light from the sun will also wreak havoc on our nation with earthquakes and great storms of hailstones, tornadoes, flooding rain and even fire from the sky. It's very likely our satellite communications and radar defense systems will be rendered useless on that day. If that is indeed, the case, it's also likely that guided missiles, like ICBM's, will not be effective when that great stormy "cloud" is over America. But does the Bible support this scenario? Yes, this is exactly the scenario we see in the Word of God.

Several passages speak of this blindness and destruction beginning at midday.[319] But when we examine the Scripture speaking of the destruction of America we find her ultimate destruction coming in the evening, not at midday. The watchman of Isaiah 21 speaks of her downfall coming during an evening feast (the king's table) which the president will host.[320] And Isaiah 17 echoes this idea when it says "Then behold, at eventide, trouble! And before the morning, he is no more."[321] So is there a disagreement among the prophets? Not at all. Remember that we're told the enemy is coming from a distant land.[322] In chapter 5 I showed that Jeremiah was commissioned to prophesy to his generation and ours, which is

---

[317] Isaiah 25:2
[318] Jeremiah 51:42, 51:64, Revelation 18:21
[319] Psalm 91:6, Isaiah 59:10, Jeremiah 20:16, Zephaniah 2:4, Amos 8:9
[320] Isaiah 21:4-5
[321] Isaiah 17:14
[322] Isaiah 5:26, 13:5, Jeremiah 51:27-28

confirmed by both Moses and Daniel. Much of what Jeremiah prophesies can be directly applied to our generation.

Twice in Jeremiah we read of a destroyer coming against God's people at noon. The first is found in Jeremiah 6 where we find the enemy's intent: "Prepare war against her; arise, and let us go up at noon. Woe to us, for the day goes away, for the shadows of the evening are lengthening. Arise, and let us go by night, and let us destroy her palaces."[323] In this passage Jeremiah is exposing the plan of the enemy coming against a nation inhabited by God's people. Notice what we're being shown. The enemy knows he must start out at noon. But he also knows that if he doesn't arrive by evening then trouble, or woe, will come upon him. What we see here is a very specific time frame. He has to leave at noon and arrive by the evening to deliver his attack. But how is it that he leaves at noon but says "let us go by night?" The answer is simple and fits perfectly with the events of that particular day. They "go by night" because while it's noon over America, it's nighttime in their land. Furthermore, the light of the sun is blotted out from the time they leave to the time they arrive.

The timing of his departure and arrival is crucial to his success. Nothing is said of the battle itself. Nothing is said of the strength of the two opponents and the losses they may incur. The only consideration we're shown of possible failure is in the timing of their arrival. They understand and acknowledge that if they arrive too late only then will they experience trouble from the land they are attacking. This further illustrates that the duration of that cloud over America will last about eight or so hours, from midday to early evening. Just as the cloud is finishing its pass over North America, the enemy arrives: "Then behold, at eventide, trouble! And before the morning, he is no more."[324]

---

[323] Jeremiah 6:4-5
[324] Isaiah 17:14

The second passage is found in Jeremiah 15. There we find written: "I will bring against them, against the mother of the young men, a plunderer at noonday; I will cause anguish and terror to fall on them suddenly. She languishes who has borne seven; she has breathed her last; her sun has gone down while it was yet day; she has been ashamed and confounded. And the remnant of them I will deliver to the sword before their enemies."[325] The Hebrew word translated as plunderer or spoiler has a definition that includes both thief and destroyer. This is exactly the picture we're given for the destruction of America. Not only will that thief[326] come upon her suddenly but the end result will be her complete destruction and demise. When does Jeremiah 15 tell us all of this will begin? Noonday. You may also find this description curious: "She languishes who has borne seven;" In Revelation 17 America is described as the mother of harlots[327] who sits upon a beast with seven heads[328] which represent seven mountains.[329] The Greek word for mountains has a definition meaning to rise or to rear.[330] This mother of harlots not only sits upon, or reigns over, all the nations of the earth but she has also raised them up under her wicked influence. She has infected the entire earth with her harlotry.[331] One doesn't have to strain too hard to see the similarities between the mother of harlots described in Revelation 17 and the mother in Jeremiah 15, of whom it's predicted that "she has breathed her last; her sun has gone down while it was yet day."

At midday something will begin to pass between the earth and the sun while America is facing the sun. That great cloud will cause untold destruction on America as it passes and will render our radar and navigational systems useless as it passes. This will allow

---

[325] Jeremiah 15:8-9

[326] Hosea 7:1, 1 Thessalonians 5:2-3

[327] Revelation 17:5

[328] Revelation 17:3

[329] Revelation 17:9

[330] Strong's Greek Dictionary entry G3735

[331] Revelation 18:3

the army "from the north"[332] to approach undetected and arrive at our northern borders just before the cloud passes. By now it should be obvious they will choose to send bombers and fighter jets with a nuclear payload, instead of guided missiles, because they know those guidance systems will not work as that cloud passes. To give you an idea of how this could play out today, consider the following: The distance from Murmansk, Russia to Chicago, Illinois is 4205 miles (6768 kilometers). The cruising speed of a Russian Tupolev Tu-95MS Bear-H bomber is 441.2 mph (715.3 kph).[333] Time from Murmansk to Chicago is about 9.5 hours. Even using an older aircraft like the one I mentioned, at just cruising speed, Russia would be capable of fulfilling the "early evening" prophecy if they leave from their "farthest border."[334]

You Are Surrounded!

That great cloud will give the enemy a decisive advantage and allow the greatest military known to man to be defeated in just one hour. Those bombers and jets will fly to their intended targets, deliver their nuclear warheads, and return to their land. I suspect, and I'm just guessing here, every city in America with a population over fifty thousand will be targeted. In all that's about 600 cities.[335] This complete and utter destruction of America will take only one hour. But this is not all we're told. A consistent theme regarding this army is that not only will they come from the north but they'll also surround that land being attacked.[336] In Jeremiah 50 we read, "Put yourselves in array against Babylon all around, all you who bend the bow; shoot at her, spare no arrows, for she has sinned against the

---

[332] Jeremiah 1:14-15, 4:6, 6:1, 22, 10:22, 50:3, 9, 41, 51:48, Zechariah 2:6
[333] Valka.cz. Retrieved March 14, 2012 from http://en.valka.cz/viewtopic.php/t/45631
[334] Jeremiah 50:26
[335] http://www.demographia.com/db-uscity98.htm
[336] Jeremiah 4:17, 12:9, 50:14-15, 50:29, 51:2, Amos 3:11

LORD. Shout against her all around."[337] While it's easy to see that a bow and arrow can represent a modern missile and its launcher, one might be puzzled to think how America could be literally surrounded by enemy forces. We know that last-day Babylon is described as being surrounded by water. America fits this description as much of her borders touch the sea. When those bombers reach our northern border, submarines all around us will join them in unleashing their nuclear payload. The same judgment we poured out on Japan and other nations will be meted back on us.[338] Their victory will be decisive and final. She who rules the earth now will have come to the end of her years.

> *"...She has breathed her last; her sun has gone down while it was yet day..." says the LORD.* Jeremiah 15:9

---

[337] Jeremiah 50:14-15
[338] Ezekiel 24:14, Ezekiel 22:31, Matthew 26:52, Luke 6:38, Revelation 18:7

Chapter 8 - Year of Recompense

For it is the day of the LORD's vengeance, the year of recompense for the cause of Zion. Isaiah 34:8

As my parents were preparing to marry they feared they may not even get to enjoy their honeymoon. The year was 1967 and the reborn nation of Israel had just established full control of Jerusalem during the Six Day War. It seems some of my parents' friends speculated this monumental event indicated the imminent return of Christ. But Yahshua (Jesus) the Christ, or Anointed One didn't return, I was born several years later, and the rest is history. There's no question in my mind that that event, along with the rebirth of Israel in 1948, were monumental events. I can understand how those must have been exciting times. But here we are, nearly forty-nine years later and time marches on. Since that time many of us have heard dozens, if not hundreds, of predictions regarding the return of Christ. But it seems the world has largely learned to tune them out. And if they aren't being altogether tuned out they are met with scorn and ridicule. After all, can anyone really know if we're two months or twenty years from the beginning of the Tribulation? And if such a thing could be known is it possible to overcome all the misconceptions and convey it in such a way that people can understand? Can we only point to events of recent history to make a solid case or do we have to rely on historians' educated guesses? As I said before, any prediction derived from the distant past is sure to fail. The dates historians have derived for events before the time of Christ are often disputed and not to be taken as absolute proof of anything. Even the year of our Lord's birth is hotly disputed.

As I showed in chapter 3, not only can we know when the Tribulation will begin, we are expected to know. We are not to be in darkness regarding that Day.[339] We have the light that exposes the coming thief.[340] With this in mind I will press on and attempt to convey the year that Day will begin, as I understand it. It's of little use to merely be told that a thief is coming "some day." After all, we have to get on with our lives. We can't wait at that window every second. Would you still break ground on a new church building if that Day were to begin in a month? Would you still divorce your wife? Would you mistreat your workers? Would you live your life as if nothing at all will change? I suppose many of us, for too long already having ignored the instructions in the Bible, would begin making drastic changes. The wise among us would begin to sense the urgency of the hour and live lives pleasing to the Father. We wouldn't allow our houses (symbolic of ourselves) to be broken into. For those not already walking in the light of his Word, I urge you to pay very close attention to the case I present in this chapter and the next. Despite everything we've been told up to this point the Bible does reveal the specific day that the Tribulation begins, if we are willing to take the time necessary to understand it.

But is it really just a matter of spending enough time in the Bible? After describing some of the events of the beginning of the Tribulation, Jehovah, through Isaiah, gives us a farming lesson. He rhetorically asks how the farmer knows how to do this or that. How does he know when to stop plowing and start planting? How does he know how to work with the various seeds? The answer is then given, "This also comes from the LORD of hosts, who is wonderful in counsel and excellent in guidance."[341] This also comes from the Lord? It's imperative we don't read whole chapters of the Bible as a disjointed collection of thoughts. The farming lesson is connected to the rest of the chapter. Just as Jehovah has created all things and instructed them in the way to live[342], so he instructs the farmer and gives us understanding as we study his Word. But if we approach

---

[339] 1 Thessalonians 5:4
[340] Psalm 119:105
[341] Isaiah 28:29
[342] Job 38-41

the Word of God with "uncircumcised ears,"[343] or the filthiness of sin, we should not expect our spiritual sight[344] to gain proper understanding. And if we fail to take the whole of prophecy into account, we should not expect to rightly understand how that Day will affect us. In every single failed prediction we find the argument either lacks proper interpretation or it's missing some piece of the puzzle. I have been guilty of this very thing. But, by using those mistakes of the past, I now put forth my understanding of <u>when</u> these things will come to pass.

Revisiting Daniel's "Ah, ha!" Moment

In chapter 4 I spent a considerable amount of time explaining Daniel's 70-Week prophecy and how it came to him as he realized the full extent of both Jeremiah's and Moses' prophecies regarding our day. Remember, it was in the "first year of Darius the Mede," which was just after ancient Babylon fell to the Medo-Persian Empire, when Daniel finally understood what those two prophets meant.[345]

He understood that both Jeremiah and Moses were speaking of similar events to occur both in their day and at the end of the age, our day. When Daniel realized this he began to offer up supplications and prayers of repentance on behalf of God's people. It was at that time that the angel Gabriel was sent to Daniel to give him understanding of the time allotted both for Christ's first coming and his second. Keep in mind that what Gabriel told him was in the context of the revelation he had just received regarding the desolations (plural) of Jerusalem.[346] What Gabriel told Daniel should be considered an extension of his revelation concerning Jeremiah's 70-year prophecy regarding the downfall of Babylon.

---

[343] Jeremiah 6:10
[344] Isaiah 6:9-10
[345] Daniel 9:1-2
[346] Daniel 9:2

When we consider that one prophecy is speaking of two generations separated by a great span of time we should be compelled to look for patterns. The pattern that our generation will follow is such that God's people, living in Babylon, will be set free to return to Zion when Babylon is defeated. After all, the land of Zion was given to God's people by God as an everlasting inheritance.[347] Even before Jerusalem fell to Babylon Jeremiah predicted that God would give all nations into Babylon's hands. Whatever nation she set out to conquer would fall to her.[348] What Jeremiah was describing was superpower status. But the rest of the story we already know. Her superpower status was to last only seventy years. History shows that Babylon fell to the Medo-Persian Empire but not in the way Jeremiah described. This is what caused Daniel to sit up and take notice regarding the full extent of Jeremiah's prophecy. Taking all of this into account we can see the pattern that our generation will follow. The Day of the Lord will begin with sudden destruction. While there are prophecies that tell us that destruction will come upon other continents as well, there is one prominent nation which will be completely destroyed on the first day. That nation, like ancient Babylon, contains a large portion of God's people. That nation is America.

70 Years a Lady

Applying that ancient pattern to our day we can begin to see what's going to happen. America's "Lady of Kingdoms" status will last only seventy years. At the end of those seventy years America will be destroyed and the Tribulation will commence. God's people, those not under his immediate judgment, will return to Zion. The prophets have much more to add to this story. It's beyond the scope of this book to examine what God's people will endure in Zion during the Tribulation so I will press on to show when these things will take

---

[347] Ezekiel 37:21-22
[348] Jeremiah 25:9

place. I will only remind God's people at this time that we are his witnesses in the earth.[349] And because we're his witnesses it makes sense, then, that we would be here during one of the most important moments in all of history, to give our witness.

Obviously, for reasons I've already explained, the Tribulation has not yet begun and America is still the reigning superpower of the world. Therefore it goes without saying, we haven't reached year seventy yet. But we're close. It so happens there was a turning point in recent history which began that great 70-year countdown and set the stage for the fulfillment of all remaining prophecies. That confluence of events, as I will show, was World War II.

If America's superpower status will only last seventy years, when, exactly, did that begin? To bring this picture into focus, we have to take a look at a few more things. While few would dispute America's rise to superpower-status at the end of World War II, many may not realize how closely those events match the pattern given in the Bible of ancient Babylon. When America dropped those atomic bombs on Japan World War II came to a close and the world awoke to a new reality; one of America at the forefront of military and industrial power. The war left Europe devastated and America gladly stepped to the forefront to fill the vacuum of power. A new "American Century" had begun and America never looked back. She has emerged from humble beginnings, outlasted all other dominate powers, and now reigns as the worlds hegemon, or hyperpower.

Few may realize 1946 was a turning point in one other important way. Jehovah, through the prophet Jeremiah, made it clear that all surrounding nations were to serve Babylon. In Jeremiah 24 we find that those who serve Babylon during her reign would be like a basket of good figs. But those who refused to bring their necks under the yoke of Babylon[350] would be like a basket of rotten figs. Jeremiah sent word to the Judean captives of Babylon

---

[349] Isaiah 43:10, 12, 44:8, Acts 1:8
[350] Jeremiah 27:11-12

instructing them to settle in for a long stay. He told them to plant gardens, build houses, continue to marry and have children. He even tells them to pray for the peace of that nation, assuring them that in its peace they would have peace.[351] Was this license to sin? Was Jeremiah giving the people permission to blend in and serve the idols of the land? God forbid! In fact, that's why the people of the house of Judah, the southern kingdom, were taken from their land in the first place. This pattern of judgment was established many years before by Moses in the book of Deuteronomy. When God's people, collectively, fall into gross sin and refuse to repent after repeated warnings, God sends a destroyer against their land and he sends his people into captivity until their hearts turn back to him. Whether for good, or for bad, we are his witnesses in the earth. When we do well, keeping his commandments and statutes, we enjoy the favor of God in the land he's given us. But when we rebel, collectively, we become a hissing and a reproach to all the surrounding nations.[352] Either way people can look at us and see the work of God in our lives. We are his witnesses, whether we are under God's blessing or his judgments.

An amazing thing happened in 1946. Just as the house of Judah, the Jews, came under the umbrella of ancient Babylon's protection, so did the modern-day house of Judah come under America's protection. By the time WW2 came to an end Hitler and the Holocaust had so devastated the Jewish population of Eastern Europe they no longer felt at home there. As one Jewish woman explained: "You know what Europe is to me? It's a cemetery. When I walk into a store and see soap on sale, I remember that this may be the body of my sister."[353] They longed to feel safe again. They longed for a land they could call their own, the borders of which they could protect themselves. They longed for Palestine. The Anglo-

---

[351] Jeremiah 29:5-7
[352] Jeremiah 44:23
[353] *REFUGEES: Exodus*, TIME Magazine, Time Inc. May 6, 1946

American Committee of Inquiry report[354] seemed to be just the catalyst they needed. A May, 1946 TIME Magazine article stated that "After three months of study in the U.S., Europe and the Near East, the twelve-man committee recommended, in effect, a new policy that would scrap the 1939 British White Paper. Salient points: 1) the immediate admission of 100,000 European Jews into Palestine; 2) Jewish D.P.'s are a responsibility of all the nations; 3) terrorism by Jews or Arabs must be sternly repressed."[355] So, with the blessing and support of the world's leading nations, the Jews began returning to Palestine en masse. It was around this same time the British Mandate over Palestine started coming to an end. Palestine, and later Israel, would soon become an American concern. There's no question that Israel has been from that time, and still is today, a close Middle Eastern partner and ally of the United States of America. One could argue from a secular standpoint that the reborn nation of Israel would not exist today without the full support of the United States. But we know that God foreordained these events to take place exactly as they did. Many of the Jews who chose not to return to Palestine chose instead to head for the shores of modern-day Babylon, America. America today boasts a Jewish population estimated near seven million[356], many of whom are prominent members of our society. And if the house of Judah has found protection under America's umbrella, the house of Israel has all the more. (I will explain this in a later chapter.) It's for this reason that we find in Jeremiah 50, which speaks of America's final downfall, "'In those days and in that time,' says the LORD, 'The children of Israel shall come, they and the children of Judah together; with continual weeping they shall come, and seek the LORD their God.'"[357]

---

[354] *Anglo-American Committee of Inquiry.* Wikipedia.org. Retrieved March 14, 2012 from http://en.wikipedia.org/wiki/Anglo-American_Committee_of_Inquiry

[355] *REFUGEES: Exodus*, TIME Magazine, Time Inc. May 6, 1946

[356] *Jewish population.* Wikipedia.org. Retrieved March 14, 2012 from http://en.wikipedia.org/wiki/Jewish_population

[357] Jeremiah 50:4

But did all of this really need to take place well in advance of the end of America? The truth is that this is exactly the scenario we find in the Word of God. Not only do we see both the house of Israel and the house of Judah fleeing a burning America but we also see the house of Judah waiting in Palestine at the beginning of that Day. The only way this is possible is if a significant part of Judah (Jews) resides in America and another significant part resides in Palestine when that Day begins. In Isaiah 29 we find these words: "But when he sees his children, the work of My hands, in his midst, they will hallow My name, and hallow the Holy One of Jacob, and fear the God of Israel."[358] One might ask who these children are that he suddenly finds in his midst. Could these be the same children that Rachel is seen weeping for at the end of the age[359] because she thinks they are no more?[360] The very next verse assures her that she is to weep no longer, for her children will return. And Ezekiel 37 shows us that Israel and Judah will be reunited at the end of the age. In Hosea we read: "Also, O Judah, a harvest is appointed for you, when I return the captives of My people."[361] What's interesting is that the house of Judah is promised a harvest of people. These people can be none other than the lost tribes of the house of Israel. Furthermore, Hosea promises that Judah will have multiplied her fortified cities by the time Israel reaps that whirlwind.[362] Since 1946 the Jews have turned the desert of Palestine into a flourishing nation with fortified cites. In one of the most telling passages indicating Judah, at least in part, must be living and reigning in Palestine when that Day begins, Zechariah tells us the governors of Judah have a heart change when their eyes are opened to the true identity of the "inhabitants of Jerusalem."[363] I'll expand on this later. But keep in mind for now

---

[358] Isaiah 29:23

[359] Jeremiah 31:1

[360] Jeremiah 31:15

[361] Hosea 6:11

[362] Hosea 8:7, 8:14

[363] Zechariah 12:5

that often times Jerusalem is used to refer to God's chosen people rather than the actual city.[364]

As we study the end-time prophecies of the Bible it becomes clear that Judah, at least in part, must be living and ruling in the land of Palestine at the start of that Day. And thanks to the events of WW2, and the dominant influence of America in world affairs, that's exactly what happened. But history shows, despite the miraculous national rebirth of a people who were scattered abroad for nearly two thousand years, life in Israel has been anything but easy. It seems the nation has survived and flourished in the face of immense obstacles. But do her national victories mean God is pleased with her? Did the house of Judah, as a whole, start obeying God's commandments and statutes in 1946? Or does the house of Judah, in part, now live and reign over Palestine because it was foreordained for such a time as this? The truth is, despite her miraculous success many consider national Israel to be largely secular today. Christians living in America might ask some similar questions. Is God pleased with us today? Are we keeping his commandments and statutes, living clean lives with pure hearts? Or have we become like all the ungodliness that surrounds us? One only need look at the divorce rate among American Christians to see that we have become just as corrupt as the nation in which we live. The canary in the coal mine is the most basic building block of society: the family unit. Zechariah chapter one, which seems to describe the time just before the beginning of that Day, gives us an indication of how God sees his people. It says: "Then the Angel of the LORD answered and said, "O LORD of hosts, how long will You not have mercy on Jerusalem and on the cities of Judah, against which You were angry these seventy years?"[365]

Restore Jerusalem! (7 x 7 = 49)

---

[364] Hebrews 12:22
[365] Zechariah 1:12

Know therefore and understand, that from the going forth of the command to restore and build Jerusalem until Messiah the Prince, there shall be seven weeks and sixty-two weeks; the street shall be built again, and the wall, even in troublesome times. Daniel 9:25

Here we find ourselves, far removed from the defeat of Nazi Germany and our youth of 1946. How have the years treated us? Are we a nation blessed by God, walking in his ways, or do we find ourselves under his judgments with troubles and evils confronting us at every turn? Do we still look like a young Lady or do we have "gray hairs here and there"; our strength depleted?[366] As you ponder those questions, let me address the very purpose of this chapter head on. If that 70-year clock began ticking down sometime in 1946, when should we expect the complete and utter demise of America? Adding seventy years to 1946 brings us to 2016. But if this really is true, certainly there must be some sort of confirmation in the Word of God, right? In fact, there is. I might be so bold to state that anyone alive in 1946, with knowledge of these things, would have been very interested in the year 1967. That person, whether they existed I have no idea, would have expected something very significant to occur that year.

> 62 Start - Restore Jerusalem
> 62 End - Messiah cut off
> 7 Start - Restore Jerusalem
> 7 End - ???
> 1 Start - Covenant with many
> 1 Middle - Abomination of desolation
> 1 End - 70 weeks concluded, Return of Christ

> 62 x 7 = 434 years
> 7 x 7 = 49 years
> 1 x 7 = 7 years

If you remember from chapter 4 I spoke of a missing marker. As you read my interpretation of Daniel 9 keep a couple things in

---

[366] Hosea 7:9

mind. America is destroyed at the beginning of Tribulation; the very first day. Therefore, all other events of the Tribulation take place after America is out of the picture. We can overlay Daniel 9 with other passages in the Bible and see that the 1 shabuwa, or week of years, is clearly speaking of a time during the Tribulation. In fact, when those seven years are finished, the 70-week prophecy will be complete and Christ will physically return to earth.

The 62 and the 1 shabuwa have starting and ending markers, or events, associated with them. But the 7 only has a starting marker. The ending marker is hidden. But we saw that this 70-week timeframe was given to Daniel within the context of his revelation about Jeremiah's 70-year reign of Babylon. I contend that though the ending marker is hidden, it's not out of view. The 7 shabuwas (or 49 years) ends at the same time the Tribulation begins. The 7 shabuwas must give way to the 1 shabuwa. The 49 years must end before the final 7 years can begin. Now, let me be clear, I'm not saying the 49 year period ends and then the last seven years begins on the very next day. Taking other prophecies into account, that simply cannot be the case. There are a series of events that must occur between the end of the 49 years and the beginning of the final 7 years, the discussion of which is beyond the scope of this book.

> Ancient Babylon Defeated
>   62 Start - Restore Jerusalem
>   62 End - Messiah cut off
>   7 Start - Restore Jerusalem
>   **7 End - Day of the Lord begins**
> Present-Day Babylon (America) Defeated

What we have then is a situation such that the downfall of the two Babylons act like a set of bookends. Babylon was defeated just before Daniel was given this timeframe. America will be defeated 49 years after a command goes forth to restore Jerusalem. I've shown that America's reign will come to an end in 2016. But, if that's true, there must be a command to restore Jerusalem 49 years prior. Was there? Subtracting 49 years from 2016 brings us to the year 1967. Was there a command to restore Jerusalem in 1967?

Before the Six Day War[367] in June of 1967, Jerusalem was divided. East Jerusalem, the Old City, was under Arab control and the remainder under Israeli control. But after the war, the whole of Jerusalem, including its coveted holy sites, was under Israeli control, as it remains this day. Since that day, rebuilding and restoration of the Old City has commenced under the watchful eye of the Israeli government. That command to restore and rebuild Jerusalem did go forth exactly as foretold in the Bible, 49 years before the end of America.

Signs in the Sky

"And there will be signs in the sun, in the moon, and in the stars; and on the earth distress of nations, with perplexity, the sea and the waves roaring" Luke 21:25

For those still unconvinced after seeing two separate time frames which point to the same year, perhaps a third sign will help. There are a couple things we have to understand before we begin. The first is that celestial events are part of God's plan. He intends them to be used to indicate signs and seasons. In Genesis 1:14 we read: "Then God said, 'Let there be lights in the firmament of the heavens to divide the day from the night; and let them be for signs and seasons, and for days and years.'"

The second thing we have to understand is that Jehovah's seven annual feasts, recorded in Leviticus 23, are his appointed times with men. It's when he personally intervenes in history. These are God's special days each year that he has marked on the calendar. He tells us these days are holy. We are to keep these appointments with him.[368]

---

[367] *Six-Day War*. Wikipedia.org. Retrieved March 14, 2012 from http://en.wikipedia.org/wiki/Six-Day_War
[368] Leviticus 23:37

Now, what happens when his celestial signs line up with his holy days? Is it something we should give some attention? Obviously, I think we should pay very close attention. So, what are these celestial events that fall on God's holidays? In 2008 Mark Blitz, pastor of El Shaddai Ministries[369], discovered that by using NASA's website, he could determine past and future lunar and solar eclipses. He then overlaid that information with the calendar of holy days. This is a summary of what he discovered:

> Lunar Eclipse - Passover - April 15, 2014
> Lunar Eclipse - Feast of Tabernacles - October 8, 2014
> Solar Eclipse - Adar 29/Nisan 1(new year) - March 20, 2015
> Lunar Eclipse - Passover - April 4, 2015
> Solar Eclipse - Feast of Trumpets - September 13, 2015
> Lunar Eclipse - Feast of Tabernacles - September 28, 2015

> *The sun shall be turned into darkness, and the moon into blood, **before** the coming of the great and awesome day of the LORD.* Joel 2:31

You should understand at this point that a lunar eclipse is also referred to as a blood red moon. Now, let's take a look at Joel 2:31. What if this verse is talking about solar and lunar eclipses? Certainly we see here four lunar eclipses and two solar eclipses occurring on six important holidays. Notice that these solar and lunar eclipses occur just <u>before</u> the year 2016. Also, keep in mind that a solar and lunar eclipse cannot occur on the same day. That would require the moon to be in two places at the same time, or a second moon. Therefore, it's very likely Joel is referring to solar and lunar eclipses occurring on various days just prior to the beginning of that Day. Four consecutive lunar eclipses on God's high holy days are referred to as a tetrad and are very rare. One might be inclined to believe Jehovah is trying to show us something. After all, this series of eclipses occur just prior to 2016. But is this a one-time event? Perhaps it's just a fluke. In fact, Mr. Blitz discovered this

---

[369] El Shaddai Ministries, Bonney Lake, WA. (http://www.elshaddaiministries.us/)

tetrad pattern at two other significant points in recent history. Once again we see four lunar eclipses on God's holy days.

> Lunar Eclipse - Passover - April 24, 1967
> Lunar Eclipse - Sukkoth - October 18, 1967
> Lunar Eclipse - Passover - April 13, 1968
> Lunar Eclipse - Sukkoth - October 6, 1968

Around the same time that Daniel's prophecy to restore Jerusalem came to pass in 1967, another rare tetrad occurred in the heavens. Notice those four lunar eclipses on God's holy days do not occur at any time between November 1968 and March 2014. But what's even more astonishing is that these lunar eclipses show up at one other key time in recent history. After nearly 2000 years without a land to call their own, the house of Judah, or Israel, officially became a sovereign nation once again in 1948.

> Lunar Eclipse - Passover - April 13, 1949
> Lunar Eclipse - Sukkoth - October 7, 1949
> Lunar Eclipse - Passover - April 2, 1950
> Lunar Eclipse - Sukkoth - September 26, 1950

Mr. Blitz discovered that these tetrads are very rare indeed. It seems the three occurrences in our lifetime are a very unique anomaly. To observe just one lunar tetrad again in history, one has to go all the way back to 1493 and 1494. It seems that the Creator of the ends of the earth[370], who has foreknowledge of all things[371], and who holds all things together by the Word of his power[372], did indeed give us signs in the sky to confirm his Word. Not only do we have three distinct signs pointing to the same year, but the third sign has three distinct signs within itself. Just as the planets orbit the sun in their respective seasons, so the events of this age have followed a predetermined path and will conclude after a predetermined duration. Without a doubt the times and seasons, years and days are appointed by our great Jehovah who exercises lovingkindness,

---

[370] Isaiah 40:28
[371] Isaiah 46:10
[372] Hebrews 1:3, Colossians 1:17

judgment and righteousness in the earth.[373] At the end of seventy years and forty-nine years, with signs in the sky confirming, America will cease to be a nation forever.

---

[373] Jeremiah 9:23-24

Chapter 9 - Day of Destruction

Alas for the day! For the day of the LORD is at hand; it shall come as destruction from the Almighty. Joel 1:15

I suppose if one stubbornly refuses to believe the Bible gives us enough information to determine the year the Tribulation begins, it quickly becomes a lesson in futility to discuss with them the timing of the actual day. But with those brave souls who remain undaunted by the absurd chorus of irrational doubters, let's press forward and settle this question of "When?" once and for all. If you've been following along closely with this book, you might notice a very deliberate progression from one chapter to the next. Each step along the way examines an important truth which is needed to understand the next. A wall is built by setting one brick atop another, brick by brick. Isaiah asks: "Whom will he teach knowledge? And whom will he make to understand the message?"[374] The answer is given: line upon line, precept upon precept.[375]

We saw that that Day will be unlike any other. It will begin with sudden destruction and will arrive at the appointed time. One prominent nation of our day, America, will receive the brunt of the fury of that first day and will meet her sudden demise after ruling over the earth for seventy years. The end of those seventy years is confirmed by a separate period of forty-nine years. Both the seventy years and the forty-nine years end on the same day and contain prophesied events which are demarcated by rare solar and lunar eclipses. But, the question remains. If we can know the year, can we also know the time of year and perhaps even the actual day? I will continue to build that wall brick by brick. Remember that a wall is

---

[374] Isaiah 28:9
[375] Isaiah 28:10

representative of a defense. Those with a strong wall will not be taken off guard by the arrival of the thief. He who understands when the thief will arrive will not allow his house to be broken into.[376] Wisdom is not found in hoping and praying that God is on our side. Rather, the wise among us will make sure we are abiding under the shadow of his wing[377] when the fierceness of his anger is unleashed on the earth.[378]

Spring in the Joyous City

> *On the land of my people will come up thorns and briers, yes, on all the happy homes in the joyous city.* Isaiah 32:13

Many people have become convinced that the Tribulation has to begin in autumn. Remember from Daniel 9 that the last seven years before Christ's return begins with the confirming of "a covenant with many for one week."[379] They reason that the whole of Tribulation is exactly seven years (which it's not) and that Christ returns on "the day and hour no one knows," the Feast of Trumpets (which I agree with). Therefore, they conclude the Tribulation must begin exactly seven years before the return of Christ, in the fall. What they don't understand is that certain predicted events must transpire between the destruction of America and the beginning of that "covenant with many." So, if that Day doesn't begin in the fall, what time of year does it begin?

If the Word of God is a lamp to our feet and a light to our path, how well are we seeing?[380] When we read the Bible do we really try to understand or do we just gloss over it? Like with everything else, we get out of it what we put into it. We're looking for two things: phrases indicating time of year within the context of

---

[376] Matthew 24:43
[377] Psalm 91:1
[378] Nahum 1:6-7
[379] Daniel 9:27
[380] Psalm 119:105

the beginning of that Day. In Isaiah we find this curious statement: "Therefore you will plant pleasant plants and set out foreign seedlings; in the day you will make your plant to grow, and in the morning you will make your seed to flourish; but the harvest will be a heap of ruins in the day of grief and desperate sorrow."[381] Clearly this is speaking of a certain time of year. It's typically in the spring when we plant our seeds and starter plants, nurture them and cause them to grow. Notice that the passage speaks of both planting and a harvest. One should not become overly confused by this. Just as we saw that a symbolic wall can be torn down by an actual storm, so this actual crop is ended by a figurative harvest. Even within this passage we see this concept presented. Those grains, grapes, and olives in verses 5 and 6 are symbolic of God's people who will be spared on that day. By examining other passages we can see that a harvest symbolically represents a supernatural preservation of God's people in the midst of destruction.[382]

However, is the context of Isaiah 17 the beginning of the Tribulation? We read that this ending, or harvest, of the land "will be a heap of ruins in the day of grief and desperate sorrow." Verses 7 and 8 tell us this will be at a time when people look up toward God, pulling their attention away from their daily lives filled with idol worship. What would cause the masses to finally think about the Creator of all things if not the quaking and reeling to and fro of the earth, the hail and mighty winds, and fire falling from the sky on that first day of the Tribulation? In Zechariah 9:1 we find a parallel passage describing a time when "the eyes of humanity, including all the tribes of Israel, are on the LORD." Also in that passage we find, just as we do here in Isaiah 17 and other places, judgment coming to the city of Damascus.[383]

The astute reader may realize that the start of spring varies greatly throughout the earth. Seeming to deliberately address this

---

[381] Isaiah 17:10-11
[382] Isaiah 1:8, 21:10, Amos 8:2, 9:8-9
[383] Isaiah 17:1, Amos 1:5, 3:12, Jeremiah 49:24

concern, the very next chapter, Isaiah 18, removes any doubt that the time of year being spoken of here is referring to spring in America. Isaiah 18 is one of the few chapters in the Bible dedicated solely to describing America and her fate. There we read: "For before the harvest, when the bud is perfect and the sour grape is ripening in the flower, He will both cut off the sprigs with pruning hooks and take away and cut down the branches."[384] While I don't grow grapes for a living, it seems this passage is indicating the time of year just after bud break. Verse 6 even informs us that whatever has grown that spring will be food for wild animals and birds during the upcoming summer and winter.

Those still unconvinced that the Tribulation begins during spring in America may want to consider numerous other passages confirming this point. America's watchman of Isaiah 21 who proclaims "Babylon is fallen, is fallen!" pegs this at the time when "whirlwinds in the South pass through."[385] Typically tornadoes rip through tornado alley during the spring in America. Habakkuk, who most clearly describes America's powerful military and current foreign policy, laments "Though the fig tree may not blossom, nor fruit be on the vines; though the labor of the olive may fail, and the fields yield no food."[386] The prophet Joel, who prophesies of that first day, says "The land is like the Garden of Eden before them."[387] This picture of the Garden of Eden, I believe, is being used to describe the time of year when new growth and new life[388] overtakes the barrenness, or void and darkness[389], of winter.

Joel begins his book by describing this time of joy (descriptive of spring) being suddenly changed to desolation, causing all the vines and fruit trees to wither.[390] It wouldn't make

---

[384] Isaiah 18:5

[385] Isaiah 21:1

[386] Habakkuk 3:17

[387] Joel 2:3

[388] Genesis 1:11

[389] Genesis 1:2

[390] Joel 1:12

much sense to describe a barren tree of fall or winter to have withered. Rather, it makes more sense to realize that this season of hope and renewal (spring) has withered before the faces of men, just as the new life seen on the trees has withered. Hosea declares that the day God's people reap the whirlwind will be at a time when the stalk has no bud.[391] Also, when speaking of the grain of the land, wheat and barley, Joel and Jeremiah describe both a sowing of seed and a harvesting of grain.[392] How could this be? Are they in contradiction? God forbid! For we know that in America, as in other lands with similar climates, there are two grain crops harvested each year. The winter crop is harvested around the same time the spring crop is sown. When that day begins, seeds already sown will "shrivel in the clods" and some of that winter crop will have not yet been harvested. This perfectly describes the overlapping wheat and barley sowing/reaping schedules in various regions of the U.S. [393]

While I could easily rest my case here regarding a spring beginning for the Tribulation, there's one more thing I'd like to bring to your attention. We should be mindful of how water is described in reference to that Day. In Hosea we read of a great wind coming against God's people, which will cause the springs and fountains to dry up.[394] Springs and creeks are most notable in the springtime when rains begin to fall and the snow begins to melt to increase the flow of those streams. Even more notably we read of one river in particular in reference to that Day. Both Zechariah and Jeremiah mention the floodplain of the Jordan.[395] The Jordan River floodplain, the depressed strip of land on either side of the river, tends to fill with water during one particular time each year. As you would expect, floodplains fill up during the spring due to excess rains and

---

[391] Hosea 8:7

[392] Jeremiah 12:13, Joel 1:11, 1:17

[393] *Usual Planting and Harvesting Dates for U.S. Field Crops*. Usda.gov. December 1997. Retrieved March 14, 2012 from http://www.nass.usda.gov/Publications/Usual_Planting_and_Harvesting_Dates/uph97.pdf

[394] Hosea 13:15

[395] Jeremiah 12:5, 49:19, 50:44, Zechariah 11:3

snow runoff. This swelling of the floodplain, as Zechariah tells us, is also referred to as the pride of the Jordan.[396] The swelling water near the banks of the river will force fierce animals, such as lions, out of those floodplains and into populated areas. We see a picture here of an actual swelling of a river, during the spring, used to represent the swelling pride of the people. When you understand where God's already prideful people end up, those who are spared certain destruction in America, these passages begin to take on added significance.

Dark Moon Over America

As we study these passages it becomes clear we're given ample Scripture to determine what time of year the Tribulation will begin. But can we narrow that down a little bit? Just as the Bible reveals the season, it also allows us to pinpoint one particular day in the near future. In the previous chapter we learned that the "lights in the firmament of the heavens" are to be used not only for discerning night from day, but they're also used for signs.[397] The One who has foreknowledge of all things is able to use them as signs, indicating when certain things will take place in our day. Many may not realize that the Bible, when speaking of end-time events, often describes the moon in one of two ways. It describes it as either being dark or as blood red. This is not just poetry. Jehovah is telling us that all the events of the coming days are according to his clock. A dark moon is a new moon. A blood red moon is a lunar eclipse.

In Hosea we read this prophecy: "They have dealt treacherously with the LORD, for they have begotten pagan children. Now a New Moon shall devour them and their heritage."[398] In a later chapter I will go into more detail regarding how the prophets identify God's people today. Suffice it to say for now that in Jeremiah

---

[396] Zechariah 11:3
[397] Genesis 1:14
[398] Hosea 5:7

141

50 and 51, two important chapters describing the destruction of America, we find two families of Jehovah fleeing the burning country[399]: the house of Judah and the house of Israel. The ancient northern kingdom, the ten tribes of the house of Israel, was identified by the lineage of Joseph, who had two sons named Manasseh and Ephraim. Although Manasseh was the elder, Ephraim was given the blessing of the first born.[400] Ephraim was considered the lead tribe, and the house of Israel, who inhabited Samaria, is sometimes referred to as Ephraim. What we find in Hosea is not just a history of ancient Israel and Judah, but also prophecies concerning our day. Just as we've seen already, Hosea describes the day of the trumpet alarm[401] when the land of Ephraim is made completely desolate[402] as God's wrath is poured out on them like flooding waters.[403]

When we read about a new moon devouring us it should spur us on to find confirming passages within the Bible. Remember that Isaiah 13 is devoted to describing how America will be destroyed at the beginning of that Day. Within that chapter we read that "the sun will be darkened in its going forth, and the moon will not cause its light to shine."[404] And Joel, who's three chapters are filled with descriptions of that Day, confirms this by saying "the sun and moon grow dark."[405] Contrast these passages with a similar description found in Revelation. There we find that "the sun became black as sackcloth of hair, and the moon became like blood."[406] Sometimes contrasting similar passages helps to further our understanding of each. We already know that some sort of celestial object will blot out the sun on that first day of Tribulation. And we can see from Hosea, Isaiah, and Joel that it will also be on a new moon, when the moon is

---

[399] Jeremiah 50:4, 51:10
[400] Genesis 48:14
[401] Hosea 5:8
[402] Hosea 5:9
[403] Hosea 5:10
[404] Isaiah 13:10
[405] Joel 2:10
[406] Revelation 6:12

dark. But Revelation is referring to a lunar eclipse because the moon is giving off a reddish hue. Therefore, while the former is describing the first day of Tribulation, Revelation is either describing a different day entirely or it's describing a period of time which begins with a dark sun and ends with a lunar eclipse.

Sunday Morning Worship Service

I suspect what I say next may be a difficult pill to swallow for many. The typical American Christian has acquired certain ideas over the years. We accept the redemptive sacrifice Yahshua (Jesus) made on the cross, believing that God raised him from the dead the third day. Through the acceptance of this new covenant offering, the final offering for sin, we acknowledge that Jehovah is adopting us into his eternal family. We willing receive this adoption, realizing that we're saved by grace, through faith; it's the gift of God.[407] But if we really do spend consistent time studying the Bible, we soon realize that things have gotten out of balance. The majority of American Christians, it seems, have used their liberty in Christ as a cloak for vice.[408] Rather than becoming that spotless bride of Christ we were intended to become, I'm afraid we've allowed Babylon, the mother of harlots, to corrupt us. So, while we think God is pleased with us, it's just a figment of our imagination, a delusion.

In perfect harmony with the Scripture I've presented so far in this book, we see described a devastation coming to one nation, in particular, which will begin at the exact moment many of the people of that nation are in their local houses of worship offering sacrificial worship to the one true God, Jehovah. One might wonder why judgment would befall a nation at precisely the moment they are worshiping God. As I'll show in a later chapter, outward acts of worship, in and of themselves, are not a good indicator of the heart of man. Through Isaiah God proclaims "I cannot endure iniquity and

---

[407] Ephesians 2:8
[408] 1 Peter 2:16

the sacred meeting."[409] As we saw earlier, that passage of Isaiah has application for our day. It seems the day will come when Jehovah will have received all the worship he can tolerate from a people "laden with iniquity."[410]

In chapter 5 we saw how Zechariah's scroll of judgment begins to go forth at the same moment in time that end-time Babylon, America, receives her double judgment. But what I didn't address is the very specific size of that scroll. We're told that the scroll is twenty cubits in length by ten cubits in width.[411] Why in the world, you may be thinking, does it matter how big that scroll is? As is often the case, God is giving us an opportunity to make a connection to one or more other passages in the Bible. These connections allow us to study the passage in proper context, decipher its hidden meaning, and gain a better understanding of what's being conveyed. In the text describing how Solomon's temple was to be constructed, we learn that the porch, or portico, acted as an entrance of the temple on its east side.[412] Its length and width was identical to Zechariah's scroll.[413] Notice also from another passage we see that the height of the porch was one hundred twenty cubits, making it more like a watch tower.[414]

Some commentators feel this measurement is an error and that it should read only twenty cubits. Whether or not it's an error I can't say. But I think it makes perfect sense that the portico of the temple would symbolically represent a watch tower. The temple was an actual physical structure where the presence of our great, all-powerful, holy Jehovah, Creator and giver of all life, would actually rest from time to time. Consider the magnitude of this and how significant it was for mankind to have a place of meeting that the

---

[409] Isaiah 1:13
[410] Isaiah 1:4
[411] Zechariah 5:2
[412] Solomon's Temple. Wikipedia.org. Retrieved March 14, 2012 from http://en.wikipedia.org/wiki/Solomon's_Temple
[413] 1 Kings 6:3
[414] 2 Chronicles 3:4

very presence of God himself would inhabit here on earth. And when we consider the many Scripture texts instructing us to be very mindful and watch carefully how we live our lives, the great height of that portico takes on added meaning. We are to be found waiting and watching to see what God will do in the earth realm. We are not to live carelessly, thinking we can do whatever we please because we are "saved by grace." No, we are to be very watchful as we "do justly, love mercy and walk humbly with our God"[415] all the days of our lives.

Therefore, with that scroll of judgment going out, there's a connection being made to our relationship with God. The conclusion of all things is at hand. The things for which many have been watching are now commencing. But are God's people where they need to be? Are God's people truly ready for the days ahead? After taking the first eleven verses of his second chapter to describe what the day will be like, the prophet Joel turns his attention to God's people just before this calamity overtakes them. Make no mistake about it. Starting in verse twelve Joel is speaking to every man, woman and young adult in America today. Jehovah, through the prophet Joel, speaks down through the ages to communicate the solution to the problem. He's telling us how we can avoid what's soon coming. In a word, the solution is repentance. But let me bring your attention to verse seventeen.[416] There he instructs the leaders of his people to "weep between the porch and the altar." Consider that this is the very same portico, or watchtower, that we just discussed, whose length is twenty cubits and width ten cubits.

Will the people of America avoid the coming calamity? Will the nation repent like Nineveh of old?[417] Will we fast and weep and mourn upon that watchtower to see if God will turn and relent and leave a blessing behind?[418] Will the rich of God's people in the last

---

[415] Micah 6:8
[416] Joel 2:17
[417] Jonah 3:6-10
[418] Joel 2:14

days, following the example of their leaders, rend their hearts and begin to weep and howl for the miseries coming upon them?[419] I'm sorry to say that we're told time and again that it will not happen (though Father extends that offer to the very end). We will not, collectively, follow the advice found in Joel 2 or James 5. That disaster will arrive on the appointed day. And no less than three times in Joel's first chapter we're told the day of week it will arrive.[420] It will arrive on the day when God's people all across the great land of America, the focus of that first day, are offering up various forms of worship. When we look beyond the types and shadows of things that were, we see here spoken things of our day: worship services in American churches when that Day begins.

In perfect agreement, both Amos and Malachi confirm that that Day will begin at midday (remember when that "cloud" arrives) when God's people are worshiping. That day is, without doubt, largely on a Sunday. Amos informs us: "'The songs of the temple shall be wailing in that day,' Says the Lord GOD— 'Many dead bodies everywhere, they shall be thrown out in silence.'"[421] And again: "I will turn your (religious) feasts into mourning, and all your songs (of worship) into lamentation; I will bring sackcloth on every waist, and baldness on every head; I will make it like mourning for an only son, and its end like a bitter day."[422] Malachi, speaking to the leaders of God's people, declares: "Behold, I will rebuke your descendants and spread refuse on your faces, the refuse of your solemn feasts (religious services); and one will take you away with it."[423] I will go into more detail in a later chapter, but suffice it to say for now that when that Day begins (on a Sunday), God is not at all pleased with his people, especially the leaders of his people. Truly judgment will have begun at the house of God.[424]

---

[419] James 5:1-3

[420] Joel 1:9, 13, 16

[421] Amos 8:3

[422] Amos 8:10, Text in parenthesis mine.

[423] Malachi 2:3, Text in parenthesis mine.

[424] 1 Peter 4:17

Exactly 49 Years to the Day

In this chapter I've tried to show that the Bible gives us the time of year, the time of month, the day of the week, and even the time of day that the Tribulation will begin. That mysterious "cloud" will begin to pass over America during the spring, on a new moon, and around midday on a Sunday. I'm afraid if this is all we had to go on, we wouldn't be able to determine with any kind of certainty when that Day would arrive. Our lamp would be rather dim. As years come and go there will always be days that match these criteria.

In the previous chapter I showed overwhelming evidence that the Tribulation will begin in the year 2016. But is there a day in 2016 that matches the criteria I've shown in this chapter? If we look into the future, let's say until the year 2025, we find no less than six individual days that meet the spring, new moon, and Sunday criteria:

> May 20, 2012
> March 30, 2014
> June 5, 2016
> June 21, 2020
> June 18, 2023
> April 27, 2025

If I interpreted Daniel 9 correctly then all we should have to do is count forward forty-nine years from the day a command went forth to rebuild Jerusalem. But what day in 1967 was that? Was it June 5 when the Six Day War started? June 7 when Israel's army began to retake Jerusalem? Or June 28 when the Knesset made a law to annex East Jerusalem? If we start at June 5, 1967 and count off forty-nine years, we arrive at June 5, 2016; the only day in 2016 which matches the criteria we're given! Coincidently, if we start with the Hebrew day of Iyar 28, 5727 (June 7, 1967) and count forty-nine years, we arrive at Iyar 28, 5776 (June 5, 2016). Using two different dates, two days apart, both bring us to June 5, 2016 using either the Gregorian or Hebraic calendar. It's almost as if God, having foreknowledge of all these things before they began, wanted to remove all doubt that the Tribulation is to begin on June 5, 2016 with the complete and utter destruction of America.

Soon after I began my journey to decipher what the Bible really has to say about our day, I came across a website called Hand of Help.[425] Hand of Help is an organization dedicated to the care of widows and orphans in Romania. Its founder, Dumitru Duduman, was a Romanian who was ruthlessly tortured for smuggling Bibles into communist Russia. After being deported to America he began receiving dreams and visions. After comparing many of his visions to Scripture, I believe Dumitru was a true prophet of God. I conclude this chapter with his own words describing one of his dreams:

> *Then I fell asleep and dreamed that I was in an American church service, when the building began to move violently. Because they did not know what was happening, the people inside panicked and quickly began to run out. I succeeded in walking out also, but with every step I tried to take, it seemed like I was sinking into the ground. I began to look around to find something to support myself with so I could walk. I heard a voice that said, "Look up, and see the heavens!"*

> *I looked up. As far as the eye could see, all the sky was blood red. I said, "Lord! What does this mean? Why is the sky red?" Then I remembered my father telling me that before the great war the sky turned blood red.[426]*

---

[425] Hand of Help Ministries. (http://www.handofhelp.com)

[426] Duduman, Dimitru. (January 24, 1994). *The Savior Returns as Judge*. Hand of Help Ministries. Retrieved March 14, 2012 from http://www.handofhelp.com/vision_29.php

Chapter 10 - What's In a Name?

"In those days and in that time," says the LORD, "The children of Israel shall come, they and the children of Judah together; with continual weeping they shall come, and seek the LORD their God. Jeremiah 50:4

When I first realized that America is end-time Babylon, my next question was "What about me?" I'm an American. I live in America. I'm a child of God, the one and only true God, Jehovah. I've been adopted into his eternal family, redeemed by his only begotten son, Yahshua (Jesus). What will happen to me when America is destroyed? Will I be raptured at the beginning of that Day like all the prophets of peace tell us we will? I had grown up on a steady diet of the pre-Tribulation rapture doctrine. I accepted it. I believed it. (I was not reading my Bible.) But it made perfect sense. God loves his people. Certainly he won't pour out his wrath on his people, right? Didn't Yahshua take all our punishment to the cross? God won't punish his people, right?

Early in my study I came across this verse in Jeremiah which says: "The children of Israel shall come, they and the children of Judah together."[427] I knew at the time that Jeremiah 50 and 51 are two chapters of the Bible that give the most detail regarding the destruction of America. Naturally, I wanted to know who this verse was talking about. And I was determined to take an honest look at the Scriptures, no longer relying on what I had been taught by the popular teachers of our day. Who are these two families mentioned by Jeremiah and all the prophets? Why are they mentioned separately in the context of America's sudden demise? Who were these people at the time of ancient Babylon and who are they today?

---

[427] Jeremiah 50:4

One God, Two Families

Discovering the ancient identities of the house of Israel and the house of Judah is not difficult at all. Scripture gives us ample backstory of how the people of Jehovah became two distinct families. And I can't overemphasize the importance of that story. If we fail to understand the distinction between the two houses, much of the Bible becomes unintelligible. Multitudes of Christians today define "Israel" in one of two ways. They either think of the nation of Israel, reborn in 1948, or they think about Jews wherever they may be living. Many don't realize that the nation of Israel is largely secular today, or that there's a huge difference between a devout Jew and one who is a Jew because their family of origin is Jewish. Popular teachers of our day have convinced the masses that Jews will endure the Tribulation while all true believers in Christ will be snatched away into heaven before the trouble begins. The problem with that teaching, besides the fact that it causes Christians to become overly confident to the point of spiritual laziness, is that it ignores much of the prophetic text of the Bible, such as this one in Jeremiah.

Who is being discussed in Jeremiah 50:4? When America is destroyed in one hour, who is this Israel and Judah who will supernaturally survive and set their faces towards Zion?[428] If this were the Jews only wouldn't it have been sufficient to just list the children of Judah? After all, only the house of Judah was taken into captivity by ancient Babylon and only the house of Judah returned to Palestine. See the books of Ezra and Nehemiah for an examination of that return. In fact, by the time Judah was taken to Babylon, the house of Israel, the ten northern tribes (10-Israel), had already been taken into Assyrian captivity more than one hundred years prior.[429] But no such return is recorded for the house of Israel. To end up with the correct answer regarding Jeremiah 50:4 we have to

---

[428] Isaiah 18:7, Jeremiah 51:10
[429] 1 Chronicles 5:26, 2 Kings 15:29, 17:3-6, 18:11-12

understand the history of Israel, the northern kingdom, and Judah, the southern kingdom.

Brief History of the Two Houses

Under the rule of King David and his son Solomon Israel was a united kingdom. But things changed when Solomon's son, Rehoboam, became king. The northern kingdom of Israel came to King Rehoboam seeking mercy. They wanted him to lighten the heavy burden his father, King Solomon, had placed upon them. They wanted less taxation and a kinder, gentler leader in Rehoboam. But Rehoboam, taking the advice of his younger counselors rather than his older, wiser counselors, chose instead to increase their burden. He told them: "And now, whereas my father put a heavy yoke on you, I will add to your yoke; my father chastised you with whips, but I will chastise you with scourges (scorpions)!"[430] And so the schism began. Israel rebelled against the kingdom of Judah (Judah, Benjamin, and Levi) and the two kingdoms became divided. It wasn't long after that that the house of Israel was taken into Assyrian captivity because of their sin and rebellion against God. The house of Judah would soon follow. But instead of being taken to Assyria, they would end up in Babylon. Both kingdoms inherited the curses spoken of by Moses in the book of Deuteronomy that come upon God's people, collectively, when they become polluted with the idolatry of the land, collectively.

Now let me ask you a question? If you had a way to somehow escape the brutality and slavery of the attacking Assyrians, would you take it? It just so happened that the tribe of Dan, whose tribal territory was situated on the Mediterranean coast, was a seafaring tribe.[431] They loved their ships and used them to trade with distant lands.[432] And when it came time to choose between

---

[430] 1 Kings 12:11, Text in parenthesis mine.

[431] Judges 5:17

[432] *Mediterranean archaeology*, Volume 16. University of Sydney. Dept. of Archaeology. 2003. p. 117

those ships and being carried away into captivity, some (I suspect as many as could fit on those ships) chose to set sail. All of this and more is detailed in one of the most amazing books I've ever read. J.H. Allen, author of "Judah's Sceptre and Joseph's Birthright,"[433] traces the migration of those ten lost tribes of the house of Israel. Using the information we're given in the Bible, in addition to available historical records of his day, Mr. Allen, in my opinion, successfully unraveled one of the greatest mysteries known to man. Being able to chart the migration of the house of Israel from the time of their Assyrian captivity gives us a clear picture of how we got from there to here. It's no coincidence that the Anglo-Saxon race, descendants of the ancient house of Israel, leads the world today. The Holy One of Israel, through the prophet Micah, makes a special point to remind us "what Balak king of Moab counseled, and what Balaam the son of Beor answered him."[434] How did that conversation go? The king of Moab hired Balaam to curse the children of Israel.[435] After several attempts all that perverse[436] prophet-for-hire Balaam could do was bless them. Balaam concludes: "How shall I curse whom God has not cursed? And how shall I denounce whom the LORD has not denounced?"[437] Despite what some may think America leads the world today because God blessed her to achieve that status. But now, after treacherously departing from her God, she has fallen under the curses of Deuteronomy.

Who Will Survive?

"They shall be Mine," says the LORD of hosts, "on the day that I make them My jewels. And I will spare them as a man spares his own son who serves him." Then you shall again discern

---

[433] J. H. Allen, *Judah's Sceptre and Joseph's Birthright,* A. A. Beauchamp, Boston, Mass. 1918
[434] Micah 6:5
[435] Numbers 22:6
[436] Numbers 22:32
[437] Numbers 23:8

between the righteous and the wicked, between one who serves God and one who does not serve Him. Malachi 3:17-18

Now, at the end of this age, every man, woman and child in America, whether they realize it or not, is facing a catastrophe of monumental proportion. A death sentence has been handed down on this land and no one will be left standing. Those who are building bunkers are wasting their time. Bunkers will buy only so much time as America will eventually sink beneath the ocean waves.[438] Nahum asks "Who can stand before His indignation? And who can endure the fierceness of His anger?" The answer is given: "The LORD is good, a stronghold in the day of trouble; and He knows those who trust in Him."[439] Likewise Isaiah asks "Who among us shall dwell with the devouring fire? Who among us shall dwell with everlasting burnings?" Or, in other words, who can survive that day when America is completely destroyed? Again the answer is given: "He who walks righteously and speaks uprightly, he who despises the gain of oppressions, who gestures with his hands, refusing bribes, who stops his ears from hearing of bloodshed, and shuts his eyes from seeing evil."[440] It's clear that those who will survive that day of destruction are those who are already in covenant relationship with the one true God when that day begins. Psalm 91 echoes this when it says "you shall not be afraid...of the destruction that lays waste at noonday."[441] Remember that the great "cloud" that passes between the earth and the sun will begin to do so at midday. But those who have placed their trust in God, and who have the proof (those bearing good fruit) of that relationship, will be spared in that day. But every tree that does not bear good fruit will be cut down and cast into the fire.[442]

---

[438] Isaiah 42:15, Jeremiah 51:42, Revelation 16:19
[439] Nahum 1:6-7
[440] Isaiah 33:14-15
[441] Psalm 91:5-6
[442] Matthew 7:19

The House of Israel

How can we be sure who Israel and Judah are today? Many Christians, only familiar with the popular teachings of the day, become very nervous when they hear fringe teachings about the identity of Israel. They cry heresy and seem to reject out-of-hand any teaching that isn't mainstream. I suppose they think all mainstream teachings must be accurate, not realizing how Satan creeps in unnoticed to deceive the masses.[443]

Replacement Theology teaches that the Church replaced Israel, who they consider to be Jews. That's not at all what I'm saying. If we look closely at the Scriptures we can begin to see that the house of Judah has, from the time of the schism, been representative of the Jewish people. And we can clearly look back through history and see that it was the devout Jews who so revered the law of Jehovah (and by extension Jehovah himself) that they diligently preserved its teachings throughout the ages, even in foreign lands wherever they went. As we've already seen, the eyes of the remnant of Judah will be opened and they will have a heart change concerning Yahshua as Messiah during the Tribulation, when Israel and Judah are reunited.[444] For it is written, that Judah, also, will be grafted in again if they do not continue in unbelief.[445]

But the house of Israel took a very different course through history. And while Mr. Allen has uncovered their path through the ages, the question remains: who is this so-called house of Israel who will survive America's destruction? Race or family ancestry has never made a man righteous or acceptable before God. The apostle Paul addressed this very issue in the book of Romans. After lamenting the plight of his Christ-rejecting countrymen, Paul explains that "they are not all Israel who are of Israel, nor are they all children because they are the seed of Abraham; but, 'In Isaac your seed shall be called.' That is, those who are the children of the flesh,

---

[443] Matthew 7:15
[444] Zechariah 12:10-14, Ezekiel 37
[445] Romans 11:23

these are not the children of God; but the children of the promise are counted as the seed." [446] In this passage Paul is showing how the prophecies of old relate both to his day and to the end of the age, our day, when "the remnant will be saved."[447] Those who "attain the law of righteousness" do so by faith.[448] These are the children of God. The righteous will live by faith.[449]

At the time of Christ many Jews did believe in him, whether his words alone convicted their hearts or because of the signs they witnessed.[450] Just as Zechariah predicted, the poor of the flock, especially, believed the teachings of Yahshua.[451] But a good portion of Judah "stumbled at that stumbling stone."[452] When we take a careful look at all the teachings of the Bible we begin to see that the law itself is not condemned, but reliance on the works of the law for justification. The kingdom of Judah, as a whole, rejected the notion that "no one is justified by the law in the sight of God."[453] In so doing they also rejected the Messiah, being blinded by the idea that the works of the law can justify. Therefore Judah was cast off by Jehovah and was subsequently cast out of their land until that turning point in 1946.

Beauty and Bonds

Zechariah predicted a time would come when "the brotherhood between Judah and Israel" would be broken.[454] This prophecy was given at the same time that God would also break the

---

[446] Romans 9:6-8
[447] Romans 9:27
[448] Romans 9:30-32
[449] Ezekiel 33:13, Habakkuk 2:4, Romans 1:17, Hebrews 10:39
[450] John 2:23, 8:30, 10:42, 12:42, Acts 9:42
[451] Zechariah 11:11, Luke 4:18
[452] Romans 9:32
[453] Galatians 3:11
[454] Zechariah 11:14

covenant which he had made with all the peoples.[455] And at the same time the thirty pieces of silver, that "princely price," would be set on him.[456] Zechariah was speaking of the time when Yahshua would be largely rejected by his own people, represented by the thirty pieces of silver that Judas, the betrayer of Yahshua, received as payment. One might find it interesting that the name Judas is derived from, and has the same meaning as, the name Judah.[457] Judas thought he was receiving something of true value for betraying Yahshua. Judah, the Jews, thought they could attain something of value, namely justification by the works of the law, by rejecting Yahshua. But Yahshua made it clear that we can't serve both money (unrighteous mammon) and God.[458] While God expects us to live clean, holy lives, we can never be justified by those works. That kind of mentality puts a holy, omnipotent God on par with weak, sinful man. When Yahshua came as the spotless lamb[459], slain from the foundation of the world[460], he established a new covenant with man, making the effect of the first covenant obsolete.[461] That first covenant was broken just as Zechariah's staff, called Beauty, was broken. And at that same moment in time Zechariah's other staff, Bonds, representing the brotherhood between Israel and Judah, was also broken.

Have you ever wondered why Zechariah's thirty pieces of silver were thrown into the house of the LORD for the potter?[462] When Christ walked the earth, the house of Israel was not living in Samaria. The tribes of Judah were living in Judea, but the tribes of Israel were long gone at that point. As I stated earlier, they were taken into Assyrian captivity and didn't return. Judah returned from Babylonian captivity but Israel didn't return from Assyrian

---

[455] Zechariah 11:10
[456] Zechariah 11:12-13
[457] Strong's Greek Dictionary entry G2455, Hebrew Dictionary entry H3063
[458] Matthew 6:24, Luke 16:13
[459] John 1:29, 1 Peter 1:19
[460] Revelation 13:8
[461] Hebrews 8:13
[462] Zechariah 11:13

captivity.[463] The New Testament account supports this. Remember that the two kingdoms were called Samaria and Judea. The ten-tribed northern kingdom of Israel dwelt in the land of Samaria. The two-tribe (plus Levi) southern kingdom of Judah dwelt in Judea. But when Assyria took 10-Israel away, they filled Samaria with a bunch of strangers. This is why the Jews of Christ's day considered them second-class citizens.[464]

At the time of Christ the schism between Israel and Judah was an established fact of life. And they were also aware of Ezekiel's prophecy about the reunification of Israel and Judah at the end of the age.[465] But, not realizing the end of the age was yet a long time off[466], they asked him: "Lord, will You at this time restore the kingdom to Israel?" [467] So, if Israel and Judah were already divided for hundreds of years by the time of Christ, why did Zechariah link the breaking of the brotherhood of Israel and Judah to the time of Christ? And why, again, were the thirty pieces of silver thrown to the potter?

The answers to these two questions are related. Even though Israel and Judah were not living side-by-side at the time of Christ, they were still under the same covenant. But when the staff of Beauty, the first covenant, was broken, so was the brotherhood "officially" broken between Israel and Judah. Why? Because Jehovah already knew that Judah, as a whole, would reject the new covenant, while Israel, as a whole, would accept the new covenant. (Christianity became the unofficial religion of the Anglo-Saxon race.) This is why Yahshua stated "I was not sent except to the lost sheep of the house of Israel."[468] And why God, through Jeremiah, in the context of the overthrow of America, states "My people have been lost sheep."[469] Remember that the schism between Israel and Judah

---

[463] Jeremiah 3:7
[464] Matthew 10:5-6, John 4:9
[465] Ezekiel 37
[466] Isaiah 42:14
[467] Acts 1:6
[468] Matthew 10:6, 15:24
[469] Jeremiah 50:6

occurred at the very time Israel was seeking mercy. They didn't receive mercy from Judah but they did receive mercy from Jehovah through the redemptive blood of Yahshua. This is why, when Israel is reunited with Judah at the end of the age, Hosea prophesies: "Say to your brethren, 'My people,' and to your sisters, 'Mercy is shown.'" [470]

A New Vessel

But why was the silver thrown to the potter in the house of the Lord? On the surface we can see this is a parallel to Judas returning the coins and throwing them into the temple before ending his life.[471] But if we stop here we won't see the whole picture. This was not just any old potter being spoken of in Zechariah. This potter, because he was in the house of the Lord, was a servant of the Lord. This potter, and by extension his work, his pottery, is being associated with a sacred work. The vessels he makes are being sanctified, made holy, set aside for the work of the Lord.[472] Now, I want to show you how this potter is connected to the identity of the house of Israel. The thirty pieces of silver, that unrighteous mammon representing supposed justification by the works of the law, are thrown to the potter. An exchange is being made between Judas (Judah) and the Potter. The false notion that works result in justification is being exchanged for a new vessel.

Allow me to digress for a moment. Mercy and grace was not a foreign concept among God's people before Christ. God's mercy was often spoken of and shown in the lives of people all throughout the Bible. But for whatever reason the leaders of God's people at the time of Christ relied on the works of the law for justification. They were delusional. They willingly rejected the whole character of God. They were willfully ignorant of a large portion of Scripture dealing

---

[470] Hosea 2:1
[471] Matthew 27:5
[472] 2 Timothy 2:21

with the mercy of God. They traded truth for falsehood because the falsehood suited their flesh. It made them happy to think that human piety earned them a place in society, and supposedly with God too. But God saw the hypocrisy and drew a line in the sand. We would do well to learn from the past. The same type of thing is now taking place among God's people today. But instead of placing ourselves on par with God, we have brought God down to be on par with us. We have embraced the mercy of God but have ignored his justice and righteousness. We think God winks at our sin and we've become polluted with all the idols of the land. The people of God today do not fear him.[473] That's a big mistake.

With 20/20 hindsight we can look back and see why Jehovah had to exchange that unrighteous mammon of false mindsets with a new vessel. But what kind of vessel did the Potter make? What did he call that vessel and who is that vessel today? When a nation of God's people enters into gross sin and rebellion, forsaking his ways and laws, he sends them warnings through his prophets. If that nation continues in their sin and rebellion and refuses to turn back to God, he sends a destroyer to that nation to conquer them and lead them into captivity. This pattern is established all the way back in the Torah, the first five books of the Bible. Just as America will soon reap the reward of a rebellious nation under that curse, so did the northern kingdom of Israel. Israel received ample warning, yet refused to return wholeheartedly to worship of the one true Jehovah. Therefore, they were conquered by Assyria and led into captivity. But unlike the house of Judah, the house of Israel decided not to return. For all that they suffered under God's hand of judgment it wasn't enough to bring them back. Like wild donkeys in their time of heat, they sniffed at the wind and sought out a life apart from God's ways and laws.[474]

Like a good parent trying to warn a rebellious teenager, God tried to warn them what would happen. In Jeremiah 18 we see one

---

[473] Isaiah 57:11, Malachi 3:5
[474] Jeremiah 2:23-24

of those warnings. But notice the very serious threat being made here. God told Jeremiah to go down to the potter's house and he would speak to him there. Jeremiah saw that the vessel the potter was making was marred in his hand so he made it again into another vessel, whatever seemed good for the potter to make. Notice what God says next: "'O house of Israel, can I not do with you as this potter?' says the LORD. 'Look, as the clay is in the potter's hand, so are you in My hand, O house of Israel!'" [475] While Judah is mentioned later, this threat is directed specifically to the house of Israel. God already knew that the house of Judah (the Jews) would survive as a distinct people throughout time. But the house of Israel is a different story entirely. Just as we saw in Zechariah that the thirty pieces of silver were thrown to the potter, so we see here the Potter (Jehovah) threatening to make the house of Israel into a different vessel if they refused to return. But is that what happened? Did God really divorce the house of Israel?

A Certificate of Divorce

> 7 "And I said, after she had done all these things, 'Return to Me.' But she did not return. And her treacherous sister Judah saw it. 8 Then I saw that for all the causes for which backsliding Israel had committed adultery, I had put her away and given her a certificate of divorce; yet her treacherous sister Judah did not fear, but went and played the harlot also."
> Jeremiah 3:7-8

Remember that God commissioned Jeremiah to "root out and to pull down" kingdoms and also "to build and to plant" kingdoms.[476] Are we to assume this is speaking only of godless nations? No, rather, this is being spoken of in the context of God's people. We should assume God is primarily concerned with his people. And right after we read of the threat to remake the house of Israel into a

---

[475] Jeremiah 18:6
[476] Jeremiah 1:10

different vessel, God reminds us of his intent to root out nations and plant other nations.[477] Not only does Jeremiah's prayer at the end of chapter 18 confirm the reality of the outcome, but we also read in Jeremiah 3 that God did, in fact, divorce the house of Israel because they didn't return.[478] Although Israel's sister, Judah, played the harlot as well, we read of no certificate of divorce being given to her. The truth is that while God hates divorce[479] Israel didn't leave him much choice. Israel left those "cold flowing waters" and chose instead "strange waters."[480] Israel embraced those strange waters and forsook the cold flowing waters for good.

Now, according to God's own law, we have every reason to believe that the divorce was final. In Deuteronomy we read that a divorced woman, after having been taken by another husband, is not to return to the first husband.[481] If this were the end of the story, it'd be a rather sad story indeed. But this was not the end, rather only a brief intermission. The house of Israel rejected that first covenant after seeking mercy but finding none. They went from mountain to hill; they forgot their resting place.[482] Ah, but the Good Shepherd went looking for his lost sheep! But while it would have been an abomination to take Israel back as she was, our great Jehovah made a new way, a better and lasting covenant.[483] But could that new wine be placed into old wine skins? Certainly not! The new wine must be placed in new wineskins.[484] The Potter knew he had to remake the house of Israel into a different vessel. So, who did Yahshua, the Good Shepherd, find when he went looking for his lost sheep? He found the Church. That lump of clay marred in the hand of the Potter was remade into a new vessel called the Church, or those who have come into right standing with Jehovah through that better covenant, the

---

[477] Jeremiah 18:7
[478] Jeremiah 3:8
[479] Malachi 2:16
[480] Jeremiah 18:14
[481] Deuteronomy 24:1-4, Jeremiah 3:1
[482] Jeremiah 50:6
[483] Hebrews 7:22, 8:6
[484] Matthew 9:17, Mark 2:22, Luke 5:38

blood of Yahshua, and who bear good fruit as outward evidence of that heart change. While the ancient house of Israel rejected the snow waters of Lebanon, the righteous who live by faith in Yahshua drink of "the waters of Shiloh that flow softly"; the very same waters that Judah rejected.[485]

But does the rest of the Bible support this? What are we to think of all the Old Testament prophetic Scripture that speaks of the house of Israel? When Isaiah wrote his prophecies, certainly God knew what the house of Israel would become. Before time began he knew all that would transpire. So why do we read of both Judah and Israel in prophecies regarding our day? Shouldn't the prophecies for our day only mention Judah, the Jews? After all, her sister Israel is now the Church. The clay was remade into a different vessel nearly two thousand years ago. What are we to think, then, when we read passages like Ezekiel 37 which tell us that Israel and Judah will be reunited in the latter days? Should we expect the prophets of old to have used the word "Church?" How could they speak of a people of whom they were not even aware?

> *Doubtless You are our Father, though Abraham was ignorant of us, and Israel does not acknowledge us. You, O LORD, are our Father; our Redeemer from everlasting is Your name.*
> Isaiah 63:16

Ah, but we see that the prophets do speak of us, though ignorant of us. Who else could Isaiah be speaking of here? Abraham didn't know about us, the Church, nor does national Israel, and the house of Judah, acknowledge us. Of course they don't now, but they will later.

> *Thus says the LORD: "Where is the certificate of your mother's divorce, whom I have put away? Or which of My creditors is it to whom I have sold you? For your iniquities you have sold yourselves, and for your transgressions your mother has been put away.* Isaiah 50:1

---

[485] Isaiah 8:6

Isaiah, confirming that the divorce did, in fact, take place, reminds us of the divorce of our mother (the ancient house of Israel), whom Jehovah put away because of her transgressions.[486] Perhaps we should begin to see this Scripture in new light, realizing the Church is being spoken of here. Even the apostle Paul, when speaking of the Church, says: "And as many as walk according to this rule, peace and mercy be upon them, and upon the Israel of God."[487] Paul rightly understood that the initiation of that better covenant changed what the Gentile converts were to be called; they were now the Israel of God.

> *Listen to Me, O house of Jacob, and all the remnant of the house of Israel, who have been upheld by Me from birth, who have been carried from the womb: even to your old age, I am He, and even to gray hairs I will carry you! I have made, and I will bear; even I will carry, and will deliver you.* Isaiah 46:3-4

Who's he talking about? Are we to believe Isaiah is referring to the ancient house of Israel here? If so, how could that be? How could God claim to carry them to old age? The house of Israel left God, mixed with the Gentiles and became Gentiles themselves. When we realize that the house of Israel was remade into a new vessel Scripture begins to make sense. I realize the majority of people today believe what the majority of their teachers are telling them. They think Israel in the Bible must always mean the Jews of today. It's true that in some cases the word Israel is being used to address all of God's people, including Jews. But these teachers fail to acknowledge the clear distinction in the Bible between the house of Israel and the house of Judah. And there is a clear distinction in both their history and destiny.

Jerusalem, God's Chosen People

---

[486] Isaiah 50:1
[487] Galatians 6:16

Is it really that strange to see how God refers to his people by various names?[488] In Jeremiah 13 God tells Jeremiah to take a sash, put it around his waist, but he's not to put it water. Later God tells him to take it off and put it in a hole near the river. After much time transpires, God tells him to go back to the river and see what that sash looks like. Obviously, the sash is ruined; it's good for nothing. So are we when we refuse to allow the cleansing water of the Word of God to wash us.[489] When we allow the Bible to sit on the shelf and collect dust for days, weeks, even months on end, we become just as polluted and useless as that sash.[490] But look what God says: "'For as the sash clings to the waist of a man, so I have caused the whole house of Israel and the whole house of Judah to cling to Me,' says the LORD, 'that they may become My people, for renown, for praise, and for glory; but they would not hear.'"[491] They wouldn't hear the Word of the Lord to them. It went in one ear and out the other. The house of Israel and the house of Judah refused to hear and obey God's instructions to them for their own good.

When God's people become spiritually lazy they become filthy and begin to believe all sorts of things. They think all bottles will always be filled with good wine.[492] Let the good times roll! God is with us! He'll never take away his lovingkindness and mercies from us! Ah, but then the truth comes out. Those bottles of wine represent a disaster that Jehovah is planning against his people for their great rebellion and refusal to hear his Word. The answer to this dilemma? "Give glory to the LORD your God before He causes darkness, and before your feet stumble on the dark mountains, and while you are looking for light, He turns it into the shadow of death and makes it dense darkness."[493] We've seen enough from Jeremiah already to recognize apocalyptic language. But let me point something out here. Look how God refers to his people: "Thus says

---

[488] Hebrews 12:22
[489] Ephesians 5:26
[490] Jeremiah 6:10
[491] Jeremiah 13:11
[492] Jeremiah 13:12
[493] Jeremiah 13:16

the LORD: 'In this manner I will ruin the pride of Judah and the great pride of Jerusalem.'" [494] In verse 9 he calls them Judah and Jerusalem. In verse 11 he calls them Israel and Judah. Could it be he's calling the house of Israel by two different names: Israel and Jerusalem?

> *"Hear this, O house of Jacob, who are called by the name of Israel, and have come forth from the wellsprings of Judah; who swear by the name of the LORD, and make mention of the God of Israel, but not in truth or in righteousness; for they call themselves after the holy city, and lean on the God of Israel; The LORD of hosts is His name.* Isaiah 48:1-2

In Isaiah 48, which follows one of the few chapters that deals exclusively with the destruction of America, we read of a people who "call themselves after the holy city, and lean on the God of Israel." In verse 1 he addresses the topic of "who." He wants to make it clear who he's talking about. Both kingdoms, Israel and Judah, came forth from the lineage of Jacob. But here he's addressing those of "the house of Jacob, who are called by the name of Israel." Of the two families, God is addressing those who are called Israel and have come out of the wellsprings of Judah. If you look at that word wellsprings[495] you may notice that it has to do with lineage. This Israel, who is also called after the holy city, Jerusalem, has come forth from the lineage of Judah. They swear by the name of Jehovah and they recognize themselves by the God of Israel. But at this particular point in time, they're not walking in the whole truth and they aren't righteous. Though they think they might be righteous, in reality they are polluted. They aren't living in the whole truth of God's Word.

So who is this being described? What people came forth from the lineage of Judah and swear by the name of Jehovah. Who came forth from the family line of Judah? Yahshua, that Good

---

[494] Jeremiah 13:9
[495] Strong's Hebrew Dictionary entry H4325

165

Shepherd sent to recover his lost sheep, came forth from the lineage of Judah.[496] In fact, one of his names is the Lion of the Tribe of Judah.[497] Therefore it can be concluded that the people of God being here described, who now swear by the name of the Lord and who came forth from the lineage of Judah, is the Church. Isaiah is speaking about the Church.

You Only Have I Known

> *Hear this word that the LORD has spoken against you, O children of Israel, against the whole family which I brought up from the land of Egypt, saying: "You only have I known of all the families of the earth; therefore I will punish you for all your iniquities." Amos 3:1-2*

If we fail to understand the extent to which the prophets spoke of our day, we're bound to miss what God is trying to tell us in his Word. The popular commentators and teachers have convinced multitudes that much of the Bible is in the past tense. But if you were God, and you wanted to write a book that would capture the attention of people all throughout the ages, wouldn't you write it in such a way that people could identify themselves in that story which speaks of the interactions, both past and future, between God and mankind? In Amos we find language that has become all too familiar in this journey we've been on. It opens with a destruction determined upon several nations which will incur God's fierce anger at the beginning of that Day. We read of pastures mourning and mountains withering. We read of fire raining down, overthrowing strong cities and entire peoples perishing. We read of "shouting in the day of battle, and a tempest in the day of the whirlwind."[498] In chapter 2 God, through the prophet Amos, turns his attention to

---

[496] Matthew 1:1-16, Luke 3:23-38
[497] Revelation 5:5
[498] Amos 1:14

Judah. Notice how short all of these judgments are. Each nation listed only receives a verse or two of condemnation.

But then God begins to speak to Israel. From chapter 2 verse 6 the discussion is directed specifically to the house of Israel. Chapter 3 opens addressing the children of Israel. Chapter 4 opens addressing those of Samaria. (One might conclude by the sheer amount of text devoted to the house of Israel, the Church, that God is especially disappointed with her. To whom much is given, much is required.) Later in that chapter we learn of lesser judgments coming upon the land, until finally she is overthrown like Sodom and Gomorrah. Yet some supernaturally survive, like firebrands plucked from the fire.[499] If you remember, Sodom and Gomorrah were destroyed by fireballs raining down from the sky. Upon which of the nations from antiquity the commentators feel this is referring, I don't know. However, it's the opinion of this author that not only is America experiencing the drought mentioned in verse 7, but she will also experience the cleanness of teeth mentioned in verse 6 before suffering that same fate as Sodom and Gomorrah described in verse 11.

This brings me to my main point. In Amos 3:1-2 we see God speak of the children of Israel in a very exclusive manner. He first makes it known that when he says "children of Israel" he's referring to the whole family which he brought up out of Egypt. The whole family includes all twelve tribes and is equivalent to saying the house of Jacob. He then goes on to say that it's only this family that he's known of all the families of the earth. It's only this family with whom he's been in covenant relationship. I suppose if one thinks the book of Amos is merely in the past tense this verse makes sense as the Church would not have existed at the time Amos wrote it. But if Amos is speaking of events only in the past one has to reconcile why Amos 5:2 says "The virgin of Israel has fallen; she will rise no more." For it's quite clear that the Israel has not yet fallen, never again to rise. What or who is that "virgin of Israel?" She is the nation of God's

---

[499] Amos 4:11, Zechariah 3:2

people who have been pushed to the farthest parts of the earth at the end of the age. She is the youngest, or hindermost, nation called by God's name. She is America.

If the Church is not to be included in that passage then we have to conclude that either God doesn't know us within the context of a covenant relationship, or Amos 3 is past tense. But if Amos 3 is past tense we have to either conclude that the virgin of Israel has already fallen, never again to rise, or that Amos 5 is future tense. But if we conclude that chapter 3 is past and chapter 5 is future, we have to somehow reconcile how one continuous story is so easily broken between past and future. Or we can bypass all of this nonsense and just conclude, as I have, that the entire book of Amos is speaking of "the day of the Lord" (Amos 5:18), and the days leading up to it, our day.

But if we conclude that Amos 3:1-2 includes the Church then we have to realize that this prophet, as well as the others, speaks of the Church using the name Israel. And it's only with the truth of this understanding that the prophetic text of the Bible begins to make sense.

The Prodigal Son

Many of us are familiar with the parable Yahshua taught regarding the prodigal son.[500] All of the same themes I've been discussing are in that parable. If you remember, the father had two sons. The younger one asked the father for his inheritance and subsequently goes out into some other land and spends it on riotous living. Seeing that his choices have resulted in eating after swine, he decides to return to his father and seek mercy, even if it means being like one of the hired servants. But his father, seeing him approach from a long way off, runs to his lost son, embraces him, welcomes him back into the family and throws a big party. But the older son,

---

[500] Luke 15:11-32

returning from his work in the field, hears the music and wonders what's going on. A servant fills him in and he immediately becomes indignant and refuses to join the celebration. The father pleads with him but the son responds by saying "these many years I have been serving you; I never transgressed your commandment at any time; and yet you never gave me a young goat, that I might make merry with my friends. But as soon as this son of yours came, who has devoured your livelihood with harlots, you killed the fatted calf for him."[501] But the father tells him: "Son, you are always with me, and all that I have is yours. It was right that we should make merry and be glad, for your brother was dead and is alive again, and was lost and is found."[502]

On the surface we can see this is a beautiful picture of redemption that Yahshua came to offer those who would humble themselves, turn from their wicked ways, believe in him, and live for him all the remaining days of their lives. But few might understand that this is also a picture of Jehovah's two families, so called the house of Israel and the house of Judah. The older son, Judah, stayed home and was obedient to the Father, Jehovah. But the younger son, Israel, treacherously departed so he could live however he pleased. But notice how Judah wasn't interested in mercy and forgiveness. No, his relationship with the Father was based on obedience to the point of blindness. He couldn't see that the Father was just as interested in mercy as he was loyalty. And the younger son, Israel, although finally reestablishing his relationship with the Father through mercy, broke the Father's heart by departing, choosing instead the pleasures of this life. Left to his own devices, and rejecting obedience and honor, he became filthy, unclean, lost, dead.

Judah represents God's justice. The scepter shall not depart from Judah, nor a lawgiver from between his feet.[503] Judah honors the law of God; and the law, with faith, produces a reverence for

---

[501] Luke 15:29-30
[502] Luke 15:31-32
[503] Genesis 49:10

God.[504] Israel represents the mercy of God. The kindness of God leads us to repentance.[505] But Judah refused God's mercy[506] and Israel refused the law.[507] Mercy without justice results in a lack of reverence. And justice without mercy misses the fruit of a repentant, contrite heart: a new creation that springs up through mercy and forgiveness. One without the other is a false balance and leads to calamity, which is where we are today.

Mercy without justice results in a lack of reverence. This is where the Church is today; at least the Church in America. We think because we call ourselves Christians God will always wink at our sin. Our land is polluted and plays the harlot, and we play along. The Church in America is nearly indistinguishable from the rest of America. We think God won't punish us. In fact, we have become so filled with pride we think God will punish everyone except us.

But now at the end of the age, Israel (the Church) finds mercy from the Good Shepherd. Judah, you rejected mercy. But your brother found mercy. Judah, you didn't reject the Torah, the law of God, which describes the very nature of God, like your treacherous brother Israel did. Judah, some of you still fear and deeply revere God because you have an understanding of God's nature. But Judah, you missed the mercy of God and instead chose to obtain salvation by the law. The law wasn't meant to provide salvation; only temporary atonement. The law points us to our need for mercy.[508] Judah, you may properly revere the Father, but you don't yet realize the work of Yahshua, the Good Shepherd. Israel, you understand the work of Yahshua but you don't fear God. Strangers have entered into your houses and have led you astray.[509] You are so comfortable in America and so detached from reality that you have forgotten the

---

[504] Malachi 1
[505] Romans 2:4
[506] Isaiah 8:6
[507] Hosea 4:6
[508] Romans 3:19-26
[509] Jeremiah 50:5, Malachi 2:8

severity of God.[510] You think you can live however you choose and God is fine with it. He's not fine with it. He's not at all pleased with you, Israel.[511] And Judah, you are no better off. In fact you are worse off because you rejected the gently flowing waters of Shiloh.[512]

The world, including and especially God's people, are entering into a time of judgment with God. It's not going to be pleasant. But those faithful to God, those who fear him and think about the honor of his name will be preserved because their names will have been written in a book of remembrance.[513] They will set their faces towards Zion[514] and the two sticks of Ezekiel 37, Israel and Judah, will be reunited. What's in a name? When it comes to Bible prophecy, everything.

---

[510] Romans 11:22
[511] Malachi 1:10
[512] Isaiah 8:6
[513] Malachi 3:16-17
[514] Jeremiah 51:10

Chapter 11 - Every Bottle Shall Be Filled

If a man walking in the spirit and falsehood do lie, saying, I will prophesy unto thee of wine and of strong drink; he shall even be the prophet of this people. Micah 2:11 KJV

Sometimes we hear only what we want to hear. Sometimes we embrace certain doctrines because it suits us. After all, it's what everyone who is anyone is teaching. All the big-name preachers are saying the same thing. It must be right, right? But is that the attitude we should take with the Word of God? Should we allow ourselves to be spoon-fed the popular teachings of the day without laboring in the Word of God for ourselves? Micah 2 describes the people of God who reject hard sayings but instead embrace prosperity teaching. In verse 6 they command the true prophets of God to stop prophesying. They don't want to hear it. Yet in verse 11 they embrace the false prophets who speak of wine and strong drink, which denotes excess. "Let the good times roll! God loves his people and will only bless them!" If you read Micah 2 in its entirety you might notice some familiar themes. The first two verses are strikingly similar to the foreign policy of Babylon discussed in the first two chapters of Habakkuk. But this is not some godless nation. No, it's clear Micah is speaking directly to the nation filled with God's people. In verse 3 we see that Jehovah himself is devising a disaster against that people. Verses 4 and 10 tell us it will result in that land being utterly destroyed. And verse 12 places this event at a time when God will assemble, or gather, all of Jacob. By the use of the name Jacob he's telling us he's referring to that same event that Ezekiel discusses[515], and many of the prophets confirm, when the two families of God, Israel and Judah, will be reunited and rejoined into one family in the latter days.

---

[515] Ezekiel 37

We've already seen this same concept taught in Jeremiah 13 regarding the sash. When the prophet came to the people and declared that "all bottles shall be filled with wine" they interpreted that message through their own fleshly pride. They had deceived themselves. Instead of receiving that message as the prophet intended, through a balanced teaching from the Word of God, they took it as a reason to party! "Do we not certainly know that every bottle will be filled with wine?"[516] Their understanding regarding the filled bottles was completely different than God's. While the people thought it represented the blessings of God, Jehovah and his true prophet understood the real meaning. "Thus says the LORD: 'Behold, I will fill all the inhabitants of this land...with drunkenness! ...I will not pity nor spare nor have mercy, but will destroy them.'"[517] Listen and look closely at the Word of the Lord to this people. It's as if Jehovah is saying to them: "It's not what you think! I'm not talking about mercy and lovingkindness. Though My Word speaks of my great lovingkindness and mercy, that's not what those bottles represent. Those bottles represent a great disaster I'm devising against My people because you are polluted and refuse to truly turn to Me. Listen and understand: Stop being prideful!"

The pride of God's people blinded them from the truth. Just as it was in Jeremiah's day, so it is today. I have no doubt many will read this book and think to themselves "Yes! In 2016 all of God's people will be raptured and 'so shall we ever be with the Lord.'"[518] But that couldn't be further from the truth. When we take a look at the whole Word of God we can see clearly that the rapture won't happen at the beginning, or even in the middle, of Tribulation. When God's people become polluted with all the idols of the land they are not deserving of a reward. Do you reward your own children when they rebel? While we show them leniency from time to time, good parents do not make it a habit of turning a blind eye to their children's bad behavior. Nor should we expect the Holy One of Israel

---

[516] Jeremiah 13:12
[517] Jeremiah 13:13-14
[518] 1 Thessalonians 4:17

to reward us, forever winking at our sin and rebellion. The first few chapters of Amos speak of the calamity coming upon the world at the beginning of that Day. After addressing the sin and rebellion of his Church, so called the house of Israel, God asks "Can two walk together unless they be agreed?"[519] God is rhetorically asking "You want me to rescue you from the coming judgment? You want me to snatch you away into heaven before the trouble begins? No, I'm sorry children, we're not in agreement." Look how he follows this comment. The next three verses explain cause and effect.[520] Our great Jehovah is trying to tell us something about his character. Despite the great love and mercy and grace he's shown us by sending Yahshua to redeem us, there's another side to God. Jehovah is a God of righteousness and judgment; and that didn't change when he sent Yahshua, the Good Shepherd, to recover his lost sheep. God does not change.

That He Understands and Knows Me

In Jeremiah 9 we read of a punishment coming to the several nations, as well as those "in the farthest corners," who will be judged at the opening of that Day.[521] After taking the entire chapter to lament the sin and treachery of God's people and the consequent punishment coming to their doorstep, we read something very curious: "Thus says the LORD: 'Let not the wise man glory in his wisdom, let not the mighty man glory in his might, nor let the rich man glory in his riches; but let him who glories glory in this, that he understands and knows Me, that I am the LORD, exercising lovingkindness, judgment, and righteousness in the earth. For in these I delight,' says the LORD." [522] Many of us, especially those raised in church, have heard our whole lives of the lovingkindness of

---

[519] Amos 3:3
[520] Amos 3:4-6
[521] Jeremiah 9:26
[522] Jeremiah 9:23-24

God. We know all about the goodness of God. We're constantly reminded of his goodness and grace.

But do we really understand his judgment and righteousness? And if we don't know about those key attributes of Jehovah, do we really know him?[523] And if we don't really know him, is it possible to rightly understand what the Bible says about our day? Or could it be we read a few versus about the rapture and conclude it must occur before the trouble begins because we won't even entertain the idea God would punish his people? All bottles will be filled with wine. Indeed they shall be. But is that wine representative of blessing or judgment? Paul in Romans 11 admonishes us to consider not only the goodness of God, but also his severity.[524] He said this not just in the context of God's people being punished, but in the cutting off of those natural branches of Judah who considered themselves beyond reproach. Yahshua called them white-washed tombs.[525] Cleary God does not always view his people like we view ourselves. Paul was admonishing Christians, those purchased and redeemed by the blood of Yahshua, to remember and understand the severity of the God we serve. Our relationship with the Creator of the universe through the redemptive sacrifice of Yahshua was never meant to be a careless one. Merely professing the name of Jesus and then living our lives however we want is a recipe for disaster. "Do not be deceived, God is not mocked. Whatever a man sows, that also will he reap."[526] The Christian walk was always meant to be one of deep introspection, purity, and obedience. The blood of Yahshua redeemed us not only from eternal separation from God, but also from a miserable life of aimless wandering and bondage to the lusts of the flesh. We are to live for

---

[523] Jeremiah 4:22, Hosea 5:4
[524] Romans 11:22
[525] Matthew 23:27
[526] Galatians 6:7

God and his purposes.[527] We are called to work out our salvation with fear and trembling.[528]

Where Judgment Begins

We read in 1 Peter 4 of a time when the end of all things will be at hand. We're admonished not to consider that "fiery trial" a strange thing. But rather, when we are reproached for the name of Christ we're blessed because the Spirit of glory and of God rests upon us.[529] We know that Yahshua taught these very same principles when he said "then they will deliver you up to Tribulation."[530] It's within this context that Peter explains that "the time has come for judgment to begin at the house of God."[531] We know this is speaking of the end of the age because Yahshua did not first come as Judge but as Savior.

We saw in a previous chapter that judgment will begin at the house of God in a very specific way: on a Sunday morning during worship service. Sometimes we read the Bible in only a general sense, not realizing that God was peering down through time at the very specific events that would befall his people in the latter days. But believers, knowing the end of all things is truly at hand, should not only be serious and watchful in prayer[532], but we should also train ourselves to become very inquisitive in our study of his Word.

In James chapter 5 we see James addressing a very specific people during the last days. He warns the rich to weep and howl for the miseries that are coming upon them.[533] Using the same theme of fire as do all the other prophets when speaking of our day, James

---

[527] 2 Corinthians 5:15, Philippians 2:13
[528] Philippians 2:12
[529] 1 Peter 4:7-12, Isaiah 48:10
[530] Matthew 24:9
[531] 1 Peter 4:17
[532] 1 Peter 4:7
[533] James 5:1

says: "Your gold and silver are corroded, and their corrosion will be a witness against you and will eat your flesh like fire. You have heaped up treasure in the last days."[534] One doesn't have to look too hard to see that America is unlike all other nations in that the richness of our lifestyle far exceeds the rest of the world. Americans today are the ones who have "lived on the earth in pleasure and luxury."[535] Isaiah, when speaking of that Day declares that "the sinners in Zion are afraid; fearfulness has seized the hypocrites"[536] A hypocrite says one thing but does another. He pretends to hold certain moral virtues or religious beliefs but doesn't actually possess them. Have we become a nation of hearers only?[537] Or do we actually read the Bible and do the things it says to do? Do we strengthen the hands of the weak and downtrodden?[538] Do we feed the poor and visit the sick and imprisoned? Are these the things the Church is known for in America? (In Matthew 25 Yahshua teaches that these things prove we belong to him.) Or are we more concerned with how we can prosper? Do we flock by the tens of thousands to hear the wealthy prosperity preachers tell us how we can all be rich too? Do we give our money to churches who distribute the majority of it to the poor and needy? Or do we hand it over to senior pastors who fund their own ideas of what it means to operate a church in America, largely ignoring the needy of the community?

Not Appointed for Wrath

I can hear the loud chorus of believers in America sing about how we can't possibly be sent through the Tribulation because "we're not appointed for wrath." I grew up in those same American churches and read the same books. I realize what we've all been

---

[534] James 5:3
[535] James 5:5
[536] Isaiah 33:14
[537] James 1:22
[538] Isaiah 58, James 1:27

told. But did any of us take time to study those Scriptures for ourselves? 1Thessalonians 5:9 says: "For God did not appoint us to wrath, but to obtain salvation through our Lord Jesus Christ." We can see here that wrath and salvation are diametrically opposed. It's either one or the other. Can a person endure hardship and still inherit eternal life? I sure hope so because Yahshua himself said "In the world you will have Tribulation; but be of good cheer, I have overcome the world."[539] Paul is not talking about the wrath or trouble of the Tribulation. He's speaking of hell: eternal separation from Jehovah. We're not appointed for those eternal hell fires but to obtain salvation through our Lord Yahshua, the Christ, the Anointed One. We would do well to understand how these words are being used within the context of the passage.

But while we're not appointed for the wrath of eternal hell fire, will God use the events of the Tribulation to punish his people? To answer this question in a general way we only need to familiarize ourselves with how Jehovah treats his people who have become overrun with sin and refuse to hear. In Deuteronomy 28 we see that the nation that obeys and fears Jehovah will be blessed. But the nation that turns from him will be cursed until they are driven off the land that God gave them. Many will protest, declaring that we are under a new covenant now. They insist that God somehow changed his very nature when he sent Yahshua to recover his lost sheep. To these I only need encourage to lift up your eyes and look around. Are your born-again friends and loved-ones being miraculously healed of all sorts of infirmities. Isn't that what's promised in Exodus 15 to a people living under God's hand of favor and blessing because they're keeping his commandments?[540] Is America currently under God's blessing or his curse? One only need read the headlines of each day to see America is circling the toilet of defilement and depravity. And as a result, we are experiencing troubles and evils at every turn, as one would expect of a nation under judgment. In the midst of those curses being poured out on the nation that has

---

[539] John 16:33
[540] Exodus 15:26

followed the dictates of their evil hearts we read: "And you shall grope at noonday, as a blind man gropes in darkness; you shall not prosper in your ways; you shall be only oppressed and plundered continually, and no one shall save you."[541] "You shall grope at noonday." When will that great, destructive cloud blot out the light of the sun? Noonday. Do you suppose Jehovah instructed Moses to write those words after looking down through history and observing the most powerful yet morally polluted country to ever exist? A nation who at one time was called by his name and filled with his people who obeyed him; but now she has "become a dwelling place of demons, a prison for every foul spirit, and a cage for every unclean and hated bird!"[542]

> *How the faithful city has become a harlot! It was full of justice; righteousness lodged in it, but now murderers.* Isaiah 1:21

But the real story isn't found on the front page. The real story is that of God's people. The truth is we allowed our country to become polluted, defiled. At one time Christians, and Christian principles, served as a moral compass for the nation. There was a time when America stood for truth and justice and held fast to certain virtues. But now America sends out pollution and filth of every sort and corrupts the rest of the world with every form of wickedness. And God's people, rather than remaining true to their holy God, being that light and salt in a dying world, has become swept away by that wave of wickedness. I could easily cite a slew of polls exposing how Christians in America, collectively, have fallen from that standard of holiness we read about in the Bible. But there's really no need. Those who are living clean lives already recognize the treachery of God's people and "sorrow over the appointed assembly."[543] But the majority of God's people in America only need look at their daily lives. How do you spend your time? How do you spend your money? What websites do you visit? What

---

[541] Deuteronomy 28:29
[542] Revelation 18:2
[543] Zephaniah 3:18, Ezekiel 9:4

movies do you watch? How is your marriage and home life? The prophets describe the Church today as completely filthy. Isaiah declares that all tables (religious services) are full of vomit and filth; no place is clean.[544]

Multitudes come into these churches every Sunday with blood on their hands.[545] We treat our spouses like wretched enemies. We divorce them and then marry unbelievers. Because of this our children are just as lost as the pagan kids across the street.[546] Our homes are dysfunctional and without true love. We celebrate all the pagan holidays. There's constant cursing (bickering, complaining) instead of blessing. There is very little true compassion. We aren't feeding the hungry and caring for the widows, orphans and the downtrodden; instead we go on shopping trips to make ourselves feel better. Multitudes of men are committing adultery within their hearts on the internet...and now women too...and our children, by lusting after the ritual harlots of our day.[547] And many of us are committing actual adultery and fornication and aborting our innocent ones.[548]

Some of us have even made idols out of our gifts and talents; even talents performed in these very same churches. Others of us have made idols out of our possessions and lifestyles. Many of us would rather waste away for hours on end, lounging on our comfy couches and beds[549] in front of the TV instead of pick up our Bible. We are gossiping and backbiting and lying and spewing out all kinds of hatred to one another. Garbage is constantly flowing into our homes via TV, radio, internet and video games. Many of our churches spend all our tithes (of those who actually still give tithes) on salaries and the mortgage (for a building that will soon be destroyed) and have none left over to even stock a food pantry.

---

[544] Isaiah 28:8
[545] Malachi 2:16, Isaiah 59:3
[546] Hosea 5:7
[547] Hosea 4:14
[548] Jeremiah 2:34, 19:4
[549] Amos 3:12

Why? What's more important: another trip to the spiritual buffet to hear Ephesians taught yet again, for the tenth time this year, or to go out into the community and serve? And don't get me started on our pride and arrogance. We are so hypocritical that we feel compelled to tell the world, through political demonstrations and the media, how sinful they are. And we are so full of pride that we actually believe we will escape judgment when the Day of the Lord begins; a lie perpetuated by the false prophets of our day and believed by the Church who listens to lies.[550]

"There is therefore now no condemnation to those who are in Christ Jesus, who do not walk according to the flesh, but according to the Spirit."[551] But are we walking according to the flesh or the Spirit? God is pleased with us as long as we don't draw back into a walk according to the flesh.[552] Are we abiding in Yahshua, in his Word, in the true Vine; and he in us?[553] Or is our walk according to the flesh; doing our own thing, living our lives however we please? "Yet they act so pious! They come to the Temple every day and seem delighted to learn all about me. They act like a righteous nation that would never abandon the laws of its God. They ask me to take action on their behalf, pretending they want to be near me."[554]

God Will Punish His People

Is God happy with his people in these last days? Will all the lovely Christians float up to heaven at the beginning of Tribulation? Quite the opposite is true. Read in Isaiah 5 how God feels about his vineyard. Or hear how Micah describes the days just before the Tribulation: "But truly I am full of power by the Spirit of the LORD, and of justice and might, to declare to Jacob his transgression and to

---

[550] Ezekiel 13:19
[551] Romans 8:1
[552] Hebrews 10:39
[553] John 15:4
[554] Isaiah 58:2 NLT

Israel his sin."[555] Micah declares that "the LORD has a complaint against His people, and He will contend with Israel."[556] And Amos confirms this by describing "the day I punish Israel for their transgressions." [557] The Church has forgotten the righteousness and judgment of Jehovah. And we don't fear him because he's held his peace such a long time.[558] Nor do we even recognize his judgments when they come upon us.

We don't realize that our holy God absolutely despises a mixture of sin and religious pretense.[559] In Revelation he makes it known that his desire is that we were either spiritually hot or cold.[560] In Amos he declares that he hates our sacred assemblies and will refuse to listen to the melody of our stringed instruments.[561] In Isaiah he says he can't stand "iniquity and the sacred meeting." [562] In Malachi he wonders out loud if someone would be so bold as to lock the doors of his house so we would stop offering worthless sacrifices.[563] Why are they worthless? Because they're polluted. How is our worship polluted? Because we are polluted. We have not taken his words to heart when he says he's pleased with us as long as we don't draw back.[564] But we have, collectively, drawn back from that balanced doctrine which leads to life. We've drawn back from purity and obedience to his Word.

The people of God today in America think God will perpetually wink at our sin. We've used our liberty in Christ as a cloak for vice.[565] We think God will overlook our little weaknesses...after all, living clean lives is hopeless, right? We don't

---

[555] Micah 3:8
[556] Micah 6:2
[557] Amos 3:14
[558] Isaiah 42:14, 57:11
[559] Isaiah 58:2
[560] Revelation 3:15
[561] Amos 5:21-23
[562] Isaiah 1:13
[563] Malachi 1:10
[564] Hebrews 10:38
[565] 1 Peter 2:16

realize that the new and better covenant is supposed to be life transforming. We don't consider that God actually meant it when he said we are to be holy.[566] While we understand that by turning to Christ we are made into a new creation[567], we think that means we're always pleasing in his sight. We don't realize God abhors our wickedness and finds no pleasure in a people overrun with sin.[568] And who has time to study his Word each day? Even though his Word is the very thing which renews the mind[569], sanctifies and cleanses his Church from the filth of the world, "that He might present her to Himself a glorious church, not having spot or wrinkle or any such thing, but that she should be holy and without blemish."[570]

The King's Tribulation

Sometimes entire chapters of the Bible foreshadow the pattern of coming events. Daniel 4 speaks of a king who had become lifted up with pride and self-indulgence. Instead of giving God the thanks and glory he was due, he was found congratulating himself for all the strength, wealth and dominion he had acquired. He was living on the earth in abundance, luxury and leisure. Little did he know his world was about to be turned upside down. Even as words of peace and security were still on his lips, he was driven into the wilderness for a very specific period of time.

Just as this king and his nation had grown and become strong, his greatness reached to the heavens, and his dominion to the end of the earth[571] so that great harlot, America, now has achieved dominion over the earth.[572] And just as the holy watcher calls for the

---

[566] Leviticus 11:44-45, 19:2, 20:7, 1 Peter 1:16
[567] 2 Corinthians 5:17
[568] Hosea 8:8, Malachi 1:10, Hebrews 10:38
[569] Romans 12:22
[570] Ephesians 5:26-27
[571] Daniel 4:22
[572] Revelation 17:9, 17:18

symbolic tree to be chopped down and destroyed[573], so the watchman of America cries "Babylon is fallen, is fallen! And all the carved images of her gods He has broken to the ground."[574] But just as the stump and roots were to be left in the earth[575] so Isaiah speaks of this stump in reference to the people of Jehovah who will be spared when America is utterly destroyed.[576] Through many of his prophets God makes it clear he will not make a complete end of his people in America when she is destroyed.[577]

But just as God caused the thoughts of that self-exalted king to become confounded like a beast[578], so God will bring the lofty thoughts of his people back down to earth and will contend with his people.[579] And just as that great king learned the ways of Jehovah "till seven times pass over him"[580] so God's people must learn his ways during a time of great Tribulation which will also last roughly seven years. During this time God's people will come to understand "that the Most High rules in the kingdom of men, and gives it to whomever He chooses."[581] In that day his people will say "Come, and let us go up to the mountain of the LORD, to the house of the God of Jacob; He will teach us His ways, and we shall walk in His paths."[582] Perhaps this is why the phrase "Then you shall know that I am the Lord" occurs so many times in regard to the last days. Just as Job was doubly blessed after his Tribulation, so this king said "my counselors and nobles resorted to me, I was restored to my kingdom, and excellent majesty was added to me."[583]

---

[573] Daniel 4:23
[574] Isaiah 21:9
[575] Daniel 4:23
[576] Isaiah 6:13
[577] Jeremiah 5:10, 5:18, 30:11, 46:28, Amos 3:12, 9:8, Joel 2:32, Amos 4:11, Zechariah 3:2, Isaiah 1:9, 6:13, Ezekiel 7:16
[578] Daniel 4:23
[579] Micah 6:2
[580] Daniel 4:23
[581] Daniel 4:32
[582] Isaiah 2:3
[583] Daniel 4:36

*Belteshazzar answered and said, "My lord, may the dream
concern those who hate you, and its interpretation concern
your enemies!"* Daniel 4:19

Does Daniel 4 really foreshadow God's people enduring the
Tribulation? Why would Daniel imply that the dream concerns his
enemies? I'm sure many will say that Daniel was trying to appease
the king before delivering the bad news. I don't think so. Daniel was
a righteous man and had no reason to fear or pander to any man. I
think Daniel was giving us a clue. Who were those enemies of the
king who hated him? You know, a lot of people died when Judah was
besieged by king Nebuchadnezzar and carried captive to Babylon;
friends and family members, loved ones. I suspect there wasn't a
whole lot of affection for this pagan king from the people of Judah.
So who are the king's enemies? The people of God at the time. And
truly this chapter is referring to what we will soon experience.

Yes, the people of God in America have become polluted with
all the idols of the land because of our exalted mindsets and spiritual
laziness. We're told time and again by the prophets that not only will
Jehovah enter into judgment with the world, but he will start at the
doorstep of the Church. "But I will correct you in justice, and will not
let you go altogether unpunished."[584] When does this take place? "In
the latter days you will consider it."[585] But our loving God does not
punish for punishment sake. He has a purpose in mind. "I will leave
in your midst a meek and humble people, and they shall trust in the
name of the LORD."[586] Despite what the majority of teachers
confidently proclaim about being snatched away into heaven before
the trouble begins, we know that the meek shall inherit the earth[587]
after that time known as Jacob's trouble.[588]

---

[584] Jeremiah 30:11
[585] Jeremiah 30:24
[586] Zephaniah 3:12
[587] Psalms 37:11, Matthew 5:5
[588] Jeremiah 30:7

Chapter 12 - A Warning to Pastors and Teachers

> *Do you not know that you are the temple of God and that the*
> *Spirit of God dwells in you? If anyone defiles the temple of God,*
> *God will destroy him. For the temple of God is holy, which*
> *temple you are.* I Corinthians 3:16-17

Isaiah 22 speaks of the very beginning of the time of world-wide judgment known as the Tribulation, or the Day of the Lord. As verse 5 states, it is "a day of trouble, of treading down, and perplexity" and of "breaking down the walls." The previous chapter gives us some insight into the watchman who is allowed to see that day approaching. And here in chapter 22 we're given a glimpse of two very different groups of people who will be overtaken by that day: those who mock and the blind ministers of the Lord's house who rejoice as that day of dread approaches. Jeremiah speaks of these two groups of people as well, saying "I did not sit in the assembly of the mockers, nor did I rejoice; I sat alone because of Your hand, for You have filled me with indignation."[589]

What was this indignation that Jeremiah was filled with by the Lord? It was none other than a great indignation for the sin of God's people. As we see in the opening chapter of his book, Jeremiah was commissioned to speak to both his generation and the last generation before the return of Christ, our day. Much, dare I say all, of what is written in his book is directed to both his generation and ours. Even when Jeremiah is directly referencing an event of his day there is application for our day as well. And such is the pattern of the prophets and all of God's Word. The Bible is a living book. It contains truth that can be understood and applied by every generation throughout history. And when the prophets speak we

---

[589] Jeremiah 15:17

can find fulfillment in our day. And sadly this is the case with Isaiah 22.

A Very Severe Rebuke

> *"Woe to the shepherds who destroy and scatter the sheep of My pasture!" says the LORD....My heart within me is broken because of the prophets; all my bones shake. I am like a drunken man, and like a man whom wine has overcome, because of the LORD, and because of His holy words....In the latter days you will understand it perfectly.*
> Jeremiah 23:1, 9, 20

I want to make clear from the beginning that this chapter should be treated as nothing less than a very severe and scathing rebuke of most of the ministers of the Gospel today in America. There should be no misunderstanding on this. However, these are not my words. These are the words in the Bible that God speaks to the leaders of his house today. My heart is broken for the blindness and rebellion of the pastors, prophets, teachers, worship leaders, elders, shepherds, priests, bishops, apostles, bloggers, authors and whatever else they want to call themselves. But even more broken is my heart for the multitudes they are misleading. I realize many people will not understand, or will even be able to fathom, what I'm saying in this chapter. The very people who many think would be at the front of the line into heaven will actually be at the end of the line, if at all. Those who should receive the greatest honor will receive great dishonor when that Day begins, as I will show from the Bible. "But many who are first will be last, and the last first."[590]

Overwhelming Evidence

---

[590] Matthew 19:30

People may conclude I have some sort of hidden bitterness against leaders in God's Church. This couldn't be further from the truth. I have not been abused in any way by any of these leaders. Nor do I hold any sort of grudge towards them. In fact, until very recently I held them in high esteem, thinking they were doing God's will by ministering to the saints and promoting the Good News of salvation through Yahshua (Jesus). But then I started reading my Bible. And I started comparing what I was hearing and seeing to the words I was reading in the Bible. And the more I read the more I kept coming across a common theme, which is just how displeased and angry God is with these ministers of his house today. In fact, there are so many passages in the Bible addressing the sin of the pastors and prophets of our day that it's very hard to miss. Open your Bible randomly to any of the major or minor prophets and it's likely you'll quickly come across one of these rebukes. The Bible has much to say on this topic and I tried to include the majority of those references. I don't take this topic lightly; therefore I want to give a clear and accurate treatment of this topic. And my prayer is that those who are misrepresenting the holiness and honor of the name of our great Jehovah will quickly see the error of their way and change their ways, and their message to the people, before it's too late. Again, I can't over emphasize the severity of judgment coming first to the house of the Lord.

> *For the time has come for judgment to begin at the house of God; and if it begins with us first, what will be the end of those who do not obey the gospel of God? Now "If the righteous one is scarcely saved, where will the ungodly and the sinner appear?"* 1 Peter 4:17-18

> *My brethren, let not many of you become teachers, knowing that we shall receive a stricter judgment.* James 3:1

Let not many of you become teachers. One would do well to take these words to heart. If you are a teacher in the Church today you had better make sure you are teaching the whole Truth, and nothing but the Truth, so help you God. The truth not as you understand it but the truth as God understands it, according to his Holy Word.

> *"Whoever therefore breaks one of the least of these commandments, and teaches men so, shall be called least in the kingdom of heaven; but whoever does and teaches them, he shall be called great in the kingdom of heaven.* Matthew 5:19

Shebna, Minister Over the House

> *Thus says the Lord GOD of hosts: Go, proceed to this steward, to Shebna, who is over the house, and say: What have you here, and whom have you here, that you have hewn a sepulcher here, as he who hews himself a sepulcher on high, who carves a tomb for himself in a rock? Indeed, the LORD will throw you away violently, O mighty man, and will surely seize you. He will surely turn violently and toss you like a ball into a large country; there you shall die, and there your glorious chariots shall be the shame of your master's house. So I will drive you out of your office, and from your position he will pull you down.* Isaiah 22:15-19

Sometimes we read a passage and think to ourselves, why in the world is that there? It's an honest question. Sometimes things just don't seem to fit so we skim over it. But God has his reasons for putting it there. First we have to look at context. What's the context? The context of Isaiah 22 is the beginning of the Day of the Lord; the very first day. Isaiah begins this chapter by describing it as the day when the people go up to the rooftops to see what's going on. (Remember the great cloud that appears at midday.) Verse 2 then informs us that some of them are slain, but not with sword, because of the terrifying thing they see on those rooftops.[591] "Men's hearts failing them from fear and the expectation of those things which are coming on the earth, for the powers of the heavens will be

---

[591] Isaiah 22:1-2

shaken."[592] I suppose many read about the partying mockers[593] and say, yes, that fits. After all, God today is calling for weeping and mourning and sackcloth and ashes...in other words, true repentance. But these godless mockers will have none of it. But what is this blurb about Shebna? Why is he being connected to the mockers by the use of the word "Thus"[594] in verse 15? He doesn't seem to be a mocker. In fact, if you search for him in Scripture, we are told nothing else of significance about him. Why is he severely judged here along with these mockers? And what is this about this tomb he's building himself? It all seems so odd on the surface.

There is some value to the commentaries on this passage, if you care to read them. History shows that it was a place of great honor to be buried "on high." Shebna was building himself a burial place of honor with the kings of Israel. These tombs were dug out of mountains and hills in high and lofty positions. They were places of honor and esteem. The only problem was that Shebna didn't deserve this place of honor. He was a scribe and we are told he was "over the house," but that's it. It's apparent that, while yet alive, he was making preparations to be greatly honored and held in high esteem, even in his death. He was ascribing himself a lasting legacy of honor, well after his death. Shebna's name means 'growth'. That in itself doesn't seem too important until we look a little further. In the Strong's Concordance his name is numbered H7644. Look at the next word, H7645. Shebaniah: Jah (Jehovah in the shortened form) has grown, prospered.

Now look at Shebna's replacement, Eliakim.[595] His name is means "God of raising."[596] It's apparent here that Shebna was all about himself, whereas Eliakim waits on Jehovah to raise him into any position in which he sees fit to use him. Shebna is named Shebna, and not Shebaniah, because God is not the one promoting

---

[592] Luke 21:26

[593] Isaiah 22:13-14

[594] Strong's Hebrew Dictionary entry H3541

[595] Isaiah 22:20-21

[596] Strong's Hebrew Dictionary entry H741

him. Shebna seeks to promote himself. We can only assume that Shebna has jockeyed himself into a position of importance within the house. He thinks of himself as a very honored servant of Jehovah. And he's even making preparations to be honored after he is long departed from this earth. On the surface this sounds all well and good. We can take away a simple lesson here that we need to remain humble and allow God to exalt us in due time, as he sees fit.

Big Red Flag

I suppose we could take this story at face value and continue on our merry way. Ah, but there's much more going on here. Does anyone else think God's response to Shebna's sin seems exaggerated for the amount of information we're given? Check this out:

> *Indeed, the LORD will throw you away violently, O mighty man, and will surely seize you. He will surely turn violently and toss you like a ball into a large country; there you shall die, and there your glorious chariots shall be the shame of your master's house. So I will drive you out of your office, and from your position he will pull you down.* Isaiah 22:17-19

Clearly God is just in whatever judgment he decides to hand down. But let me tell you something. Many have suffered far less judgment though they seemingly committed far greater sin. King David committed adultery and murder yet retained his throne. Just look at the mockers, spoken of earlier in this same chapter. They suffer a similar fate at the beginning of Tribulation, but the language is very different. This alone should set off bells in our head that something much greater is happening in this text. However, we must study our Bibles to see the rest of the picture here.

We're told that Shebna is "over the house." The word "house" here is used in a wide variety of applications. We're not told exactly what his duties were, or where they were, but we know that he was a learned man and would have been valuable in both civil and religious matters. There are some interesting commentaries on this subject. One says:

> *Jerome explains this in his Commentary as meaning, 'go to him who dwells in the tabernacle, which in Hebrew is called Sochen.' He understands by this some room, or recess in the temple, where the treasurer or the prefect of the temple dwelt.*[597]

So there is definitely some reason to believe that Shebna served in the temple. What I find interesting is that his duties could have been related to that of a treasurer. Or one who is a steward over the treasure. And what is the treasure of God? Is it not his people? His elect? His bride? Remember that the context of Isaiah 22 is the start of the Tribulation. So why is Shebna's judgment listed here, on the very first day of Tribulation? Besides the godless mockers of our day, is there any other group of people in the Bible, serving in a role similar as that of Shebna, who have a severe judgment levied against them when God stands up to judge the world? In fact, there is. Those who are so named the "priests and prophets."

Points of Comparison

Let's take a closer look at Shebna. We're going to try to draw out some similarities. Just as Isaiah 28 tells us to set "line upon line," Hosea 12:10 says God has given us "symbols through the witness of the prophets." That word "symbols" means points of comparison. So first we have to identify some points to consider about Shebna and later we'll see if we can compare those points to other texts speaking of the coming judgment against the pastors and prophets of our day.

---

[597] *Analysis of Isaiah 22:15-25. - Vision 20.* Barnes' Notes on the Bible. Retrieved March 14, 2012 from http://bible.cc/isaiah/22-15.htm

Shebna's Position in the House

- He was THE leader of the house, in that he was set over the house
- In most churches today, Shebna would be referred to as the Senior Pastor
- As a leader he had a certain authority to rule over others
- To obtain the position of a steward he would have had to have shown a level of trust-worthiness
- People trusted him
- As a steward he had a dominion and decision-making authority over certain places and things
- As a leader he would have been an example to others
- As a leader in the temple he would have been a representative of God and all that that entails
- As a scribe he would have been expected to be very knowledgeable of the Word of God
- As a scribe he would have been expected to know God's ways
- As a scribe he would have been expected to answer questions regarding, and to teach from, the law of God and the prophets

Shebna's Sin

- His actions betrayed the true character of the God he represented
- He attempted to carve out for himself a lasting legacy of honor
- He tried to promote himself to a very lofty and honorable position
- He thought very highly of himself
- He was very prideful
- His pride was on open display for everyone to see
- He saw no need to conceal his pride but rather wore it like a badge of honor

- His public sin was an indication of greater iniquity at work, hidden in his heart
- He most likely used the resources of the house to promote his own agenda
- His pride would have affected his thoughts and how he taught from the Word of God
- His sin and teachings would have been like a cancer in the body; effecting all those he taught
- He most likely jockeyed himself into a position within the house
- He was self-seeking
- He was more concerned about his own honor in the after-life than giving God honor in the present life
- He felt very secure about his position in the after-life
- He was at ease and had ample leisure time to make sure everyone knew just how deserving of honor he thought he was
- He was oblivious to how God really felt about him
- He did not take God's words to heart by living the kind of life God expects of leaders
- He did not fear God
- He likely did not consider that he had reason to fear God
- He had become comfortable under the mercy and blessing of God
- He did not respect and live up to the high standards God has for his leaders
- He had deceived himself into believing he was something he was not
- He had deceived himself into believing he was deserving of something he was not
- He was an impostor...someone who misrepresented God and the office of a true leader
- As an impostor in the house, he would have most likely misled others with a mixture of truth and falsities
- He was oblivious to the season in which he was living

- He was oblivious to the coming judgment
- He didn't see it coming
- His pride blinded him from the truth
- In the face of impending doom he was going about his business as if nothing was wrong
- In the face of impending doom he was rejoicing in his own perceived present honor and expectation of an elevated future

Shebna's Judgment

- His judgment is very severe
- Unlike the mockers who are denied atonement for their sin, nothing is said about atonement for Shebna's sin
- His judgment is a violent casting down or out
- His judgment is a mighty overthrow or rejection of his service and person
- His judgment includes a double violent casting out (as repeated in verses 17 and 18)
- His judgment includes being covered with a veil
- His judgment includes being tossed like a pile or ball
- His judgment includes being tossed into a broad, open country
- His judgment includes dying in this broad, open country
- His judgment includes his glorious chariots (lofty doctrines) resulting in the shame of his master's house
- His judgment includes his position or office being taken away from him violently
- His judgment includes his position or office being given to another who is faithful

Partaker of Double Judgment

Notice his double judgment in verses 17 and 18. Now let's compare this with a text in Zechariah.

> *Indeed, the LORD will throw you away violently, O mighty man, and will surely seize you. He will surely turn violently and toss you like a ball into a large country; there you shall die, and there your glorious chariots shall be the shame of your master's house.* Isaiah 22:17-18

> *Then he said, "This is Wickedness!" And he thrust her down into the basket, and threw the lead cover over its mouth.* Zechariah 5:8

As I described earlier, Zechariah 5 is speaking of the destruction of America at the beginning of Tribulation, when the scroll of judgment goes forth. The language is indeed very similar. We see here in both texts a double judgment, a casting down twice, and a veiling of iniquity. I want to point out here that the priests and prophets, those who meet the conditions of Shebna's sin, will suffer this judgment alongside the godless, Christ-rejecting people of America. It will be a horrifying time of hunger, depravity, and hopelessness. My heart breaks for the pastors who think they're doing a good job but have not taken God's words to heart. It will be a time of great sorrow and regret.

His Glorious Chariots

> *Chariots are very frequently mentioned in the Word, but hardly anyone knows that they signify doctrinal things of good and truth, and also the memory-knowledges belonging to doctrinal things. The reason is that when a chariot is mentioned nothing spiritual enters the idea, but only the natural historical, and it is the same with the horses in front of the chariot; and yet by horses in the Word are signified things of the understanding...,*

and therefore by a chariot are signified doctrinal things and the memory-knowledges belonging thereto.[598]

Keep this in mind for later. We will see how the "glorious doctrines" of the pastors will be the very reason for their demise. There is a very high price to pay for misleading God's people.

Roomy In Every Direction

Isaiah 22:18 tells us they will be tossed like a ball into a large country. I want to key in on one of the words used here. Strong's entry H7342 literally means "roomy in every direction." This fits the narrative perfectly. For when America is destroyed, all the major population centers will be desolate, save a few poor souls. However I believe some of the smaller cities, say with a population less than fifty thousand (and I'm just guessing here) will suffer much less damage. I suspect a great number of cities[599] will be destroyed instantly with nuclear missiles. However I envision many smaller cities will be left to suffer a dismal death of starvation. And this is the picture we're given in Scripture of America's demise, after the initial one-hour destruction.

> *If I go out to the field, then behold, those slain with the sword! And if I enter the city, then behold, those sick from famine! Yes, both prophet and priest go about in a land they do not know.*
> Jeremiah 14:18

These pastors will go about in a land they don't even recognize. It will seem like a foreign land. When they wake up on that last Sunday and prepare to give their sermon, everything will seem quite normal. But the next day, desolation. Joel 2:3 says the

---

[598] Swedenborg, Emanuel. Bible Meanings. *Spiritual Meaning of Chariot, Horse*. Retrieved March 14, 2012 from http://www.biblemeanings.info/Words/Artifact/Chariot.htm
[599] *US Municipalities Over 50,000*. Demographia. (2000). Retrieved March 14, 2012 from http://www.demographia.com/db-uscity98.htm

land will seem like the Garden of Eden before them, and behind them a desolate wilderness. The conglomerate of nations coming to destroy America will make this great land desolate. And these leaders of the flock will go about in a land they don't know. They will witness the horrors of depravity as they watch the people grasp for life by any means possible. They will at that moment realize the full extent of their error. They could have prevented all of this. If only they had uncompromisingly preached the whole Word of God. If only they had insisted their flocks obey the written Word. If only they had themselves taken God's words to heart.

> *But if they had stood in My counsel, and had caused My people to hear My words, then they would have turned them from their evil way and from the evil of their doings.* Jeremiah 23:22

When? What's the context of Jeremiah 23? Verse 20: In the latter days you will understand it perfectly. "Oh, but this isn't all our fault. The whole nation is wicked." Yes, but had God's people kept his commandments none of this would have happened. And who does Jehovah hold accountable for the polluted body of Christ in America? The leaders of his house. Micah 1:5 says: "All this is for the transgression of Jacob and for the sins of the house of Israel." All of what? The Tribulation. "I don't believe it. The Tribulation is for the wicked of the world."

> *Oh, that you had heeded My commandments! Then your peace would have been like a river, and your righteousness like the waves of the sea. Your descendants also would have been like the sand, and the offspring of your body like the grains of sand; His name would not have been cut off nor destroyed from before Me."* Isaiah 48:14-15

Whose name would not have been cut off? Babylon...America.

> *Go forth from Babylon! Flee from the Chaldeans! With a voice of singing, declare, proclaim this, utter it to the end of the earth; say, "The LORD has redeemed His servant Jacob!"* Isaiah 48:16

Had God's people remained pure the curse would have never come. The land would not have to be judged. God would have taken care of the wicked. In fact, the wicked would never have gained traction in the first place.

Rulers of God's People, Leaders of the Flock

Is Shebna really a type of pastor today? I suppose this may be the hardest thing for people to believe about the last days prophecies. Folks, I'm not even talking about "bad" pastors here. Or what we would consider bad. You know, those who have written books that deny that there is eternal separation even for the wicked God-haters of the world. Or those who have so watered down the gospel that many may mistake them for a secular self-help coach. Or those who use their position to abuse children. Or the infidel I recently learned about. A youth pastor with a wife and small children who had an affair with a college student. Or those popular televangelists who live in mansions. (Whatever happened to "let your moderation be known to all men?"[600]) I'm talking about respectable, born-again pastors who think they're in the will of God. So who are these rulers of God's people?

> *The priest and the prophet have erred.... Therefore hear the word of the LORD, you scornful men, who <u>rule</u> this people.* Isaiah 28:7, 14

What's the context of Isaiah 28? As we saw earlier, the destroying storm and overflowing scourge of the Tribulation.

> *The prophets prophesy falsely, and the priests <u>rule</u> by their own power; and My people love to have it so. But what will you do in the end?* Jeremiah 5:31

---

[600] Philippians 4:5

> *Let the elders who <u>rule</u> well be counted worthy of double honor, especially those who labor in the word and doctrine.*
> 1 Timothy 5:17

Certainly those who "rule well," those who are doing a good job by God's standards, are worthy of double honor. Are there many today? I have not come across any Scripture that would lead me to believe they are very many who rule well today. The Bible seems to address the pastors and prophets of our day as one large group, meaning most of them. In an email discussion with an elder, I told him I respectfully disagreed with him on whatever we were discussing. He then, strangely, felt it necessary to remind me that he was worthy of double honor. It was also in that conversation that he said he had learned such and such in seminary but he didn't "know how it was being taught today on the internet." As if the internet is the source of my revelation! Oh, what treachery in the house of God! How the sheep are scattered by men of such vanity. How I wish that he really was worthy of double honor. My heart is broken for what's coming to these elders of the house.

> *"Wail, shepherds, and cry! Roll about in the ashes, you leaders of the flock! For the days of your slaughter and your dispersions are fulfilled; you shall fall like a precious vessel. And the shepherds will have no way to flee, nor the leaders of the flock to escape. A voice of the cry of the shepherds, and a wailing of the leaders to the flock will be heard. For the LORD has plundered their pasture.* Jeremiah 25:34-36

What's the context of Jeremiah 25? The prophecy of the 70 year reign of America: 1946-2016.

Hananiah, Prophet of Peace (Jeremiah 28)

I want to point out here an underlying principle. And that is, when a nation and a people sin against God, as we have in America and in the church of America, we fall under a curse. When this happens, God will send prophets and warnings (lesser judgments) to that nation for the purpose of repentance. God does this with the intent that the people will turn from their wickedness before the final judgment falls on that nation. Such is the case today in America and as outlined in Amos 4. And such was the case in Jeremiah's day. But look at this confrontation recorded in Jeremiah 28 between Jeremiah and the false prophet, Hananiah:

> *"The prophets who have been before me and before you of old prophesied against many countries and great kingdoms--of war and disaster and pestilence. "As for the prophet who prophesies of peace, when the word of the prophet comes to pass, the prophet will be known as one whom the LORD has truly sent."* Jeremiah 28:8-9

He's saying here that the normal thing to expect is a prophet of doom. For this is the very thing of which the people are worthy, because of their sin. The precedent in this situation is a message of doom. A message that says "Hey, you better turn from your wicked ways or God is going to bring disaster." In a round-about way I believe Jeremiah is conveying the message here that anyone who recognizes the sin of the people would then be well within the bounds of normality to predict impending judgment. And he goes on to say that the prophet who predicts peace in such times would be going against the grain of what is considered normal in that situation. And in so doing, if that prophet turns out to be correct, then it would be evident to everyone that God had sent that prophet of peace because it would be such an aberration.

Jeremiah is confirming a basic precept of the Bible. We can go all the way back to the Torah and see how God established this principle. Just read through Deuteronomy. When a nation sins and turns from the Lord that nation can expect judgment from the Lord. And America is under that curse today. Anyone who takes God's words to heart and is familiar with how God responds to gross sin and rebellion can easily predict doom for a nation. But that's not what Hananiah is doing here. Hananiah is predicting peace. And I can tell you, folks, this is exactly what the majority of pastors and end-time teachers are doing today. Even well-known, honorable pastors, pastors I grew up listening to on the radio and admiring, are predicting peace for God's people today, even though God's people are polluted.

Pastors today have wrongly concluded that faith in Yahshua equates to unrestrained mercy forever, which they call 'grace.' It's true that we have found mercy and are reconciled to the Father through his grace and our active, living faith in Yahshua (Jesus). But it's also equally true that God will punish his people who have become just as polluted as the land in which they live. Unlike the partying scoffers of Isaiah 22, God's people can still receive atonement unto eternal salvation but that does not mean we get off scot-free when the Tribulation begins, as many would have you to believe. There is a very high price to pay for misleading God's people. Hananiah died two months after this exchange. God killed him.

> *Then the prophet Jeremiah said to Hananiah the prophet, "Hear now, Hananiah, the LORD has not sent you, but you make this people trust in a lie. Therefore thus says the LORD: 'Behold, I will cast you from the face of the earth. This year you shall die, because you have taught rebellion against the LORD.'" So Hananiah the prophet died the same year in the seventh month.* Jeremiah 28:15-17

The Crown of Pride, the Drunkards of Ephraim (Isaiah 28)

> *The pride of Israel testifies to his face; therefore Israel and Ephraim stumble in their iniquity; Judah also stumbles with them.* Hosea 5:5

> *Woe to the crown of pride, to the drunkards of Ephraim, whose glorious beauty is a fading flower which is at the head of the*

verdant valleys, to those who are overcome with wine!
Isaiah 28:1

Ah, what a beautiful tomb you've dug for yourself Shebna! It's a lovely idea, that you will be so elevated at your departure. But you don't realize what's coming. You are blind because you don't take God's holy words to heart and give him the glory he is due.[601] God has a destroying storm in store for this wicked nation, and you will partake. Yes, you will drink of it. Yes, he will bring you down with it!

> *Behold, the Lord has a mighty and strong one, like a tempest of hail and a destroying storm, like a flood of mighty waters overflowing, who will bring them down to the earth with His hand.* Isaiah 28:2

Just a few short chapters after this blurb about Shebna we come to Isaiah 28, a chapter that gives much more detail about the sin of Shebna. All of the same themes are represented in this chapter: the leaders of God's people, filled with pride and drunk on false doctrine, blind to the coming judgment, thinking they will escape the Tribulation unharmed. In fact, like Shebna, they believe they will be elevated (raptured) above and out of the "overflowing scourge" that is to come upon the world. But in reality, like Shebna, they will be trampled down by that overflowing scourge. Their covenant with death and hell will be annulled. In other words, it will not happen the way they think it's going to happen. You won't be exalted, Shebna, you will be abased; you will be trampled down as the mire of the streets.

Do you see what's going on here? Shebna had made a covenant with death. Shebna had determined that when he died he would be greatly honored. That was his agreement with his death. But the word used here goes beyond just death. The word here is Strong's Concordance H4194. It carries with it a sense of violence or ruin. Multitudes of pastors and end-time prophets (expositors,

---

[601] Malachi 2:2

teachers of end-time prophecies) are telling people "hey, there's no need worry about the overflowing scourge, the Tribulation, we have the promise of the rapture. Before the trouble begins we'll all be snatched away to the safety of heaven." So life carries on uninterrupted for a people laden down with sin.[602] People don't feel the need to get right with God and live clean lives. The priests and prophets of our day have come into agreement with hell (verse 18). But how? Because this pre-trib notion of rapture is a doctrine of demons. Those who would teach such things are in agreement with hell. And such is the folly of the pastors and prophets of our day. But is it just the rapture teaching or is something else going on here?

Why does this chapter say they are drunk? And what does that mean? Verse 7 reveals that they are "out of the way," they error in vision and stumble in judgment. Wine and drunkenness is used here to denote something of excess. These teachers are "out of the way" of Truth, as they are teaching destructive doctrines to their congregations. These doctrines are at the core of their beliefs. At the very point in time when the sin of God's people has so filled to fullness the "valleys of fatness," the rich low places of profane worship, these leaders of the flock are telling them, in various ways, that they don't need to repent. They treat the sin of the people as a very light thing. The people of God, spiritually, have terminal cancer and these drunkards of Ephraim are treating it as if it's a scrape on the knee.

> *They offer superficial treatments for my people's mortal wound. They give assurances of peace when there is no peace.*
> Jeremiah 6:14 NLT

This crown of pride, the leaders of God's people are so very blind to the sin of God's people because they think God is blind to this sin. They don't realize what God says about us, our day:

---

[602] Isaiah 1:4

They do not consider in their hearts that I remember all their wickedness; now their own deeds have surrounded them; they are before My face. Hosea 7:2

And they are so exceedingly drunk on the mercy and blessing that God has shown us in America. "Let the good times roll! Sure, things are getting harder in America, but everything's going to be alright. Don't worry. Just trust God. No need to repent of your gross sin and blatant rebellion. Once saved, always saved. Just one drop of the blood covers all sin, past, present and future.[603] God is with us."

Her heads judge for a bribe, her priests teach for pay, and her prophets divine for money. Yet they lean on the LORD, and say, "Is not the LORD among us? No harm can come upon us." Micah 3:11

Or as one pastor told his congregation, without qualifying it: "God is pleased with you! The angels love to see us all gathered here in one place so they can gaze upon us." Woe to the crown of pride! The bride of Christ in America is filled to the full with pride, and here sits on her head the crown of pride, the pastors and prophets, ministers over the house. Woe to the crown of pride, it won't end well for you. At this very same moment in time, while the pastors and prophets dig their graves with doctrines of demons, God pleads with us:

"How can you say, 'I am not polluted, I have not gone after the Baals'? See your way in the valley; know what you have done: you are a swift dromedary breaking loose in her ways. Jeremiah 2:23

There is a very high price to pay for misleading God's people.

As often as it goes out it will take you; for morning by morning it will pass over, and by day and by night; it will be a terror just to understand the report." Isaiah 28:19

---

[603] Hebrews 10:26-27

Both Prophet and Priest Are Profane (Jeremiah 23)

"For both prophet and priest are profane; yes, in My house I have found their wickedness," says the LORD. Jeremiah 23:11

Do pastors today even read their Bibles? Jeremiah 23 of the King James Version starts out "Woe be unto the pastors..." If ever there was a clear wake-up call to the pastors, this is it. Do you care to know what that woe is? Do you desire to know how the story ends? It ends the way Shebna's life ended. That woe is the same woe that Shebna received at the hand of the Lord. In verse 2 God says, "Behold, I will attend to you for the evil of your doings." Just as Shebna was replaced by Eliakim, so we see in verse 4, "I will set up shepherds over them who will feed them." And just as Shebna was cast out into a desolate wilderness, so we read of these shepherds and prophets in verse 12:

"Therefore their way shall be to them like slippery ways; in the darkness they shall be driven on and fall in them; for I will bring disaster on them, the year of their punishment," says the LORD.

And just as Shebna was cast out and forsaken, we read in verse 39 this woe against the pastors and prophets and the land in which they live: "therefore behold, I, even I, will utterly forget you and forsake you, and the city that I gave you and your fathers, and will cast you out of My presence." And just as Shebna's "glorious chariots," his lofty doctrinal beliefs, became the shame of his master's house, so we read in verse 40: "And I will bring an everlasting reproach upon you, and a perpetual shame, which shall not be forgotten."

It is a fearful thing to fall into the hands of the living God.
Hebrews 10:31

But when? Is Jeremiah 23 really speaking of us, our day, our country, our pastors, our pre-trib rapture teachers? Is there anything in this chapter that would lead us to believe this is the case?

> *The anger of the LORD will not turn back until He has executed and performed the thoughts of His heart. In the latter days you will understand it perfectly.* Jeremiah 23:20

And who is this spoken of in verse 5?

> *"Behold, the days are coming," says the LORD, "That I will raise to David a Branch of righteousness; A King shall reign and prosper, and execute judgment and righteousness in the earth."* Jeremiah 23:5

"Oh, this is clearly Jesus, so it must be speaking of his day." Sorry, no, Yahshua came first as the suffering Servant[604], but his second coming is that of a righteous Judge[605], as shown here in verse 5. And what about this? When does the great ingathering of God's people take place?

> *But I will gather the remnant of My flock out of all countries where I have driven them, and bring them back to their folds; and they shall be fruitful and increase.* Jeremiah 23:3

Clearly this great ingathering is a common theme in the Bible in reference to the last days, when the two sticks, the house of Israel and the house of Judah, are reunited into one stick.[606] This is the time when Judah (the Jews) will find salvation through Yahshua, who the house of Israel, the Church, already knows as The Lord Our Righteousness.

> *In His days Judah will be saved, and Israel will dwell safely; now this is His name by which He will be called: THE LORD OUR RIGHTEOUSNESS.* Jeremiah 23:6

---

[604] Isaiah 42:2
[605] Isaiah 42:13
[606] Ezekiel 37

Scattering the Sheep

> *"For both prophet and priest are <u>profane</u>; yes, in My house I*
> *have found their wickedness," says the LORD.* Jeremiah 23:11

pro·fane[607]
adjective
1. characterized by irreverence or contempt for God or
sacred principles or things; irreligious.
2. not devoted to holy or religious purposes; unconsecrated;
secular (opposed to sacred).
3. unholy; heathen; pagan: profane rites.

Strong's Concordance H2610, chânêph, khaw-nafe'
A primitive root; to soil, especially in a moral sense: -
corrupt, defile, X greatly, pollute, profane.

And what exactly is the profane wickedness of the majority
of pastors and prophets that God has discovered in his house today?
In short, they have corrupted the flock of God with false doctrines.
Just as Hananiah, they have, this very day in which we live, week
after week, year after year, caused the people of God to believe a
lie.[608] They have taught rebellion against the Lord of Hosts. They
have polluted the bride with false teaching. And the people of God
believe them because they don't read their Bibles.[609] The people of
God cannot themselves discern between the truth and a lie. These
teachers of false doctrines have mixed truth with lies and then fed
that to the sheep. And now, after the people of God in America have
committed great sin and treachery against their Holy God they feel
no need to truly turn from their wicked ways and live clean lives
before the Father, whose eyes are so pure that he can't even look
upon wickedness:

---

[607] Dictionary.com. *Profane*. Retrieved March 14, 2012 from
http://dictionary.reference.com/browse/profane
[608] Ezekiel 13:19
[609] Jeremiah 6:10

You are of purer eyes than to behold evil, and cannot look on wickedness. Habakkuk 1:13

Insulting the Spirit of Grace

And herein is the lie: "When God looks at us he sees the blood of Jesus. All my sin, past, present and future, is under the blood of Christ." So people think: God understands my weakness. He's already forgiven all the sin I will ever commit. I'm acceptable in his sight. God doesn't care about perfection. He will tolerate this little weakness. But God says:

Of how much worse punishment, do you suppose, will he be thought worthy who has trampled the Son of God underfoot, counted the blood of the covenant by which he was sanctified a common thing, and insulted the Spirit of grace?
Hebrews 10:29

Now the just shall live by faith; but if anyone draws back, My soul has no pleasure in him." Hebrews 10:38

Grace:
Strong's G5485, charis, khar'-ece
From G5463; graciousness (as gratifying), of manner or act (abstract or concrete; literal, figurative or spiritual; **especially the divine influence upon the heart, and its reflection in the life**; including gratitude): - acceptable, benefit, favour, gift, grace (-ious), joy liberality, pleasure, thank (-s, -worthy).

And what is that Spirit of Grace that we have insulted? It's the working of the Holy Spirit, producing in us the fruit of the Spirit[610], activated by our faith and determination to live for God, resulting in a vessel consecrated to God and made acceptable in his sight. It is nothing short of the miraculous restoration of a person

---

[610] Galatians 5:22-23

who becomes pleasing to God through a living faith in Yahshua and the work of the Spirit of Grace as our will comes into agreement with God's. Thy will be done. Lord, your will be done in my life. Your will be done on earth as it is in heaven. Let my life be a pure reflection of you. I submit to you.

But can this work of the Spirit of Grace take place in a willfully polluted vessel? No, it cannot. We are made clean by the washing of the water of the Word.[611] We are made clean by faith in Yahshua when we turn to him and turn away from the world. We are then to live for him, being transformed day by day, by the Spirit of Grace. But when we choose to ignore his Word, despising his commandments, and do our own thing and walk in our own ways, we become polluted with the ways of the world and we frustrate the Spirit of Grace. Now, IF we sin, we have an advocate with the Father.

> *My little children, these things I write to you, so that you may not sin. And if anyone sins, we have an Advocate with the Father, Jesus Christ the righteous.* 1 John 2:1

"If we sin." The intention of the Father was never to cause us to believe that he winks at our blatant disobedience and willful ignorance of his Word. What I'm telling you today is consistent with the whole Word of God, cover to cover. But what we've been taught all our lives by the pastors and prophets is contrary to the whole Word of God. They would have you believe Jehovah somehow changed his very nature when he sent Yahshua after us, the lost sheep. Do you see how truth and lies have been mixed together to create this hybrid mess of a doctrine they call "grace?" And the people of God, complicit in this corruption of the gospel, love to be told that God winks at their sin, which is exactly the message coming down from pulpits all across the land and plastered across the pages of books in the Christian book aisle.

---

[611] Ephesians 5:26

> *"How can you say, 'We are wise, and the law of the LORD is*
> *with us'? Look, the false pen of the scribe certainly works*
> *falsehood.* Jeremiah 8:8

And now at the end of this age the bride of Christ in America
is absolutely filthy. But our pastors and prophets treat this filth as a
very small thing while they chant "Peace, peace!" They insist that all
the lovely Christians will float up to heaven when the trouble begins.
They don't take it to heart that God asks in Amos 3:3 "Can two walk
together unless they be agreed?" God is saying, "You want me to
snatch you away into heaven before the trouble begins? Sorry, we're
not in agreement. I'm a holy God and you are a mess. You are filthy,
my bride. You have chosen to reject the cleansing water of my Word.
You don't keep my commandments which I gave you for your own
good. You have polluted yourself. I'm coming back for a spotless
bride, not a bride that's been out whoring with the world."

Your Hollow Wall Will Come Crashing Down (Ezekiel 13)

It's for this very reason, this defilement of God's Word, and
by extension both his character and his bride, that the pastors and
prophets will learn first-hand of the severity of God.[612] They have
misrepresented the holy nature of God's name; his character. By
teaching this defiled doctrine they have caused many to miss that
narrow door. They have scattered the sheep of God, making them a
prey for every devouring beast of the field. They have seduced the
people of God.

> *Because with lies you have made the heart of the righteous sad,*
> *whom I have not made sad; and you have strengthened the*
> *hands of the wicked, so that he does not turn from his wicked*
> *way to save his life.* Ezekiel 13:22

---

[612] Romans 11:22

And what is this defiled doctrine? It's the exact opposite of what God's Word teaches. Do these teachers spend any time at all in God's Word? Or do they just pull a verse here or there and expound on it from the vain imaginations of their hearts? Isaiah tells us their doctrine is a like bed that you can't stretch out on and like a cover that's too small, which leaves you cold at night.[613] There simply is not enough Biblical truth in their arguments to be considered strong and solid. Ezekiel says it's like building a wall without mortar. When the great storm of Tribulation finally arrives the wall that they've built using half-truths will come crashing down around them.

> *Because, indeed, because they have seduced My people, saying, 'Peace!' when there is no peace--and one builds a wall, and they plaster it with untempered mortar-- say to those who plaster it with untempered mortar, that it will fall. There will be flooding rain, and you, O great hailstones, shall fall; and a stormy wind shall tear it down.* Ezekiel 13:10-11

When does this happen? What's the context of Ezekiel 13?

> *You have not gone up into the gaps to build a wall for the house of Israel to stand in battle <u>on the day of the LORD</u>.* Ezekiel 13:5

Folks, this is the long-awaited Day of the Lord being talked about here. The Tribulation. Who is the house of Israel? The same lump of clay in Jeremiah 18 that had to be remade into a different vessel. Why? Because the northern kingdom left and never returned. They rejected God and his law so God divorced them. These are the lost sheep whom Yahshua said he was sent to recover.[614] But how? They mixed with the Gentiles and became Gentiles themselves. They migrated and filled the face of the earth. That promise to Abraham, that his seed would be as the sand of the sea and the stars of the sky, that was fulfilled by the house of Israel, the descendants of Abraham,

---

613 Isaiah 28:20
614 Matthew 15:24

his seed. But the Good Shepherd went looking for them. And who did he find? The Church.

Look at the indictment in verse 5. You have not gone up into the gaps to build a wall for God's people. In fact, the wall you did build you built with untempered mortar; with false doctrines that mislead people "so that he does not turn from his wicked way to save his life." And how is it that you didn't build a strong wall for God's people? That's your job! For many of you it's your full time job! You are supposed to tell people the truth and let God worry about the rest. Your teaching should have been like a fortress to the people in the day of their visitation. You were supposed to be like an assayer of metals who removes the impurities so they can stand before the King blameless, without fault.[615]

> *I have set you as an assayer and a fortress among My people, that you may know and test their way.* Jeremiah 6:27

Compare the word 'fortress' here with Ezekiel 13:5. Notice the contrast. The false pastors and prophets who "speak peace when there is no peace" are doing harm. They are preventing people from repenting of their sin and turning to God with their whole heart. But this voice of truth is like a fortress; a defense. How? Because he preaches about sin and repentance. He says the Day of the Lord is about judgment first for God's people. Those who repent and are clean before God have a sure defense in that day. They are the just who live by their faith. Those who turn away from sin and turn to him are God's children and God will preserve his people on the day America is destroyed by nuclear fire. They will be like firebrands plucked from the fire.

But that's not what these pastors and prophets are doing. They are causing the people of God to believe a lie. They are working against God by teaching false doctrines. And in so doing they become the enemies of God and receive the reward of the wicked.

---

[615] Philippians 2:15

Woe To the Shepherds Who Feed Themselves (Ezekiel 34)

> *Son of man, prophesy against the shepherds of Israel, prophesy
> and say to them, Thus says the Lord GOD to the shepherds:
> Woe to the shepherds of Israel who feed themselves! Should not
> the shepherds feed the flocks?*   Ezekiel 34:2

Woe to the shepherds who feed themselves! Here, yet again,
we have a woe to the pastors. But is this talking about our day? Is
there anything in this chapter that would cause us to believe this is
the case? Here's an interesting phrase in verse 12: "on a cloudy and
dark day." This couldn't possibly be the same cloudy and dark day
mentioned in other places in reference to the beginning of
Tribulation, could it?

> *What good is the day of the LORD to you? It will be darkness,
> and not light.*   Amos 5:18

> *A day of darkness and gloominess, a day of clouds and thick
> darkness.*   Joel 2:2

And what about this great last-days ingathering of God's
people in the very next verse. Didn't we just see this same thing
when discussing Jeremiah 23?

> *And I will bring them out from the peoples and gather them
> from the countries, and will bring them to their own land; I will
> feed them on the mountains of Israel, in the valleys and in all
> the inhabited places of the country.*   Ezekiel 34:13

Do you view the Bible as some sort of random collection of
thoughts? Or do you think maybe God has a purpose for putting
these thoughts together in the same chapter? What's happening
here is that God wants to make it clear that this passage is to be
applied to our day. This is why these clues were placed here.
Certainly there could have been only one chapter in the Bible for
each event of the latter days. But that's not how the Bible was

written. Isaiah 28 asks, "who can I cause to understand the message?"[616] Then he gives the answer. He tells us how we are to understand the message of the last days. Line upon line, precept upon precept.[617] And at the end of the chapter he gives us a farming lesson. He's saying we must compare all the messages of the prophets. We must set line upon line. And just as the farmer receives instructions from God, who is wise in counsel, so we must depend upon God for understanding and not rely on our meager understanding. God instructs us in right judgment and teaches us.[618] Our understanding must be divinely inspired. We must set precept upon precept. The whole Word of God must agree. We can't find ourselves in a position like Hananiah did, contradicting the basic precepts of the Word of God.

Woe to the shepherds who feed themselves. Just as Shebna was concerned about his status, his reputation, his vain glory, so we see this warning in Ezekiel 34. Woe to the shepherds who are more concerned about their own glory than they are about God's honor. I'm reminded of a church whose pastor divorced his wife. Nothing was said about infidelity on the part of either spouse. Without giving details it was conveyed that, after attempts at reconciliation, they just couldn't get along. Not only did this pastor try to justify divorcing his wife using Scripture, but after his wife posted something in the local post office about the pastor, he then stated that God was trying to humble him by "dealing with his reputation." What about God's reputation!?! What about the honor that belongs to our holy Jehovah which this pastor drug through the mud for all the world to see? Should he not have been more concerned about God's reputation, even if it meant stepping down? Should he not have been concerned how the people would view the God he claims to represent? This pastor later remarried and is still pastoring the same church. Although, he's given himself several increasingly puffed-up titles since then, even though Yahshua himself said let not

---

[616] Isaiah 28:9
[617] Isaiah 28:10
[618] Isaiah 28:26

yourselves be called by a title, as you are all brothers.[619] Whatever happened to the Scripture that says a man must be blameless to be qualified to oversee God's people?[620] I guess we can throw out that verse too.

There is a very high price to pay for misleading God's people. Just as Shebna was thrown out of office and replaced by another, so we read and understand here in Ezekiel 34 the same judgment is handed down to the pastors of our day. And just as that faithful shepherd Eliakim took Shebna's place so we read that Yahshua himself will see to it that his sheep are sought out, gathered, protected and well fed during the Tribulation.

> 'Thus says the Lord GOD: "Behold, I am against the shepherds, and I will require My flock at their hand; I will cause them to cease feeding the sheep, and the shepherds shall feed themselves no more; for I will deliver My flock from their mouths, that they may no longer be food for them." 'For thus says the Lord GOD: "Indeed I Myself will search for My sheep and seek them out. "As a shepherd seeks out his flock on the day he is among his scattered sheep, so will I seek out My sheep and deliver them from all the places where they were scattered on a cloudy and dark day. "And I will bring them out from the peoples and gather them from the countries, and will bring them to their own land; I will feed them on the mountains of Israel, in the valleys and in all the inhabited places of the country. "I will feed them in good pasture, and their fold shall be on the high mountains of Israel. There they shall lie down in a good fold and feed in rich pasture on the mountains of Israel. Ezekiel 34:10-14

There really should be no confusion of what's coming. As do all the prophets, Jeremiah confirms what Ezekiel is saying here. We see in Jeremiah 50:4-6, when America is destroyed, God's true

---

[619] Matthew 23:8
[620] Titus 1:6

people, the just who have lived by faith, will set their faces toward Zion. With weeping they shall come. And they will ask the way to Zion. This last day mass exodus, this Exodus II, is confirmed all throughout the Word of God. When America is destroyed, those whom God preserves will supernaturally end up in Zion; the land God promised our forefathers. But what about the shepherds who mislead God's people today?

> *My people have been lost sheep. Their shepherds have led them astray; they have turned them away on the mountains. They have gone from mountain to hill; they have forgotten their resting place.* Jeremiah 50:6

What a scathing indictment of the shepherds today. Under their care God considers us lost sheep who are being led astray. What is the penalty for misleading God's people? These shepherds will go about in a land they don't even recognize. Like Shebna, they will reap the reward of a wicked steward. There will be no way of escape. They will not be allowed to leave this desolate land.

> *Wail, shepherds, and cry! Roll about in the ashes, you leaders of the flock! For the days of your slaughter and your dispersions are fulfilled; you shall fall like a precious vessel. And the shepherds will have no way to flee, nor the leaders of the flock to escape. A voice of the cry of the shepherds, and a wailing of the leaders to the flock will be heard. For the LORD has plundered their pasture.* Jeremiah 25:34-36

Faithful Shepherds vs. Today's Impostors (Malachi 2)

> *"And now, O priests, this commandment is for you. If you will not hear, and if you will not take it to heart, to give glory to My name," Says the LORD of hosts.* Malachi 2:1-2

I'm always amazed when pastors today preach from Malachi 3, yet they are so profoundly blind to the rest of Malachi and how it applies to our day. They aptly scold the congregation for robbing God of the tithe while conveniently turning a blind eye to their own treacherous thievery. Not only do they rob God by misusing the funds of the house, ignoring the downtrodden of the community, but they steal from God the very thing for which they are there in the first place: to give glory to God, declaring the truth about his character and ways, and leading the people in right living. In other words, to exalt the great name of Jehovah, proclaiming his whole truth, and leading by example. They are representatives of God but they profane his great name by dealing treacherously. Like Shebna, they honor themselves, preach falsehood and thereby pollute the body of Christ. And those who are lulled into complacency by their soothing words fall away through the wide door leading to perdition. They rob God of the people who would otherwise worship him in truth, which is the reason he created this world in the first place: to find those who would worship him in spirit and in truth.

> *Then you will know that I have sent this commandment to you.*
> Malachi 2:4

Every chapter of Malachi offers context that would lead us to believe the entire book is speaking of our day. Yet, for some reason, it seems pastors today either don't teach on Malachi, or when they do, they teach it as historical in nature only (other than the bit about tithing). The day is coming, and it's here now, that all things hidden will be revealed. The day is coming when these pastors will realize that God's Word really is the truth. The day is coming when they will realize Malachi 2 was talking about them. But it didn't have to be like this. They had a choice in the matter. If only they would listen. If only they would take his words to heart and give glory to his name. And herein is the problem: you can praise the name of Jesus all you want. Sing all the hymns you want. Teach the same basic principles of forgiveness through Jesus a million times. But if you are not preaching the whole Word, the whole truth, you are dishonoring his great name. Your half-truths invariably must be mixed with lies.

My covenant was with him, one of life and peace, and I gave them to him that he might fear Me; so he feared Me and was reverent before My name. Malachi 2:5

The law of God was supposed to produce a godly fear and reverence in those who declared it, those who listened, and those who obeyed. But God's people in America don't fear their God today. That's obvious; just look at how American Christians live their lives. One doesn't have to look very hard to see that our lives don't line up with the commandments of God's Word. The Church in America is hardly distinguishable from the wicked country in which we live. America is under Deuteronomy's curse today and so is the Church. God is heaping disasters upon us and the Church is partaking right alongside the wicked.[621] The day is fast approaching when that final judgment will strike America. And who in the Church will God hold most accountable on that first day? Just like Shebna, these impostors in the house today will be taken away with the polluted solemn feasts; their Sunday morning worship service.

Behold, I will rebuke your descendants and spread refuse on your faces, the refuse of your solemn feasts; and one will take you away with it. Malachi 2:3

The law of truth was in his mouth, and injustice was not found on his lips. He walked with Me in peace and equity, and turned many away from iniquity. "For the lips of a priest should keep knowledge, and people should seek the law from his mouth; for he is the messenger of the LORD of hosts. But you have departed from the way; you have caused many to stumble at the law. You have corrupted the covenant of Levi," Says the LORD of hosts. Malachi 2:6-8

We're told very plainly what God expects of a faithful minister over the house. The law of truth is in his mouth and he turns many away from sin. There is no injustice, no iniquity found on his lips. He teaches no false doctrines or half-truths. His words

---

[621] Deuteronomy 32:23

219

are the pure words from God. There is no mixture of truth and lies in his teachings. He doesn't care what everyone else is teaching. He teaches the whole truth of God's Word uncompromisingly and leaves the outcome to God. He doesn't lead people to that point of forgiveness through Yahshua and then teach them how to insult the Spirit of Grace like the pastors do today. No, the faithful steward keeps knowledge and trains the people in the whole Word of God. He doesn't deceive them by preaching mainly of the goodness of God. He declares the whole truth of God's Word. His teaching is balanced; teaching of the goodness of God but also training the people in all fear and reverence of our holy God who is returning as a righteous Judge to give to each man according to what his deeds deserve.[622]

But we're told time and again in Scripture that these unfaithful stewards over the house today have corrupted that original standard of the priesthood. Just as Isaiah 28 says they are "out of the way," Malachi 2 says they have "departed from the way." They are teaching a hybrid false doctrine of truth and lies. In so doing they have caused many to stumble at the law of God: the very words that speak of his character, his holiness and the reverence he is due.

And we're told in this very chapter what the end result of this corruption of God's people is at the hands of those teaching false doctrines. Simply stated: broken homes, broken lives, and children who want nothing to do with our God. After taking half the chapter to rebuke and warn the impostors over the house today, the second half deals with the families who have become corrupted by these false teachers. Starting in verse 10 is a description of the heart-wrenching behavior of God's people who break all restraint and trample down the very people whom they love dearest: their spouses and children.

These husbands and wives have heard all their lives, in various ways, that God is only good and loving and gracious and

---

[622] Romans 2:6

forgiving. They have not been properly taught to fear God and give him the honor due his holy name, both in words and actions. They have become comfortable with their sin. They have pushed the boundary of decency to its breaking point. They are most likely products of broken homes themselves. As children they witnessed and learned firsthand the destructive power of divorce and treating loved ones treacherously. And yet they are powerless to prevent this same destruction in their own marriages. Then, with utter disdain for God's Word, and on display for all the world to see, they divorce their spouses and marry unbelievers. Then they come to church, covering the alter with tears instead of giving our holy God what he deserves: pure worship from a believer who is dwelling under the protective wings of the promised blessing and favor of a righteous God who has made that person acceptable in his sight by the Spirit of Grace. And then after acting so treacherously God's people ask, "Where's the God of justice? Why am I so beaten down? Why is all this happening to me? Where's God when I need him?"

The whole land has become polluted. And while all this is going on the leaders of God's people, so blind to the truth of God's Word and the reality of our day, give false reassurances that God is with us; even declaring that everyone, regardless of whatever kind of life they are living, is pleasing in his sight, and that he delights in us. "God delights in you! Come just as you are. God is waiting to bless you"; speaking this to everyone, regardless of whatever kind of life they're living. In truth, God has no pleasure in us because we have counted the blood of the covenant a common thing by living such polluted lives.[623] We have drawn back from that pure word of truth that cleanses, and we have grieved the Spirit of Grace who desires to make us an acceptable vessel for God's honor and glory. God is weary of it all.

You have wearied the LORD with your words; yet you say, "In what way have we wearied Him?" In that you say, "Everyone

---

[623] Hebrews 10:29

who does evil is good in the sight of the LORD, and He delights in them," Or, "Where is the God of justice?" Malachi 2:17

I suppose what I've written thus far is enough. It's clear God has a controversy with the pastors and prophets of our day. That nail fastened in a secure place now will soon be removed and cut down and fall and the burden it's holding will fall as well.[624] It seems to me, in regard to the last day prophecies of the Bible, there is more written about this topic than any other. Do you think maybe God intentionally went the extra mile for those serving in his name? It's hard to miss the warnings, and yet they have, thereby affirming the righteous judgment of God. So far I've covered many separate chapters from the three major prophets and one minor prophet. And for good measure I've used Scripture from both Old and New Testaments to support this case. And this is how it should be. Anything we teach should be supported by the whole Bible, cover to cover. But in the interest of completeness, I'd like to point out that there are additional texts besides those mentioned thus far. Let's take a look.

Confirming Text (Isaiah)

For behold, the Lord, the LORD of hosts, takes away from Jerusalem and from Judah the stock and the store, the whole supply of bread and the whole supply of water; the mighty man and the man of war, the judge and the prophet, and the diviner and the elder; Isaiah 3:1-2

As for My people, children are their oppressors, and women rule over them. O My people! Those who lead you cause you to err, and destroy the way of your paths. Isaiah 3:12

---

[624] Isaiah 22:25

> *The LORD will enter into judgment with the elders of His*
> *people and His princes: For you have eaten up the vineyard;*
> *the plunder of the poor is in your houses.* Isaiah 3:14

If you read through the first 12 chapters of Isaiah you might notice that it's a narrative of God's people in America as the Tribulation begins. Look at the description of our country in chapter 1. He says there was a time when faithfulness, righteousness and justice were found in her. But now she's a harlot. Truly America has become Babylon, that great mother of harlots. Then chapter 13 is a flashback, going into much more detail of the destruction of America, which we learned about especially in the first three chapters, and mentioned again in 6:11. Chapter 14 is a taunt against the President of America at the time of her demise. It's clear that chapter 2 sets the context as the "latter days." Therefore, while Isaiah's words may have been applicable to ancient generations, certainly these words are meant for us today. And we see again in Isaiah 3 that the destruction coming to America will be complete and final, taking away the prophet and elder.

> *Therefore the LORD will cut off head and tail from Israel, palm*
> *branch and bulrush in one day. The elder and honorable, he is*
> *the head; the prophet who teaches lies, he is the tail. For the*
> *leaders of this people cause them to err, and those who are led*
> *by them are destroyed.* Isaiah 9:14-16

Here again in chapter 9 we see the judgment repeated: both elder and prophet, those who teach lies, will be cut off. Their time on earth will come to an end. "For the leaders of this people..." Who are the people mentioned here? The people of God. Who are the leaders? The pastors and prophets who caused them to err.

> *Pause and wonder! Blind yourselves and be blind! They are*
> *drunk, but not with wine; they stagger, but not with*
> *intoxicating drink. For the LORD has poured out on you the*
> *spirit of deep sleep, and has closed your eyes, namely, the*
> *prophets; and He has covered your heads, namely, the seers.*

The whole vision has become to you like the words of a book that is sealed, which men deliver to one who is literate, saying, "Read this, please." And he says, "I cannot, for it is sealed." Then the book is delivered to one who is illiterate, saying, "Read this, please." And he says, "I am not literate." Therefore the Lord said: "Inasmuch as these people draw near with their mouths and honor Me with their lips, but have removed their hearts far from Me, and their fear toward Me is taught by the commandment of men. Isaiah 29:9-13

Many of the same themes we discussed regarding Isaiah 28 are repeated again in 29. And here again we see the judgment against those who should know what's going on, the leaders of God's people. Is it any wonder there's so much confusion regarding the prophecies of the last days? God describes our day as blind, illiterate men trying to understand. The Book is sealed to these men because their hearts are not right. They draw near to God with their lips but their hearts are far from him. Their reverence for God doesn't exceed the lies they learned as children.

Your first father sinned, and your mediators have transgressed against Me. Therefore I will profane the princes of the sanctuary; I will give Jacob to the curse, and Israel to reproaches. Isaiah 43:27-28

What's the context of this passage? Go back one chapter. Chapter 42 begins discussing Yahshua's first coming. He came first as the gentle servant. A bruised reed he will not break. He will not cry out or make his voice heard in the street. But look at the change in language starting in verse 13. He will go forth like a mighty man. He shall cry out, yes, shout aloud. He has held his peace a long time. Now he will cry out like a woman in labor. These are the birth pangs of a new age...a new era. This is the beginning of the Tribulation.

And at the end of this age, where does "Jacob" dwell, a large portion of God's people, both the house of Judah and the house of Israel?[625]

> *Thus says the LORD, your Redeemer, the Holy One of Israel:*
> *"For your sake I will send to Babylon, and bring them all down*
> *as fugitives--the Chaldeans, who rejoice in their ships.*
> Isaiah 43:14

Notice Jehovah is saying here: "For your sake, my people, I will do this. You must be set free from bondage."[626] This is why Micah 4:10 says, "And to Babylon you shall go. There you shall be delivered. There the LORD will redeem you from the hand of your enemies." Does God consider this wicked, polluted land of America enemy territory, holding his children captive? Absolutely.

> *His watchmen are blind, they are all ignorant; they are all*
> *dumb dogs, they cannot bark; sleeping, lying down, loving to*
> *slumber. Yes, they are greedy dogs which never have enough.*
> *And they are shepherds who cannot understand; they all look*
> *to their own way, every one for his own gain, from his own*
> *territory. "Come," one says, "I will bring wine, and we will fill*
> *ourselves with intoxicating drink; tomorrow will be as today,*
> *and much more abundant."* Isaiah 56:10-12

Chapter 56 is a prelude to the Tribulation, as the context is established in verse 1: "My salvation is about to come, my righteousness is about to be revealed." And who are the self-proclaimed "watchmen" today? Those looking for the coming of the Tribulation, the majority of whom think they will be raptured at the start of that day. "And they are shepherds" who look only to their own gain, blind to their coming judgment, thinking tomorrow will be just like today.

---

[625] Jeremiah 50:4
[626] Isaiah 42:22

Confirming Text (Jeremiah)

And their houses shall be turned over to others, fields and
wives together; for I will stretch out My hand against the
inhabitants of the land," says the LORD. "Because from the
least of them even to the greatest of them, everyone is given to
covetousness; and from the prophet even to the priest,
everyone deals falsely. They have also healed the hurt of My
people slightly, saying, 'Peace, peace!' When there is no peace.
Jeremiah 6:12-14

As Daniel learned and recorded in his ninth chapter[627],
Jeremiah was commissioned by God to prophesy to two separate
generations that would both be held captive for seventy years by a
nation referred to as Babylon. And just as there were false prophets
of his day, like Hananiah, so there are today leaders of God's people
who speak falsehood. In addition to feeding the sheep false
doctrines of half-truths, they wink at the sin of God's people.

From the sole of the foot even to the head, there is no
soundness in it, but wounds and bruises and putrefying sores;
they have not been closed or bound up, or soothed with
ointment. Isaiah 1:6

Ever wonder how God really sees his people in America
today? Our gross sin and immoral behavior causes God not to see a
lovely bride that he's about to marry, but a person who's covered in
open sores and bruises and filth. He says the sores haven't been
closed or bound up, meaning the pastors of our day haven't nursed
us back to health. How? By teaching us to live right! By teaching us
to turn away from sin and be holy, for God is holy. The people of God
have terminal cancer and these impostors in the house treat it as if
it's a scrape on the knee. "There, there, little Johnny, everything will
be alright." Little Johnny is on life-support and the pastors of
America are reaching for a box of band-aids.

---

[627] Daniel 9:2

For the shepherds have become dull-hearted, and have not sought the LORD; Therefore they shall not prosper, and all their flocks shall be scattered. Jeremiah 10:21

So we see there is a dullness that has overtaken the shepherds of our day. There will be a season when the flocks are scattered during the Tribulation, before God gives them faithful shepherds, as we see in Jeremiah 33:12.

Confirming Text (Ezekiel)

Disaster will come upon disaster, and rumor will be upon rumor. Then they will seek a vision from a prophet; but the law will perish from the priest, and counsel from the elders. Ezekiel 7:26

We learned that both Ezekiel 13 and 34 deal with the pastors and prophets of our day. And Ezekiel chapter 7 fits the same pattern as all the other texts discussing the ultimate and final destruction of the land where God's people primarily dwell at the beginning of Tribulation, America. And herein we find this text. The people will ask the prophets and shepherds what in the world is going on, but they will have no clue.

Her priests have violated My law and profaned My holy things; they have not distinguished between the holy and unholy, nor have they made known the difference between the unclean and the clean; and they have hidden their eyes from My Sabbaths, so that I am profaned among them. Ezekiel 22:26

Verse 4 of Ezekiel 22 establishes the context of this chapter. "You have come to the end of your years." I challenge you to find anything in this chapter that can't be applied to America today. Herein is spoken of idol worship and government corruption and making light of father and mother (civil unions). "They will mock her as infamous and full of tumult."[628] The word infamous[629] has to do with defilement from a religious point of view. The whole land has become polluted. Just as Revelation 18:2 tells us, she has become a dwelling place of demons and a prison for every foul spirit and a cage for every unclean and hated bird. And in verse 26 the same theme we've been discussing is present. Her priests, her pastors, have violated the law and profaned (there's that word again) his holy things. The pastors willingly chose to not distinguish between the clean and unclean. The pastors have no idea how to honor our holy God, nor do they regard the fourth commandment: honor the Sabbath and keep it holy. Pastors today know only of the goodness and forgiveness found in the name of Yahshua (Jesus). They have willing chose to ignore the rest of God's Holy Word, describing his character and nature.

> *And they shall teach My people the difference between the holy and the unholy, and cause them to discern between the unclean and the clean.* Ezekiel 44:23

But we see in Ezekiel 44 that the day is coming when God's people will once again learn how to tell the difference between the clean and unclean, the holy and the unholy. God's people will have to learn about God's character and the fear and reverence he is due from faithful shepherds who will replace today's impostors.

Confirming Text (Hosea, Zechariah, Zephaniah, Malachi, Lamentations, Amos, Micah, Revelation)

As do all the prophets, so these also speak of these last days in which we're living. And in perfect agreement, here is some of what these prophets have to say about the pastors and prophets of our day, their blatant disregard for the Word of God and their rebellion.

---

[628] Ezekiel 22:5
[629] Strong's Hebrew Dictionary entry H2931

Hosea

Therefore you shall stumble in the day; the prophet also shall stumble with you in the night; and I will destroy your mother. Hosea 4:5

My people are destroyed for lack of knowledge. Because you have rejected knowledge, I also will reject you from being priest for Me; because you have forgotten the law of your God, I also will forget your children. Hosea 4:6

And it shall be: like people, like priest. So I will punish them for their ways, and reward them for their deeds. Hosea 4:9

Hear this, O priests! Take heed, O house of Israel! Give ear, O house of the king! For yours is the judgment, because you have been a snare to Mizpah and a net spread on Tabor. Hosea 5:1

As bands of robbers lie in wait for a man, so the company of priests murder on the way to Shechem; surely they commit lewdness. Hosea 6:9

Set the trumpet to your mouth! He shall come like an eagle against the house of the LORD, because they have transgressed My covenant and rebelled against My law. Hosea 8:1

I have written for him the great things of My law, but they were considered a strange thing. Hosea 8:12

The days of punishment have come; the days of recompense have come. Israel knows! The prophet is a fool, the spiritual man is insane, because of the greatness of your iniquity and great enmity. The watchman of Ephraim is with my God; but the prophet is a fowler's snare in all his ways--Enmity in the house of his God. Hosea 9:7-8

Zechariah

> *Yes, they made their hearts like flint, refusing to hear the law and the words which the LORD of hosts had sent by His Spirit through the former prophets. Thus great wrath came from the LORD of hosts.* Zechariah 7:12

> *My anger is kindled against the shepherds, and I will punish the goatherds. For the LORD of hosts will visit His flock, the house of Judah, and will make them as His royal horse in the battle.* Zechariah 10:3

> *There is the sound of wailing shepherds! For their glory is in ruins. There is the sound of roaring lions! For the pride of the Jordan is in ruins. Thus says the LORD my God, "Feed the flock for slaughter, whose owners slaughter them and feel no guilt; those who sell them say, 'Blessed be the LORD, for I am rich'; and their shepherds do not pity them.* Zechariah 11:3-5

> *And it shall be in that day that every prophet will be ashamed of his vision when he prophesies; they will not wear a robe of coarse hair to deceive.* Zechariah 13:4

Zephaniah

> *I will stretch out My hand against Judah, and against all the inhabitants of Jerusalem. I will cut off every trace of Baal from this place, the names of the idolatrous priests with the pagan priests.* Zephaniah 1:4

> *Her prophets are insolent, treacherous people; her priests have polluted the sanctuary, they have done violence to the law.* Zephaniah 3:4

Malachi

A son honors his father, and a servant his master. If then I am the Father, where is My honor? And if I am a Master, where is My reverence? Says the LORD of hosts to you priests who despise My name. Yet you say, 'In what way have we despised Your name?' Malachi 1:6

You also say, 'Oh, what a weariness!' And you sneer at it," Says the LORD of hosts. "And you bring the stolen, the lame, and the sick; thus you bring an offering! Should I accept this from your hand?" says the LORD. Malachi 1:13

But you have departed from the way; you have caused many to stumble at the law. You have corrupted the covenant of Levi," Says the LORD of hosts. "Therefore I also have made you contemptible and base before all the people, because you have not kept My ways but have shown partiality in the law." Malachi 2:8-9

Remember the Law of Moses, My servant, which I commanded him in Horeb for all Israel, with the statutes and judgments. Malachi 4:4

Lamentations

He has done violence to His tabernacle, as if it were a garden; He has destroyed His place of assembly; the LORD has caused the appointed feasts and Sabbaths to be forgotten in Zion. In His burning indignation He has spurned the king and the priest. Lamentations 2:6

See, O LORD, and consider! To whom have You done this? Should the women eat their offspring, the children they have cuddled? Should the priest and prophet be slain in the sanctuary of the Lord? Lamentations 2:20

Amos

> *They lie down by every altar on clothes taken in pledge, and drink the wine of the condemned in the house of their god.*
> Amos 2:8

Here we see Christians (of the house of Israel) drinking the wine of those who are condemned. And they are drinking it in the house of their god. Most translations render it "god," little g. However, this word, Strong's H430, can mean god or the one true God. It really depends on the individual, whether they are worshiping their gods or they are worshiping the one true God. Nevertheless, who are the condemned and what is the wine they are sharing with these people in the house of God? Those who are condemned today are the pastors and prophets who are feeding the sheep false doctrines. Isaiah 28 says they are themselves drunk on this wine. And week after week, year after year, they have shared their false doctrines with the people of God. They have caused the people of God to become drunk on the same wine on which they have become drunk.

> *That in the day I punish Israel for their transgressions, I will also visit destruction on the altars of Bethel (the house of God[630]); and the horns (signifying power, rulership[631]) of the altar shall be cut off and fall to the ground.* Amos 3:14

Micah

> *And I said: "Hear now, O heads of Jacob, and you rulers of the house of Israel: Is it not for you to know justice? You who hate good and love evil; who strip the skin from My people, and the flesh from their bones; who also eat the flesh of My people, flay their skin from them, break their bones, and chop them in*

---

[630] Strong's Hebrew Dictionary entry H1008
[631] Strong's Hebrew Dictionary entry H7161

*pieces like meat for the pot, like flesh in the caldron." Then
they will cry to the LORD, but He will not hear them; He will
even hide His face from them at that time, because they have
been evil in their deeds.* Micah 3:1-4

Why are we given such a graphic picture of what the leaders of God's people are doing to them? Because of the soothing words and treacherous example of these pastors, multitudes are entering into that wide door that leads to perdition. And even if they make it through that narrow door that leads to life, they do so at great cost, experiencing a life on earth far removed from what Jehovah intended for them. The lies and half-truths of these leaders have destroyed the flock of God in America.

Revelation

*And in her was found the blood of prophets and saints, and of
all who were slain on the earth.* Revelation 18:24

Here found in the detailed description of the downfall of America, we read of those who will not make it through to the next day. Notice the use of the word "saints" in this verse. Thayer's Lexicon includes in its definition of this word as "1. properly reverend" and "a. of things which on account of some connection with God possess a certain distinction and claim to reverence" and "b. of person whose services God employs."[632] Given the multitude of Scripture references it should be apparent this verse is referring to pastors and teachers in America who are worthy of God's judgment on the day America is destroyed.

---

[632] Strong's G40 - hagios. Thayer's Lexicon. Retrieved March 14, 2012 from http://www.blueletterbible.org/lang/lexicon/lexicon.cfm?Strongs=G40&t=NKJV

Rest for Your Souls

> *Thus says the LORD: "Stand in the ways and see, and ask for*
> *the old paths, where the good way is, and walk in it; then you*
> *will find rest for your souls. But they said, 'We will not walk in*
> *it.'* Jeremiah 6:16

I suppose many pastors will protest, accusing me of trying to bring people into bondage by exalting the law and making it honorable.[633] Rather, what I have attempted to do is present a balanced doctrine. Jehovah is both merciful and just. And it's evident that the people of God in America are already in bondage. The truth is that we need to be set free. Set free from lies, half-truths, corruption and sin. Just I have shown that these unfaithful stewards over the house will be swept away, so by the Word of God I can show that the people of God in America will be set free. The day is coming when we will be delivered out of the bondage of this polluted land.

God himself, in the last chapter of the Old Testament, speaks expressly to our day, telling us to remember the law of Moses.[634] Why? Because we have gotten so far away from those "old paths, where the good way is."[635] We have corrupted ourselves by walking in the ways of the world. And our leaders have shown blatant disregard for much of the truth of God's Holy Word, and in so doing, are leading multitudes astray.

The day is fast approaching when the restitution of all things will begin. The day is fast approaching when everything hidden will be shouted from the rooftops. God pleads with us today:

> *"Wash yourselves, make yourselves clean; put away the evil of*
> *your doings from before My eyes. Cease to do evil, learn to do*
> *good; seek justice, rebuke the oppressor; defend the fatherless,*

---

[633] Isaiah 42:21
[634] Malachi 4:4
[635] Jeremiah 6:16

plead for the widow. Come now, and let us reason together"
says the LORD. Isaiah 1:16-18

Chapter 13 - Prelude to Destruction

The day of your watchman and your punishment comes; now shall be their perplexity. Micah 7:4

The Bible is a very large collection of books with much more detail than I can present here. While it is impossible to address every single prophecy in a book this size, I tried to thoroughly address the main issues surrounding the beginning of that Day, the Tribulation. This book is intended to be read from start to finish as each chapter expands on the arguments that came before it. I hope the information was presented in a clear and logical manner, but I also realize these are very heavy topics and not easily understood and digested. I can't overestimate the value of looking up and studying the passages referenced in the footnotes. My desire is that this book would act as a guide, or possibly even a launching point, for your own study rather than a study in and of itself. While I believe I have presented the correct interpretation of the Scriptures, I'm not infallible. May the Spirit of God be your guide as you rely on him as the final authority for your understanding of the Holy Bible, Jehovah's message to mankind.

It's quite possible many, having read and understood the arguments I've presented, now have some very practical questions. You may be wondering "OK, what next?" Or, if this guy is right, what can we expect over the next few years? Are we supposed to flee America now? Isn't that what Scripture tells us to do? Or shouldn't we at least stock up on canned goods? Before I attempt to answer these questions, let me be clear. This is not a book about fleeing end-time Babylon, America. I do not believe you need to flee ahead of time in order to survive the day of America's destruction. Those whom God preserves[636] will be like firebrands plucked out of the

---

[636] Jeremiah 50:20

fire.[637] They will be like those three men who survived the fiery furnace heated seven times hot.[638] Today in America the average Christian looks and acts like everyone else, but when that next morning arrives, "you shall again discern between the righteous and the wicked, between one who serves God and one who does not serve Him."[639] That being said, do whatever God is telling you to do. Maybe you are to be one of the rams before the flock.[640]

Should I leave America now?

But what about all the Scripture that speaks of fleeing?[641] A dear sister in Christ wrote me to ask if I'm going to be leaving the U.S. "What about the commands to leave?" she asked. She noted the urgency of those commands and that it must be a command to get out now. OK, so are we told to get out of the country? Yes, we are. But when? When are we to flee? I think another question will answer this one. When is the command given? Is the command given today, in 2012? Are we all to start fleeing when we come to realize that America is Babylon? That's going to be tricky because we're also told that Babylon, as a whole, won't even know she's Babylon. So how many will actually leave before this judgment comes to America? A couple hundred maybe? A thousand? Is that all that will make it out? Actually, we're told that 10% will survive.[642] Ten percent of 300 million, roughly the population of America, is 30 million. I propose that the command to flee is given as the destruction is taking place. If you go back and look at the context of those verses you'll see that Babylon is being destroyed when the command to leave is being given. Jeremiah 51:50 says: "You who

---

[637] Amos 4:11, Zechariah 3:2
[638] Daniel 3
[639] Malachi 3:18
[640] Jeremiah 50:8
[641] Isaiah 48:20, 54:11, Jeremiah 50:8, 51:6, 45, 50, Zechariah 2:7, Revelation 18:4
[642] Isaiah 6:13, Amos 5:3

have escaped the sword, get away! Do not stand still! Remember the LORD afar off, and let Jerusalem come to your mind." Look closely. It says "you who have escaped the sword." Or, in other words, you who just miraculously survived a nuclear holocaust. God promises that those not under his immediate judgment will not be forsaken by him.[643] One would do well to make sure they are not under his immediate judgment when that Day begins.[644]

Should I stock up on food and supplies?

If we don't leave the country, should we at least stock up on canned goods and such? Again, do whatever the Lord puts on your heart to do. But do it in faith. Without faith it's impossible to please God.[645] If you stock up then do so with the hungry in mind, knowing we are commanded to share with those in need. If you don't stock up then do so in faith, knowing God is pleased with you because you obey him in all things, believing God will provide when the store shelves go empty. But if you still refuse to live a clean life, instead following the dictates of your heart and the idols of the land, I suggest you stock up. Those who follow idols should expect their idols to rescue them. Good luck with that.

Will the grocery store shelves really go empty for a time in America?

Seems impossible, right? When the nation called by his name rebels against God, he will send that nation a series of wake-up calls. Those lesser judgments are intended to shake the sleepy, rebellious people out of their stupor. When the people continue in their rebellion and refuse to hear, God sends a destroyer against their land to conquer them and drive them from it. This pattern was

---

[643] Jeremiah 51:5
[644] Isaiah 27:5
[645] Hebrews 11:6

established from the beginning and we can see it was put into practical application all throughout history. In Amos 4 we see this pattern described once again, but this time, I believe, spoken about our day. In verse 11 we see the nation completely destroyed just as Sodom and Gomorrah. Those whom God spares from that disaster are like firebrands plucked from the fire. Note that this chapter is not speaking of a people who ignore God entirely. They bring tithes every three days (weekend and mid-week services).[646] Furthermore, they offer God thank offerings and freewill offerings but those offerings are mixed with leaven, which is representative of sin.[647] God hates a mixture of worship and pollution. Leading up to that final disaster we read of a series of lesser judgments intended to cause the people to return to God and repent. Verses 6 through 10 describe drought, crop blight and mildew, a plague after the manner of Egypt, and cleanness of teeth in all our cities. Hosea echoes that cleanness of teeth by saying we will eat, but not have enough.[648] There's no telling how long it will last, but I believe we'll see unprecedented hunger in America before mid-2015. And do not underestimate the severity of that "plague after the manner of Egypt." Pray without ceasing for the health of your unsaved loved ones and their families.

Will the economy collapse and society descend into chaos?

From what I can tell this seems to be the question people care about the most. Money is an important part of our daily lives but we are not to be overly concerned with it. Yahshua said we should be focused on storing up treasures in heaven. We are to continually bear good fruit from a clear conscience. "For where your treasure is, there your heart will be also."[649] That being said, I would be surprised to see the economy collapse. While certain regions may

---

[646] Amos 4:4
[647] Amos 4:5
[648] Hosea 4:10
[649] Matthew 6:19-21

experience periods of chaos and lawlessness, to address the question about the economy we only need look at what we're told. When America reaches her end there's still a whole lot of buying and selling going on. So much so that the merchants of the earth, those selling all that stuff to America, actually weep at her demise because they just lost their best customer.[650] Furthermore, Zephaniah informs us that "they shall build houses, but not inhabit them; they shall plant vineyards, but not drink their wine."[651] The economic life of the nation is still quite vibrant when America is destroyed. While many of us can hardly believe America's economy is still standing, Habakkuk implies the reason for this continued prosperity is because of America's aggressive foreign policy and military.[652] There seems to be an unlimited number of tricks up her sleeve. But that day will come to an abrupt end.

Will Christians be persecuted in America?

I've heard it said that our Christian brothers and sisters in China are praying for this very thing because they see how far we've fallen. It's often the case that those outside of a situation can see more clearly than those in the midst of it. As the early Church learned, nothing brings spiritual renewal and growth like persecution. While I can't answer this question definitively, there are some things to consider. If you remember from a previous chapter I showed how America's final judgment will begin on a Sunday when religious services are taking place. Therefore we can conclude that Church services will not be banned. However, there are numerous passages which should give us pause.[653] While some of the language can be interpreted in a general sense, Babylon

---

[650] Revelation 18
[651] Zephaniah 1:13
[652] Habakkuk 1:17
[653] Isaiah 47:6, 51:13-14, 52:5, Jeremiah 50:11, 17, 28, 33, 34, 51:24, 34, 35, 44, 49, Zechariah 2:8

contributing to the pollution found in God's people, other passages should cause us to sit up and take notice.

John describes that he saw her "drunk with the blood of the saints and with the blood of the martyrs of Jesus."[654] Isaiah speaks of a time when "those who rule over them make them wail." [655] But after that oppressor has been dealt with God feels a need to remind his people that "you have feared continually every day because of the fury of the oppressor, when he has prepared to destroy."[656] The very next verse describes a people whose only concern is getting out of prison because if they don't they're going to starve to death.[657] It seems the daily rations to those prisoners suddenly comes to an end. This is exactly what we would expect when a nation is suddenly destroyed. However, Jeremiah reassures us that God will bring out those whom Babylon has swallowed.[658] I believe what the Bible is showing us is there will be some form of persecution coming to Christians in America over the next few years. Some may be imprisoned. Some may become martyrs. Will it soon become a crime to do or say certain things we take for granted now? Time will tell.

Will our troops come home first?

> *Woe to you who plunder, though you have not been plundered; and you who deal treacherously, though they have not dealt treacherously with you! When you cease plundering, you will be plundered; when you make an end of dealing treacherously, they will deal treacherously with you.* Isaiah 33:1

I believe what we see here is a prophecy regarding America's military in our day. In 2011 many of our troops in Afghanistan and

---

[654] Revelation 17:6
[655] Isaiah 52:5
[656] Isaiah 51:13
[657] Isaiah 51:14
[658] Jeremiah 51:44

Iraq were brought home and I believe we'll see this trend continue. This effort to bring our soldiers home fits perfectly with the scenario concerning a time of "peace and safety" and also that of America being completely destroyed in one hour. There simply will not be enough of a force outside our borders to mount a significant retaliation. Nor will we be able to fend off that attack even if our troops are able to fight. The prophecies seem to indicate a "stand down" order may even be given.[659] When all is said and done "the ambassadors of peace shall weep bitterly."[660] They would only weep bitterly if an unprecedented time of peace preceded this destruction of America.

It also seems to me that, in order to absorb the returning soldiers into our job force, unusual steps will have to be made to make room for them. Jeremiah tells us "Cut off the sower from Babylon, and him who handles the sickle at harvest time. For fear of the oppressing sword everyone shall turn to his own people, and everyone shall flee to his own land."[661] It looks to me like the migrant workers, illegals, and maybe even H1B's, will be sent home before the trouble begins in 2016. I say "before" because how can one flee nuclear war; a devastating destruction that will last only one hour? In examining this verse more closely, the translation may be a little misleading. Look at this phrase: "for fear of the oppressing sword." The Strong's definitions are:

H4480: from
H6440: the face
H3238: to be violent
H2719: drought; also a cutting instrument (from its destructive effect), as a knife, sword, or other sharp implement

I'm not sure how H6440 was translated into "fear." I'm not claiming to be smarter than the translators, but it definitely raises

[659] Ezekiel 7:14, Jeremiah 51:30
[660] Isaiah 33:7
[661] Jeremiah 50:16

questions in my mind. Could it be that this verse is really predicting a scenario where these migrant workers are sent home to free up jobs for the returning troops? What else would cause them leave ahead of time? Even if the whole nation is warned ahead of time of what's coming, what would cause these people to heed the warning more so than the more established residents of America? It makes more sense to me that these people are being forced to leave. The first scenario seems to be more of a fit. Also, the phrase "and they shall flee"[662] can mean "to chase away." It seems they are being chased away in order to make room for the returning soldiers.

Listen to the Sound of the Trumpet

> *Also, I set watchmen over you, saying, 'Listen to the sound of the trumpet!' But they said, 'We will not listen.'* Jeremiah 6:17

I believe those of us who make it through the next few years will enter into a time of unprecedented world-wide peace and security. I believe that period of peace will begin by the middle of 2015 and end on that dreaded date the following year. In Isaiah an unknown messenger begins his warning to the people, telling them that "in a year and a few days you will be troubled."[663] His speech fits the pattern of the things discussed in this book. Not only does he know the day they will be troubled but I suspect the "year and few days" phrase is significant because it's his first time addressing the assembly of people.

Just as God brings disasters upon his people, he also sends messengers, or prophets, to warn them of the coming calamity. We can see that Jeremiah was called to warn ancient Judah of her impending calamity. God tasked him to "take out the precious from the vile."[664] God is seeking those who will worship him in spirit and

---

[662] Strong's Hebrew Dictionary entry H5127
[663] Isaiah 32:10
[664] Jeremiah 15:19

in truth.[665] Ezekiel 33 gives an in-depth look at the purpose of a watchman and we see in Isaiah 21 that America is indeed assigned a watchman to warn the people of the approaching calamity. Ephraim, whose name is representative of the house of Israel, has a watchman who walks with God[666] and who proclaims wickedness from Mt. Ephraim, which represents America.[667] "The day of your watchman and your punishment comes; now shall be their perplexity."[668] But we're told time and again that the people, as a whole, will ignore those warnings. In fact, we know they will hate the one who rebukes in the gate.[669] Nevertheless, the watchman must put trumpet to mouth in hope that some will heed. Whether or not they listen and heed is of no consequence to the purpose of the watchman. He who has the Word of the Lord must speak it faithfully.[670] The trumpet must be blown.

> *Cry aloud, spare not; lift up your voice like a trumpet; tell My people their transgression, and the house of Jacob their sins.*
> Isaiah 58:1

Before the day of the Lord's fierce anger comes upon us, we'll be assembled together to hear that trumpet.[671] Let the people be assembled. Who among them can declare this?[672] Who can proclaim it? Let him declare it and set it in order.[673] For with stammering lips and another tongue he will speak to us.[674] Truly the people will hear a voice of trembling, of fear, and not of peace.[675] The people will be brought near to hear the verdict.[676] Even the nations will draw near

---

[665] John 4:24

[666] Hosea 9:8

[667] Jeremiah 4:15

[668] Micah 7:4

[669] Amos 5:10

[670] Jeremiah 23:28

[671] Zephaniah 2:1-2

[672] Isaiah 43:9

[673] Isaiah 44:7

[674] Isaiah 28:11

[675] Jeremiah 30:5

[676] Isaiah 41:1, Habakkuk 3:1, Hosea 7:12, Jeremiah 6:24, 30:5

to hear. Let all the earth hear.[677] Yes, the people will be assembled to hear that trumpet, and he will come with a company of watchmen who will lift up their voices.[678] But who is this servant? Who among them has declared these things already? Who did Jehovah cause to understand the message[679] and instruct in right judgment?[680] He will do his good pleasure towards us (healing), but his strength will be against us, to show us our sins. God has called him and made his way prosperous. God will have brought him.[681] The vision would have already been written down and made plain by this time.[682] This one will have told us these things already, from the time they began to happen. And he knows God has sent him.[683] I suspect this servant will exalt the law, which has been forgotten by God's people.[684] After all, God is well pleased, or shows favor[685], for his righteousness sake, that his law, which describes his character, would once again be understood and revered by his people; it will be exalted and made honorable again.[686] But what is that message from the law we're admonished to remember before that Day comes upon us?[687]

> *Thus says the LORD of hosts: 'Execute true justice, show mercy and compassion everyone to his brother. Do not oppress the widow or the fatherless, the alien or the poor. Let none of you plan evil in his heart against his brother.' But they refused to heed, shrugged their shoulders, and stopped their ears so that they could not hear. Yes, they made their hearts like flint, refusing to hear the law and the words which the LORD of hosts had sent by His Spirit through the former prophets. Thus*

---

[677] Isaiah 34:1
[678] Isaiah 52:8
[679] Isaiah 28:9
[680] Isaiah 28:26
[681] Isaiah 48:14-15
[682] Habakkuk 2:2
[683] Isaiah 48:16
[684] Hosea 8:12
[685] Strong's Hebrew Dictionary entry H2654
[686] Isaiah 42:21
[687] Malachi 4:4

> *great wrath came from the LORD of hosts. Therefore it*
> *happened, that just as He proclaimed and they would not hear,*
> *so they called out and I would not listen, says the LORD of*
> *hosts. But I scattered them with a whirlwind among all the*
> *nations which they had not known. Thus the land became*
> *desolate after them, so that no one passed through or*
> *returned; for they made the pleasant land desolate.*
> Zechariah 7:9-14

The Lord confirms the word of his servant, and performs the counsel of his messengers.[688] But how will their words be confirmed? Why does he need to tell the people about their sin? A wicked generation, devoid of God's holy Word, and by extension ignorant of his ways and character, needs a sign before they'll believe. After seeing so many powerful and wonderful signs a disciple came to Yahshua, asking him to show him the Father so he could believe. Yahshua said: "Believe Me that I am in the Father and the Father in Me, or else believe Me for the sake of the works themselves. Most assuredly, I say to you, he who believes in Me, the works that I do he will do also; and greater works than these he will do, because I go to My Father."[689] I suspect we have not yet seen the fullness of the fulfillment of this prophecy. The day is coming when the Sun of Righteousness will arise with healing in his wings to those who fear his name.[690] And who is to be found hiding under the shadow of his wings but his servant.[691] At the same time God brings healing to his people, their wickedness will also be exposed.[692] That servant will do his good pleasure towards us, healing us of all sorts of afflictions by the thousands in front of large assemblies of people. But his strength will be against us, to tell God's people about their transgression.[693] "But truly I am full of power by the Spirit of the LORD, and of justice and might, to declare to Jacob his transgression

---

[688] Isaiah 44:26
[689] John 14:11-12
[690] Malachi 4:2
[691] Psalm 91:4
[692] Hosea 7:1 Young's Literal Translation
[693] Isaiah 48:14

and to Israel his sin."[694]   Why? Why not just heal people and share the gospel message? Because God desires his people to repent and turn from their wicked ways so he can spare them on the day America is destroyed.[695]

> *Blow the trumpet in Zion, and sound an alarm in My holy mountain! Let all the inhabitants of the land tremble; for the day of the LORD is coming, for it is at hand: A day of darkness and gloominess, a day of clouds and thick darkness, like the morning clouds spread over the mountains. A people come, great and strong, the like of whom has never been; nor will there ever be any such after them, even for many successive generations.* Joel 2:1-2

> *The earth quakes before them, the heavens tremble; the sun and moon grow dark, and the stars diminish their brightness. The LORD gives voice before His army, for His camp is very great; for strong is the One who executes His word. For the day of the LORD is great and very terrible; who can endure it? "Now, therefore," says the LORD, "Turn to Me with all your heart, with fasting, with weeping, and with mourning." So rend your heart, and not your garments; return to the LORD your God, for He is gracious and merciful, slow to anger, and of great kindness; and He relents from doing harm.*   Joel 2:10-13

---

[694] Micah 3:8
[695] Micah 6:11

Made in the USA
Charleston, SC
21 March 2013